Waiting for Gospel

Waiting for Gospel

An Appeal to the Dispirited Remnants
of Protestant "Establishment"

Douglas John Hall

CASCADE *Books* • Eugene, Oregon

WAITING FOR GOSPEL
An Appeal to the Dispirited Remnants of Protestant "Establishment"

Cascade Books
An Imprint of Wipf and Stock Publishers
199 W. 8th Ave., Suite 3
Eugene, OR 97401

www.wipfandstock.com

ISBN 13: 978-1-61097-672-5

Cataloging-in-Publication data:

Hall, Douglas John, 1928–
    Waiting for gospel : an appeal to the dispirited remnants of protestant "establishment" / Douglas John Hall.

    xxx + 196 p. ; 23 cm.—Includes bibliographical references and indexes.

    ISBN 13: 978-1-61097-672-5

    1. Church and the world. 2. Christianity and modern culture. 3. Theology. I. Title.

BR121.2 .H315 2012

Manufactured in the USA

For Six Younger Theologians—
Pamela McCarroll
Harris Athanasiadis
Nicholas Athanasiadis
Michael Bourgeois
Marilyn Legg
Donald Schweitzer

And for Five Whose Memory Sustains Us—
Alan E. Lewis
Arthur VanSeters
Anne Hall
Robert Bater
Benjamin Smillie

". . . necessity is laid upon me.
Woe to me if I do not preach the gospel."
—St. Paul, 1 Corinthians 9:16

"Christianity is certainly not melancholy.
it is, on the contrary, glad tidings—for the melancholy.
To the frivolous it is certainly not glad tidings,
for it wishes first of all to make them serious."
—Søren Kierkegaard

Contents

Introduction

Waiting for Gospel[1]

THE ESSAYS IN THIS volume are all expressions of their author's concern for the critical situation of the so-called mainline Protestant denominations, especially (though not exclusively) in the North American context. That situation, in my view, is redolent of a challenge unprecedented in the history of Christianity on this continent, and perhaps throughout the Western world. To speak only for the United States and Canada, the once most established churches here have been upheld by sociopolitical conventions that, though they had little enough to do with the biblical and theological foundations of Christianity, were nonetheless strong enough to bolster the ideational, organizational, and economic structures necessary to the churches' preservation. But these conventions no longer pertain—or, more accurately, their *seeming or partial* reality in the still visibly Christian sectors of our continent are pathetic bulwarks against the secular, pluralistic, and frankly antireligious tendencies of the present. They cannot prevent the continued decline and decay of denominational religion as we have known it. It is entirely possible (and thinking Christians can no longer avoid this conclusion) that most of the once-powerful ecclesiastical institutions of North America will disappear entirely within the near future.

That conclusion has recently been corroborated by a team of researchers in the USA, which predicts that religion will be "driven towards

1. I will explain in the first of the thirteen essays, "The Mystery of Gospel," why I am using the noun *gospel* without the definite article (*the* gospel).

extinction" over the next century in several Western countries, including my own.[2] This conclusion of the researchers draws chiefly upon two
"sociological principles," especially as these are manifested in societies
where a steadily increasing number of citizens indicates that they have
"no religious affiliation." The principles named in the report are "that it
is more attractive to be part of the majority than the minority, and that
there are social, political, and economic advantages to being unaffiliated
in countries where religion is in decline. The researchers say they cannot
make predictions about the United States because the U.S. census doesn't
ask questions about religion."[3]

The typical institutional response to such data (which has been
served up to us now for decades in one form or another) is to look for
more effective means of preserving the churches: for example, by bol-
stering their economic viability through financial and philanthropic
("stewardship")[4] drives; by devising "new forms of ministry that fit the
times,"[5] by exploiting modern technologies for the promotion of the
churches and churchgoing. After a century of more or less frantic efforts
on the part of Christian churches to discover new ways of staving off the
decline of organized Christianity, however, serious Christians should realize that altering the packaging of religion usually achieves little and may,
proverbially speaking, be little more than "rearranging the deck chairs on
the *Titanic*."

The only thing that can salvage a moribund religion is a lively recovery of its life-giving essence. If that which first excited human interest
cannot be rediscovered and communicated in some tangible and timely
way, a religion is likely doomed. A church will not be kept from the ash
heap of history by promoting some of its peripheral aspects and alleged
advantages. And a religion preoccupied with death—its own death!—as
so much contemporary Protestant Christianity patently is—is unlikely to

---

2. See the *United Church Observer* 74/11 (2011) 36ff; also the *Christian Century* 128/8
(2011) 9. The countries named, besides Canada, are Ireland, Australia, New Zealand, the
Netherlands, Austria, the Czech Republic, Finland, and Switzerland.

3. *Christian Century*, 128/8 (2011) 9.

4. In my work on the theology of stewardship, however, I have argued that using this
biblical office and metaphor as exclusively for *church support* as we have done in North
America constitutes a serious reduction of the metaphor, which is more broadly to be applied to the human vocation in the world. See Hall, *The Steward*; and Hall, *Imaging God*.

5. *United Church Observer* 74/11 (2011) 37.

bring light and life to a society that is also fixated on the many faces of failure and possible extinction that confront it on a daily basis.

Christianity, as faith centered in Jesus as the Christ came to be called, got a foothold in the world, and for a vital and vocal minority *changed* the world, because it proclaimed a message that awakened men and women to possibilities for human life that they had either lost or never entertained. That message the first Christian evangelists (and Jesus himself, according to the record) called *euangellion*—good news, gospel. For its first two or three hundred years, Christianity was largely dependent for its existence upon the new zest for life that was awakened in persons who heard and were, as they felt, transformed, by that gospel; and at various and sundry points in subsequent history the Christian movement has found itself revitalized by the spirit of that same "good news" in ways that spoke to the specifics of their times and places.

The lesson of history is clear: the challenge to all serious Christians and Christian bodies today is not whether we can devise yet more novel and promotionally impressive means for the transmission of "the Christian religion" (let alone this or that denomination); it is whether we are able to hear and to proclaim . . . *gospel*! We do not need statisticians and sociologists to inform us that religion—and specifically *our* religion, as the dominant expression of the spiritual impulse of *homo sapiens* in our geographic context—is in decline. We do not need the sages of the new atheism to announce in learned tomes (and on busses!) that "God probably does not exist." The "sea of faith"[6] has been ebbing for a very long time.

But what many of us fail to notice is that this great teleological recession has left in large numbers of Westerners an emptiness that neither consumerism nor social activism nor entertainment nor sex nor any other substitute for religion can fill. Not only lapsed Catholics and Protestants, but countless human beings who heretofore had little use for religion are waiting for something—something no doubt ill-defined, intangible, vague—*something* to correspond to the spirituality so many of them insist they have even when they loudly disclaim any religious affiliation. The

6. The phrase is from Matthew Arnold's poem "Dover Beach":
   The Sea of Faith
   Was once, too, at the full. . .
   But now I only hear
   Its melancholy, long, withdrawing roar . . .

general public dissatisfaction (not to say apprehension) about what is, and is coming to be, begets a longing (*Sehnsucht*) that is often palpable today in a once-secular society that, a few decades ago, imagined itself the zenith of humankind's most heroic collective ideals. That longing announces itself in every memorable film of the era; it cries out mindlessly in the repetitious and barbarous pop songs of the age, and it is detailed in the often crushingly negative tenor of every honest newscast. There was a time when I distrusted those who found God-forsakenness (or perhaps hidden obsession with God) beneath the surface of every secular city; but lately I find myself wondering whether there has ever been a moment in modern history when Augustine's most famous pronouncement has been as true of humankind as it is today: *Tu fecisti nos ad te, Domine, et inquietum est cor nostrum donec requiescat in te* (w).[7] We are truly an "inquiet" people!

Yet the old church bodies, the once-established denominations, seem to me to fail—and to fail *conspicuously!*—to speak to this inquietude. They appear trapped in another time warp. They seem incapable of uttering "good news"—as well as being honest about the *bad news* that must be contemplated if this *good news* is to have any prophetic bite in it! If they attempt "gospel" (and some do) it usually sounds like the language of another era, and it is for the majority of those who are found within hearing distance of this language—boring! Many wait for something, yet . . . "The sheep look up but *are not fed.*"[8]

I know of course: *there are exceptions!* Some of them are even *glorious* exceptions. But they are few, all too few; and in any case the point is to try to comprehend the norm in relation to which they are exceptions. To do so, we must rise above accusation and blame. The generally unsatisfying, sometimes stultifying character of our poor old churches, our once-vaunted "major denominations," is not to be laid at the feet of inadequately educated clergy, or seminaries that are out of touch with the churches, or congregational apathy. None of these can be accounted blameless, yet factors are consequences of a much larger reality. What we are dealing with is an historical condition, a sweeping and far-embracing trend centuries in the making. Many now trace its roots to the fourth-century beginnings

---

7. Augustine, *Confessions* 1.1.

8. Compare Milton's "Lycidas," line 125, which reads, "The hungry Sheep look up, and are not fed."

of "Christendom," In short, to use the jargon of the epoch, our problem is "systemic." Therefore a mood of complaint or accusation must be strictly avoided in a work like this. Contrary to the cryptic advice of Casius to Brutus in Shakespeare's *Julius Caesar*, "the fault" *is*, in some real sense, "in our stars," not "in ourselves."[9] Willy-nilly, we are part of the winding down of the great cultic clock of Western history called Christendom, i.e. the power and majority status of the Christian religion in the Western world. The pendulum of this clock is still swinging of its own momentum, here and there, though the mechanism of the clock has certainly worn out. Some say that it ceased to function effectively already two or three centuries ago—perhaps even longer. We simply cannot expect a dysfunctional system like Christendom suddenly to ring out "glad tidings of great joy." To be honest, as Søren Kierkegaard was on this subject well over a century ago, there was *always* a fundamental disconnect between Christendom and gospel.

Nevertheless some of us—perhaps we are a minority, but we are a significant minority!—know, or think we know, that precisely this enormous and fractured and battered old mechanism, reduced now to silence or something worse than silence, has been the unworthy (mostly unwilling and unimaginative) bearer of things that can "gladden the heart of man" (Ps 104:15). Whether out of hope or sheer doggedness, we are not ready to let it be carted off to the landfill pit of Western culture. The *Sehnsucht* (longing) of those who "look up" waiting to be "filled" *is too serious a matter for such a dismissive approach.* They are waiting for gospel!—or at least that is how *we* should see them, though the vast majority of them certainly would not put it that way! But their need, if we have any compassion at all—their need for meaning, for hope, for a calling as humans!—compels us to explore the wreckage of Christendom for any sign of something remembered that it not just 'religion.' Not just 'the same old same old!'

We are not interested in numbers! Let us eschew all that! What does it matter if thousands or tens of thousands pour into our neogothic or "Akron plan" sanctuaries only to be bombarded with the Christian religion—perhaps electronically hyped up?[10] Though they may seldom be able to articulate it, what the people in and around our old churches are

---

9. Act I, scene 2, lines 140–41.

10. The great Karl Rahner wrote essentially the same thought in his essay on "Christians in the Modern World," 20ff.

seeking is not just friendliness or communality or exhortation to moral improvement or a little blessed quietness in the midst of a world become ever noisier or stirring displays of the rhetoric of American optimism or the assurance of *ultimate* happiness (heaven!), etc., etc. To be sure, some will snatch at anything that is well advertised! But what the sensitive and the "quietly desperate," of whom the sagacious Thoreau spoke, both want and need is something far more radical than novelty and hype. They are waiting for gospel!

It may not be *our* gospel, of course. There is no need to indulge in vainglorious, exclusivistic, chauvinistic, and obnoxiously "evangelical" behavior in a Christian Movement that has moved beyond the Christendom phase! Christians who are still of a mind to turn the sad immensity of human need into a whole proselytizing system that assumes it is the Christian mission to make the entire world Christian have simply not been listening to the divine Spirit that has been addressing the Christian West for several centuries. The world-conquering phase of the Christian religion, the worst aspects of which, for the most part, are thankfully behind us, only succeeded in making the planet a more violent place than it might otherwise have been. When was it promised us that only *we* would be able to find the words and deeds capable of supplying the very Answer for which this ancient human "restlessness" begged? "Other sheep I have," said Jesus, "who are not of *this* fold" (John 10:16). However these words were intended originally, today we must hear them as a rebuke of all Christian "evangelical" aggressiveness. We have been shown plainly enough that among these "others" there are those who also, in their way and according to their own lights, can and do offer viable tokens of the same compassion, acceptance, meaning, and grace that we have glimpsed here and there, now and then, in our own evolving traditions and experience.

No, the challenge for us today is more accurately stated in our Lord's never-irrelevant exhortation to the self-righteous: "First remove the beam from your own eye" (Matt 7:3)!

Being translated and applied to the present question, this exhortation might be expressed as follows: "What is it, dear old Christian establishment, that has been preventing *you* from proclaiming gospel to this nearly despairing 'First World' in relation to which you have imagined yourself chief priest? Remove the beam from your own eye! Why, with all your quest for numbers, your claims to influence in high places, your endless recitation of past victories—why are you so little capable of *gospel?*"

It is not difficult, I think, to answer this question. Two observations immediately suggest themselves:

First, the old, established churches are prevented from proclaiming gospel precisely on account of their establishment, or the remnants of the same! That is, they are impeded primarily by the cloying habits of their cultural 'belonging.' The assumption of entitlement has blinded them to their vocation, as ambassadors of the crucified One, to divest themselves of the aura of officialdom and subject themselves, unprotected by their seeming status, to the stark realities of the human condition as it has come to be whilst they slept in their pews. At their best, they have been able to draw the attention of some to the more obvious bad news of the epoch. But they are too nicely cushioned by their perceived social position to explore the deeper causes of these ills, the questions beneath the questions, the anxieties below the surface ills—the ills to which the drug industry, whether legal or clandestine, addresses itself so assiduously and so effectively. If what our possessing nations are confronted by is indeed a loss of *meaning* (and the most astute diagnosticians of the age have been saying that for decades now),[11] then there will be little to be gained by offering the usual opiates, "religion," as Marx rightly said, being the most familiar of these. Only if Christians can go down into the depths that opiates cannot reach will they become "serious" (Kierkegaard) enough to open themselves to the radical new word that is gospel.

The truth, dear friends, is this: We are shallow! Not "frivolous" (Kierkegaard), I think, but shallow. We must go deeper—much, much deeper. If we are to become visible again, or anew, we must "swallow some darkness"![12] We have been satisfied with the superficial, the routine. We've replaced thought with ideas, wisdom with six-minute meditations, theology with slogans and sentiment. No one is to blame; everyone is to blame. It is not that our leaders are bad priests or banal preachers; it is only that they have inherited social functions that contain their own inner logic, their own agendas, their own daily demands. They are busy with

11. See, e.g., the analysis of my McGill University colleague Charles Taylor in *A Secular Age*, especially part 3, pp. 299ff.

12. I am using here a wonderful poem by the Swedish poet Tomas Tranströmer: "Friends, You drank some darkness and became visible." See the poem "Elegy," in Tranströmer, *The Half-Finished Heaven*.

the inherited business of Christendom. It is no longer a lively or even an interesting business, but it comes together with its own well-rehearsed demands and duties. Most Christian leadership today is undertaken seriously and conscientiously by ministers, teachers, and administrators schooled in the duties of established religion, and drawing upon centuries of its organizational refinement.

Gospel, however, is another matter altogether. It does not ask first whether church finances are in order or community relationships congenial or parishioners contented and active. To be sure, the vocation to proclaim gospel does not despise good order and decency, but its first concern is understanding of the character of the human predicament and the quest for a truth that is searing enough and modest enough to speak to that predicament. It is far more important that a candidate for the Christian ministry should himself or herself be exposed to the "shock of non-being" (Tillich) than that he or she should be indoctrinated in the latest "leadership skills." It is far more important that the preacher should himself or herself have experienced (and still be experiencing!) the grace of sin's forgiveness than that he or she should achieve a reputation for 'pastoral counselling.'

Even to *hear* gospel—to say nothing of proclaiming it—those of us who have been conditioned by fifteen centuries' Christendom will have to start all over again, at the beginning, where "the Word of God" is both strange and new (Barth).

The second most salient reason why the once-established churches fail as heralds of gospel is perhaps more complex even than the first. The plain truth is that nearly all the language of gospel, including the word *gospel* itself, has been taken over lock, stock, and barrel by "evangelicalism"—or whatever it may call itself (everyone knows what is meant)!

With the near collapse of theological seriousness and refinement, which was sustained by the remnants of classical Protestantism, biblical and traditional religious language was subjected to a process of simplification and sloganization that would have astonished Jonathan Edwards and the learned divines of our Protestant past. Key concepts of the faith were reduced to formulaic ideas lacking in depth and incapable of dialectic. The advent of electronic media that favored instant communication and deplored nuance ensured that religious discourse in the public realm, so far as it existed at all, would be brought down to the most immediately graspable thoughts—thoughts that could be expressed in sound bites. The two-hour sermons of eighteenth-century American Congregationalism, bristling with scriptural references and employing the high-flown language of Calvin and the Enlightenment, would not only have to be rejected by the modern media; they would not be *comprehended* by modern audiences. But without a modicum of linguistic sophistication, religious thought is inevitably turned into formulae, code language, and finally . . . entertainment. Mysteries as profound as the crucifixion of the incarnate Word cannot be talked around in sermonettes! Reduced to portable lists (like the five so-called Fundamentals of the Niagara Conferences of the late nineteenth century), originally profound doctrines sound like jokes to contemporary ears. They *are* jokes! But when such "jokes" take over the religious realm, and when (as in the United States today) these jokes can occupy the revered attention of millions of "true believers," those for whom the language of gospel is not in the least jocular are left wondering how they can use that language now, without betraying at once themselves, their traditions, and the thinking public they hope to address.

For example, how can serious Christians in North America today employ a term like *rebirth* without conjuring up a whole religious ideology, complete with stage directions, that is inimical to the truth they want to profess? When an extraordinarily large percentage of the American public claims a born-again status for itself; and when what this means for most, apparently, is a rhetorically dramatic personal religious experience, perhaps clearly datable, perhaps entailing glossolalia, perhaps including spectacular physical healing, and certainly separating off its recipients from all who cannot claim such ecstasies, yet manifesting in the reborn few or no discernable changes in lifestyle, political affiliation, or economic assumptions (nay, in all likelihood hardening in them the most questionable racial, creedal, political, sexual and other assumptions)—when, I ask, *rebirth* connotes such specific results as these, how, in this context, can it be used meaningfully to connote profound biblical teachings as repentance, justification by grace through faith, the simultaneity of sin and justification (*simul justus et peccator*), the inclusivity of divine love ("there is no longer Jew or Greek, there is no longer slave or free, there is no longer male or female" [Gal 3:28])? How can even the term *gospel* be employed by mainline Christians on this continent when for the majority of those using this term, the gospel is reducible to "fundamentals" or to sentimentalism, or to pathetic little greeting-card ideas that are only slightly more sophisticated than gross superstition?

Apropos this difficulty (and in a spirit of confession), I had to conduct a long argument with myself over the decision whether or not to title this book *Waiting for Gospel*. For I know that this title will please some whom I have no wish to please—for instance those who have always known that the old Protestant mainline had given up on gospel long ago! I am aware that such persons might well feel vindicated by the confessions of a so-called mainstream theologian who now, apparently, has chosen to adopt *their* language. This has indeed been part of the fate of Karl Barth, whose biblical language and concern have caused many American evangelicals to rank him as one of their own, despite the fact that Barth's theology is a far cry from evangelicalism. In my opinion, the evangelical, biblicist, fundamentalist takeover of biblical and theological language is one of the most deplorable aspects of contemporary North American Christianity. It constitutes an almost insurmountable barrier to all thoughtful Christian theology that wishes to be true to the best insights of biblical scholarship, Reformation theology, and sound theological work during the past century and more. One doubts that European and other Christians can appreciate fully the extreme difficulty of speaking about gospel today in a context as self-righteously and simplistically Christian as that of the United States of America (with its inevitable spill over into sectors of vulnerability in Canada and elsewhere).

This *apologetic* dilemma, however should not lead to neglect or silence on the part of those who attempt to preserve or recover Protestant Christianity in its best and most indispensable aspects. *Gospel, evangelical, rebirth, repentance, justification, obedience, grace, sin,* and hundreds of other biblical as well as historically important concepts like *sola Scriptura, atonement, Trinity, revelation, theologia crucis / theologia gloriae,* and the like belong to the very essence of Christian faith, and any attempt to jettison them, however understandable in the face of their public misuse, constitutes a diminution of the faith. Those who feel that Christianity will escape the winnowing of Western civilization by accentuating some of the more notable *ethical* or generally *spiritual* associations of this faith are sadly deluded. It is the *core* of the faith that must be preserved if anything recognizably Christian is to endure. The point then, I contend, is not to behave as if these ancient biblical and historical categories were optional.

It is rather to find ways of thinking, speaking, and writing about them that at once puzzles and intrigues those who are . . . *waiting for gospel.*

In this connection, it is one of the most unfortunate eventualities of recent church history that the work of the greatest theologians and biblical scholars of the first part of the twentieth century has had so little lasting effect on Christianity in North America. To be sure, a handful of Christians (mainly professionals) remember the names of Reinhold and Richard Niebuhr, John Coleman Bennett, Paul Tillich, Dietrich Bonhoeffer, Rudolf Bultmann, Helmut Thielicke, Karl Barth, Suzanne de Dietrich, and others of their generation; but for the most part this blossoming of Protestant theology, which for sheer brilliance rivals the Reformation and outshines even the High Middle Ages, was practically shunted aside on this continent and counts for very little in ecclesiastical discourse today. Its neglect (or was it dismissal?) was due to a great many factors in our common life: the anti-intellectualism (dumbing down) of our religion; the failure of preachers to *read* most of the more serious works; the short-lived character of anything "new" in our fast-moving culture; the failure of North Americans to *contextualize* theologies made in Europe; the fact that so much of this thought was antithetical to the optimistic outlook of the New World; the takeover of programmatic theologies in the 1960s and beyond, and on and on. The neglect of this theological renewal is a matter of sorrow, however, because *had we listened to these* (wrongly called) *Neo-Orthodox thinkers, we might have learned how to do justice to the great and most essential elements of our faithwithout having to capitulate to American evangelicalism—or to silence!* For they could talk about traditional biblical and historical Christian concepts without reducing them to simplism. Tillich could describe justification by grace through faith in a way that could make that primary Protestant teaching accessible to modern people. See his sermon "You Are Accepted," if you doubt that assertion.[13] Barth could speak of rebirth without any of the semimagical or excessively ecstatic connotations that it has in today's evangelical circles. Bonhoeffer could describe costly grace and its relation to the cross of Jesus Christ without acting as though Anselm of Canterbury (in a boiled-down form!) had had the last word on the subject. And Reinhold Niebuhr could write (daily!) on the ubiquity of human sin without reducing the whole of hamartiology to peccadillos of the bedroom.

13. Tillich, *The Shaking the Foundations*, 153–63.

Because we paid so little attention to these 'remembered voices'[14], and instead, in our preaching and public rhetoric, continued to concern ourselves with 'topics' and 'local pastoralia,' and psychobabble, we did not learn how to speak about gospel without always using the word *gospel*, or rebirth without using the word *rebirth*, or sin without moralism, or grace without sentiment, or heaven without science-ignoring make-believe.

But it is still not too late to learn such lessons!

Two Specific Problems

We could begin by recognizing two problems that pinpoint quite concretely, I believe, the failure of liberal and moderate Protestantism to address the human quest for gospel: 1) the substitution of moral or ethical counsel for gospel; and 2) the neglect of personal life in favor of attention to the public sphere.

Law is Not Gospel!

At their best, the liberal churches in North America have concentrated on social and political problems that surely ought to be the concern of every responsible citizen—and every serious Christian! Problems of the environment, world peace, economic justice, race, ethnicity, gender, public health, and the like need to be high on the agenda of every Christian community.

The unfortunate side of this concentration, however, is that it too often becomes the whole reason for church life and existence. The language of the church becomes *primarily* the language of exhortation. We shout about justice and peace; we insist people should be more inclusive; we plead for greater environmental concern; we deplore the extent, still today, of racism; we decry homophobia; we press for greater compassion in social programs, medical care, education, and so forth. Let me be quite clear: I am not asking for less activism. To the contrary, compared with churches that escape into liturgy or personal spirituality or tradition or innovation, Christians who *act* (and act for "Justice, Peace and the Integrity

14. See my book *Remembered Voices*.

of Creation")[15] must be recognized as being "not far from the kingdom of God" *even if 'the usual language of religion' is missing in such.*

It remains, however, that law (even when it is not called law; even when it is contextually pertinent) *is not gospel.* At best it is the *consequence* of gospel. Gospel requires the *indicative, not the imperative mood.* As every parent knows, imperatives ("Do this!" "Don't do that!") *always* incite in their hearers the question, why? Activist preachers who believe that their congregations are just waiting every Sunday to be told, once again, what they must, should, and really ought to be doing, simply have not heard the deafening *why?* that is being shouted (silently, of course) by the polite people in front of them.

For good reason the Reformers insisted that *gospel precedes law*, and it is gospel, not law (whether in traditional or contemporary form) that we are first called to proclaim. To be sure, law, as Calvin insisted, *God's law*, is implicit in gospel.[16] If what is heard is truly gospel, it will issue in obedience to God's law—or at leas approximations of such. But law, on the other hand, is *not* implicitly gospel; on the contrary, the constant iteration of the imperative only demonstrates how far human beings are from the perfection our Creator asks of us, and therefore, in the sensitive, only reinforces the guilt we feel as we contemplate our actual estate. In today's skeptical apologetic atmosphere, it also tends to increase incredulity; for few can believe that the truly rigorous laws of God (beginning with the law of love!) can be attained by our efforts. And, as Jesus constantly insisted, what God requires of us is not simply the right act but the right motivation; and motive is built on foundations far deeper and stronger than exhortation. It is built, for Christians, on gospel.

In order for human beings (that is, sinners, whose egocentrism and implicit skepticism are notorious) to be turned towards their fellow creatures with something like love in their hearts (so the Reformers insisted) a radical transformation is needed: scripturally it is called *metanoia*, a near-complete turnaround. That is what gospel is all about. And where gospel is missing law, however reasonable, relevant, and requisite it may be, can accomplish nothing by way of such transformation. The law of God, Jesus said, is summed up in the commandment to love God fully and one's

15. The title of the World Council of Churches' program throughout the 1980s.

16. The essays of the third part of this book assume just that affirmation, as the subtitle states explicitly.

neighbor "as oneself"; and Jesus knew just as well as did Paul that *such love* cannot be engendered by commandment. Love—whether it means the love of one's closest friend or of one's community or nation or of the planet Earth (or, ah!, one's enemy!)—requires a movement of the soul (*psyche*) that is so radical that it may be compared to being born all over again—a possibility, incidentally, that even the rather slow-witted among Jesus's disciples recognized as being humanly impossible and absurd. But, said Jesus (Matt 19:26), "with God all things are possible."—even the reorientation toward the good of an inveterately selfish and perverse soul.

It is precisely this *divine* possibility—the grace of human transformation—that our ancient denominations are being asked to contemplate, study, and pray for! Can we confess—do we even *profess?*—the possibility of gospel? Are we stuck with halfhearted or bold or stirring or boring regurgitation of Law—which however new and relevant it may be is still law? Can we through authentically theological, biblical, and spiritual renewal recover the sense of evangelical urgency that inspired the initial Protestant reformation and later movements of regeneration here and there? There are many—many!—still, in this "secular age" (Charles Taylor) who do not and cannot hear gospel from the Christian Right and are waiting to see what may become, finally, of the classical Protestant alternative. Is it reasonable to expect gospel from that sector? From the edges of the dominant culture will these old churches be able at least to rise from their own dry bones and announce *kerygma* that can stir significant minorities within our midst to open themselves to kind of change that is more radical than all the radical *ethical imperatives* put together: a change of human perception and expectation?

A Failure of Dialectic: The Individual and the Body

Biblical thought maintains a quite consistent and balanced dialectic of concern for the individual and concern for the collectivity (the church, the world, humankind, etc.). But it would appear that historical Christianity fluctuates uncertainly between these two poles of faith's concern, emphasizing one or the other of them rather than showing their interaction, tension, and dialogue. An overemphasis on the collective in some powerful strains of post-Reformation Protestantism led to a reaction in the eighteenth and nineteenth centuries, and in the early decades of the twentieth—individuals took over the spotlight with such heart-tugging sentiments as "the ultimate value of the human personality." Almost predictably, the most provocative theological reflection of the twentieth century, especially following the political tensions of the First World War, was at least in part a reaction to the personalism and privatism of much Liberal-Pietist theology. The Social Gospel was already an early aspect of this reaction. The most formative events of the era (two world wars preceded by and intermingled with an economic catastrophe) reminded thoughtful Christians of the fact that individual life is lived in a socio-political context, and that no private suffering can be understood, let alone healed, apart from attention to the "spirit of the age" (*Zeitgeist*) and the machinations of the powerful. As a wise woman once reminded a seminar that I was leading in Atlanta some years ago, personal life is profoundly and immediately affected by societal conditions. She had made it her business to assume primary care for some twelve older women of her acquaintance and, she said, "If I follow even one of my old ladies around for twenty-four hours, I encounter all the problems of our society at large."

There can be no disputing the truth of such an observation. Nevertheless, the opposite overemphasis and neglect is also possible, namely, that the Christian community may become so undialectically attentive to social issues that the life of the person is sorely neglected. This, I suggest, is what has occurred in many liberal-activist Christian circles in our own time. Many churches—perhaps the most engaged of all the Protestant denominations—have been so concentrated on the needs and possibilities of collectivities that they fail to speak to individual persons, including their own members, who are never just members of a specific race, gender, economic stratum, or marginalized majority, but are human beings who must live and die, for the most part, *alone*. Christian activism achieves many honorable social goals—the betterment of economic conditions for the poor, the greater acceptance of difference, and the like; but it fails often and perhaps characteristically to speak of the loneliness, foreboding, hopelessness, and emptiness in the lives of individuals.

It may seem an odd thing to claim, but it seems to me that in many ways it is *easier* to address social ills than to speak meaningfully to the individual person. To be sure, confronting the terribly entrenched assumptions of unchecked capitalism or racial superiority or male chauvinism or homophobia requires great courage. I have no wish to minimize that courage. The theologies of liberation that have helped non-Caucasian persons in our White-dominated society to experience a new sense of worth; the Gay Pride marches that have helped homosexually oriented men and women to slough off the humiliation they have had to endure for centuries; the various (and extremely difficult!) attempts of Christians and others in North America to create better conditions for our own First Nations peoples: all such causes deserve the support and encouragement of every serious Christian.

Despite the challenges that must be confronted in the struggle for a more just society, however, the Christian vocation to speak to the great, subtle, recurrent, and permanent problems of personal life requires an even deeper commitment—one that is intellectually more rigorous and spiritually more sympathetic. While for most of us there are indeed joys and laughter and moments of great happiness, human life is also filled with sorrow and pain at every stage, from childhood through to old age and death. The excruciating struggle for survival, which is both physical and spiritual, is often carried on by ordinary people quite silently, for, especially in our rhetorically upbeat society, there is a strong pressure on individuals to seem content and in charge even when they are decidedly not so. It is said that one in four persons in our comparatively affluent and healthy society is clinically depressed. Great social problems such as poverty, crime, drug addiction, suicide and the like, may and must certainly be studied objectively and addressed by legislation and public action. But behind each of these immense social problems there are individual men, women, and children whose lives *cannot* be studied objectively or addressed by remedial legislation. They are bearers of stories that, no matter how common may be the themes and patterns of them, are never simply commonplace—never easily namable as "the human condition" or "human nature." Great novels and films take us into these unique lives in a way that no social science can do. So it is not for nothing that literature and the arts have become newly interesting to the most imaginative and searching theology in our time. The life of the human person is so mysterious, so poignant, and often so filled with pathos that biblical faith stands in awe of it. "God created man," says the great Jewish author of our age, Elie Wiesel, "because He likes stories."[17] But far from being a flippant or merely quotable *bon mot*, Wiesel's intention here is identical with that

17. Wiesel, *The Gates of the Forest*, frontispiece.

of the Bible: "What *is* man [the human being] that thou art mindful of him?" (Ps 8:4, KJV) The biblical God, as one may say, is so much in awe of his creature—and more particularly at the suffering such a creature must endure—that he asks himself whether this alleged pinnacle of creation might not have been a mistake—or experiment that went too far, because it asked far too much of its subject. The story of the great flood is no primitive tale, and it is not primarily about an *angry* God, though it is perhaps about a God who is angry with himself. It shares with the expulsion from the garden, David's anguish over the slaying of Absalom, the trials of Job, the psalms of lament, the crucifixion of Jesus, and much else, the Scripture's most hidden (yet in subtle ways most insistent) question: Is a creature as self-conscious and as fragile as humankind possible—without disaster, without tragedy, without dismal failure? For unlike the creatures that "seek their meat from God," living by ingrained, unerring instinct, the human creature *knows* its condition with remarkable, fearful clarity. It knows on the one hand that it ought somehow to affirm and make good (fulfill) its creaturehood (even the faithless know this!), yet it also knows that an ever present question mark is written over all its achievements, however good, beautiful, and true. "For all flesh is as grass, and all the glory of man as the flower of grass. The grass withereth, and the flower thereof falleth away . . ." (1 Pet 1:24, KJV).

The Christian gospel must speak to this *permanent* dilemma of human being, and not only to the social ills that occur in specific historical contexts. Can this gospel address the human sense of futility ("vanity," emptiness) of which "the Preacher" (in the book of Ecclesiastes) speaks so eloquently? Can it provide for mortals some hints of *purpose* that can at least challenge their innate cynicism and melancholy? Is there any divine antiphon to counteract and relieve, in Wordsworth's phrase, "the still, sad music of humanity"? Can the youths who are just now, as I write, burning houses and busses and cars in London be made to feel by some hearing of gospel that they *do* have a future, even if their future in this world will always, perhaps, be vastly uncertain? Is our gospel profound enough to reach the psychic depths of those who are starving today in Sudan or Somalia? Even when the West fails them, will the God the West has worshipped (and denied!) come to their aid? Can old people, alone and neglected in cities that do not even know of their existence, find comfort in the gospel of the cross?

It is, I think, this *personal* side of the dialectic of "the member" and "the body" (Romans 12; 1 Corinthians 12) that calls for our greatest faith and theological acumen. If our gospel addresses only collectivities, we must ask ourselves whether it is yet gospel. There is an uncanny link between the tendency of liberal Christian activism to accentuate imperatives (law) and its failure to address the fundamental human problems of identity, meaning, and vocation. "What are human beings *for*?"[18] If we cannot speak to the great questions of ontology (What does it mean to *be*?) and teleology (Does human being have any credible purpose?), then our answers to the question of the Good (i.e., our ethic) will always remain superficial and foundationless—even if we "give our bodies to be burned" (cf. 1 Cor 13:3)!

Conclusion

It is tempting for me, as it is for many committed and serious Christians known to me, to give up on the churches. Many have done so publicly, conspicuously; many more do so quietly and without fanfare, simply voting with their feet. Yet however tempted I may be to follow them, I cannot do so, in the end. Whatever folly and vice Christendom may have caused in two millennia of history, whatever insipidities it may represent in its present, reduced state, the church, in a variety of shapes and sizes and guises, has been for many a bearer of a message of grace, truth, and hope in a world that is often bleak. I know this, because it has been such also for me. I became a Christian in a serious way because I heard in and around this unlikely community of faith and unfaith what came to me as *gospel* and changed my life. As I confessed in a recent book,[19] I first heard this gospel in a compelling way through the life and witness of a young minister who saw in the callow and introspective youth that I was, a certain potential for understanding and service. Later I heard the same gospel from my great teachers at Union Theological Seminary in the 1950s: so powerfully did they, collectively, build on my insipient understanding of this faith that more than sixty years later I am still learning from them. I have only to read one of Paul Tillich's or Paul Scherer's sermons, or a few paragraphs of Reinhold Niebuhr (e.g., in his *Beyond Tragedy*) to be

18. See the important book of Wendell Berry, *What Are People For?*
19. See my book *The Messenger*.

reminded of the enthusiasm with which I received their ideas decades ago. I have heard gospel, too, in countless great theological works of the past—in Augustine, Aquinas, Luther, Calvin, Kierkegaard, Barth, and other writers with whom, as a teacher of the history of Christian thought, I have lived quite intimately. I have heard that gospel too in the speeches, writings, and lectures of my more articulate contemporaries—Phyllis Trible, Walter Brueggemann, Dorothee Soelle, Barbara Brown Taylor, Jürgen Moltmann, Friedrich Hufendiek, Kosuke Koyama, Gregory Baum, Jon Sobrino, David Bentley Hart, Marit Trelsted, Patricia Kirkpatrick, and many others. I have heard it, here and there, in unexpected places, and often in times when I had grown jaded or dejected and looked only for the commonplace.

And if I had not heard it, and heard it again and again, I would certainly not have become—and remained—what I gladly confess I am: a Christian. The imperatives of the activists might have pricked my conscience or inspired periodic outbursts of well-doing. Good liturgy, pageantry, and music would have sent me to church occasionally—especially during the high festival seasons. Personal and family occasions—the rites of passage—would likely have ensured that I would not have turned my back completely on this faith of my fathers and mothers. Along with almost the majority of my fellow citizens, I'd probably have told the census takers, decade after decade, that I was Christian and a Protestant. But none of these conventions and affiliations would have kept me Christian in anything but name. Only gospel could do that. Only the faith that "comes by hearing" (Rom 10:17) has made me a lifelong listener to the unique and intriguing story that is told in the continuity of the biblical texts—for me, as for many, past and present, "the greatest story every told," because it touches *my* story and gives me a past and a future that my story, by itself, could never produce.

For that reason, I cannot join my contemporaries who turn their backs on Christianity and the strange admixture of faith and folly called the church. My own faith is mixed with folly too, and worse faults; but in all that I have written and taught I have wanted to remind all who live in some proximity to the Christian movement that the gospel, carried so precariously in this "earthen vessel" (cf. 2 Cor 4:7) is worthy of the greatest efforts of mind and spirit that human beings can muster. Without gospel, the churches are little more than the insubstantial remnants or rumors of past spiritual forms and preferences, ineffectual and often pathetic ghosts of other ages and generations. As such, their reduction and possible disappearance can cause a certain nostalgia in all of us; but only if they can still appear now and then bearers of "glad tidings of great joy" (Luke 2:10) can their present-day humiliations and losses become the source of deep sorrow—*and of the courage to change, still, what can be changed* (Reinhold Niebuhr).

The Essays

The thirteen essays assembled here, most of them revised versions of recent papers or lectures, are all grouped around that single aim: that is, they are intended to stimulate and refine the courage to seize the present metamorphosis of Christendom and let it become, in truth, what its best representatives have always striven for: the messenger of gospel!

The essays are arranged in three sections representative of three stages in the discernment of gospel. The first group, under the heading **The Mystery and Meaning of Gospel**, addresses questions of a preliminary nature; that is, they (1) take up the theme begun in the introduction ("The Mystery of Gospel"); (2) explore the nature of theology as the "service-science" of gospel ("Theology and the Quest for Gospel"); (3) consider the character of truth, biblically and theologically understood ("Who Can Say It as It Is?: Karl Barth on the Bible"); and (4) inquire about the present state of the Christian movement in a post-Christendom world ("Where in the World Are We?")

The second grouping, under the heading **The Basics of Gospel**, contains essays that consider four of what I regard as the most rudimentary—as well as the most contextually pressing—aspects of the Christian message: (1) "The Identity of Jesus Christ in a Pluralistic Society"; (2) "The Theology of the Cross: A Useable Past"; (3) "The Identity and Meaning of the Self"; and (4) "What Are People For?: Stewardship as Human Vocation."

The third grouping is titled **The Law within Gospel**. It concerns some of the most salient ethical and practical questions facing the churches today: (1) the relation between gospel and ethic/law ("Beyond Good and Evil"); (2) the nature of Christian ethics ("The Ethics of Participation: Dietrich Bonhoeffer"); (3) the relation of Christianity to power ("Christianity and Empire"); and (4) Christian ecumenism and its implications for interfaith dialogue ("Many Churches, Many Faiths, One Planet"); and (5) appropriate and inappropriate forms of Christian witness ("A Latter-Day Kierkegaardian Attends a Megachurch").

PART 1

The Meaning
and Mystery of "Gospel"

1

The Mystery of the Gospel

Pray also for me, so that when I speak, a message may be given to me to make known with boldness the mystery of the gospel, for which I am an ambassador in chains. —EPHESIANS 6:19–20 (NRSV)

The Gospel as Mystery

"THE MYSTERY OF THE gospel"! This intriguing phrase leapt off the page as I was reading (in a rather desultory way, I confess) this famous passage of Scripture. Is the gospel then really a . . . "mystery"—*mysterion?* For many of our contemporaries, it would seem, such an idea would have to be accounted strange. An entire segment of the Christian religion in North America—perhaps the largest segment, certainly the noisiest one— experiences the gospel not as mystery but as the plain truth, capable of statement in straightforward propositions: in doctrines and formulae and slogans; in fundamentals that can be named with as much certitude as proven scientific data; in unchanging dogmas that can be imbibed by the faithful and proclaimed everywhere without regard for the diverse circumstances in which they are announced. But the biblical author speaks of the gospel as "mystery," and it is clear from its context that he is not using the term casually or merely out of pious reverence for established religious language. His reference to the gospel's mystery suggests, rather, a high degree of both personal modesty and sensitivity to the ever changing circumstances of his hearers. The Apostle does not think of himself as already possessing the truth he is called to proclaim. Were that the case, he would hardly have to ask his Ephesian readers earnestly to pray that he might receive inspiration and understanding at the point of need. Nor does he assume that messages he has delivered before (and so often!) will be right for this present occasion. Gospel is always new. Old sermons—as all of us know who in desperation or indolence have resorted to them!—are never satisfactory, never quite appropriate, always a little . . . embarrassing.

Were the phrase "the mystery of the gospel" to be found anywhere but in Holy Scripture (say, in the writings of some allegedly liberal theologian!) those who regard themselves as the most vigilant custodians of the gospel in our society would be quick to pounce upon it. They would probably quote other Scripture to prove their point—for example, Galatians 1:8: "though we, or an angel from heaven, preach any other gospel unto you, than that which we have preached, let him be accursed."[1] This is a

---

1. This particular passage has inspired many (usually very conservative) doctrinal and ethical studies, tracts, and movements—as the reader will discover by consulting the Internet under the heading, "No Other Gospel." One of the most popular of recent movements of this kind occurred in Dortmund, Germany, in 1966, under the banner '*Kein anderes Evangelium*'. It was organized by American evangelical groups with some input from Europeans, and its special target was the theology of Rudolf Bultmann and Ernst Käsemann. Predictably enough, the organizers sought the endorsement of Karl Barth. Barth's response to them ought to serve as a model for all Christians who wish to preserve what is great and good in the biblical and theological traditions of the church, while refusing to allow them to be used in the service of a traditional-*ism* that impedes *gospel* for the here-and-now.

> Are you willing and ready," asks the old Barth of these gospel enthusiasts, "to start and attend a similar 'movement' and 'great demonstration' against the wish to supply the West German army with atomic weapons; against the war in Vietnam and against the way in which the Americans allied with the West Germans lead this war; against the outbreaks of a new phase of Antisemitism in West Germany. [Are you willing and ready to support] peaceful negotiations with eastern European states, including the acceptance of the borders which have existed since 1945?
>
> If your right confession of the Lord, crucified and risen according to the scriptures, does include and comprehend these things, then it is a good, precious and faithful confession. If it does not include and provide a rationale for these things, then, despite its [doctrinal] correctness, it is not right, but a dead, cheap, gnat-sieving, camel-swallowing statement, that is, a pharisaic confession.
>
> That is what I have to say to the 'happening' in the Westfalen Hall in Dortmund on the 6th of March. (As reported in *Der Spiegel*).

favorite verse among all those who believe that they have already deciphered whatever mystery may be associated with the gospel, and that alternative readings of the Christian message are anathema.

Yet it is not only Christian fundamentalists and the ultraconservative who should find a phrase like "the mystery of the gospel" baffling or provocative. We all, if we pause to reflect on the phrase, are surely somewhat surprised by it. For after two thousand years of Christian rhetoric—two thousand years of (sometimes even attentive!) Bible reading; two thousand years of familiar or somewhat familiar doctrinal debate, two thousand years of theology—we, especially, who work at all this professionally, hear a term like *the gospel* without pause or puzzlement, simply assuming that we know pretty well what is meant. It doesn't seem to us to be terribly mysterious. To the contrary, it belongs to the language we expect to hear and to use in and around churches, seminaries, and ecclesiastical councils.

Part of the problem (a rather large part, I suspect) has to do with the definite article. The definite article can be very . . . definite. When we hear the term *the gospel*, we are apt (if we give it a thought) to conjure up a rather definitive body of ideas, historical references, words, phrases, claims. We liberal and moderate Christians, unlike the more doctrinally explicit segments of Christendom, may be somewhat vague as to particulars; but for most of *us* too, *the gospel* suggests a given something or other, a package deal, a set of concepts that we could, if we were asked to, set down in words, ideas, illustrations, moral directives, and so on. Yes, for us too the phrase "the *mystery* of the gospel" must be considered an unusual expression—hopefully, it could be unusual *enough* to prove provocative. It could even cause us to ask again in all seriousness . . .

What *Is* Gospel?

Let us think for a moment about this word *without* the definite article: *gospel, godspell*. It originated with the late medieval attempt of English-speaking Christians to find an adequate English equivalent of the Greek word, *euangellion:* evangel, good news, good message. Or perhaps "glad [or good] tidings"—as in the sixty-first chapter of Isaiah, which Jesus himself quoted in his inaugural sermon at Nazareth, applying it specifically to himself and his mission: "The Spirit of the Lord is upon me, because he has anointed me to bring *good tidings* to the poor . . . , to proclaim release to the captives . . . recovery of sight to the blind . . . liberation of the oppressed . . . the year of the Lord's favor" (Luke 4:18–19). Glad tidings. Good News.

This hardly suggests that *Gospel* is the nomenclature for a theological formula or a codification of religious truths. Nor does it sound like a moral code. The words *preach* and *sermon* have moralistic connotations for most people because, alas, that is how preaching has been used—as a form of exhortation, cajolement, pep-talk. If you listen carefully to the linguistic mood of most sermons, you almost invariably find that they are full of *should*s and *ought*s and *must*s: laying down the law, sometimes bombastically, more often today nicely, with gentle persuasion—but still, the law. It is not accidental that preaching, for most people, connotes admonition: "Don't preach at me! Don't sermonize!" we tell those who would have us alter our ways. But for the New Testament the proclamation of gospel in the biblical sense is a completely different matter—in fact it's almost the antithesis of laying down the law—as we can see in the Isaiah passage Jesus quoted. It's more nearly a matter of *releasing* people from the law— social laws, penal systems, economic laws, moral laws, gender and sexual laws, dehumanizing ideologies, conventions and man-made injunctions by which human beings have been falsely bound.

More important, gospel is not in the first place something that *we* do, either as preachers or preached-to, but something that has been done for us (*pro nobis*) by a just, gracious, and loving God. As George Buttrick, the unforgettable twentieth-century preacher of Madison Avenue Presbyterian Church in New York City, used to tell us in his homiletics classes, the whole mood of the sermon should be "The most wonderful thing has happened!"—not (as so many sermons seem to have it) "You had better get to work, you underachievers, and make something wonderful happen!"—make yourself into that superb individual the promotional language of our officially optimistic society insists you should be, or that you think you really are, underneath it all! Gospel is always in the *indicative*, not the *imperative* mood. It assumes an activity, an event, a new or greatly altered condition that precedes us and has already transformed our real situation, appearances notwithstanding. Our task as ambassadors of this gospel is to formulate it in a manner that speaks to the minds and hearts of those to whom we address ourselves—or at least does not get in the way of their hearing. We cannot bring about that hearing in others;

when it occurs, it is always in reality the work of the divine Spirit, who causes our poor words to testify to a Word that we can in no sense manipulate. Yet, for all that, our words matter.

As such, Gospel is always *news!*—and never just *yesterday's* news. Moreover, it is always *good* news! But of course news is only good when it confronts or engages whatever it is in our lives that seems wrong, demeaning, fearful, enslaving, humiliating, debilitating. To be "*glad* tidings of great joy" gospel must take on that in one's life that keeps reducing one to fatalism, future-shock, sadness, or perhaps just to a quiet, unspoken sorrow that colors all we think and do. To be *good* news, gospel must confront and do battle with the *bad* news.

Ergo: whoever wants to become the *bearer* of good news must know, as intimately as possible, the bad news that is just now, in this place, this time, this community at work keeping human beings in their various kinds of prisons. And of course *the bad news always keeps changing.* It is never the same from one time to the next, from one place to the next, from one person to the next. Never quite the same. Every sensitive pastor knows this. And therefore he knows that he must find different words, different messages, for different occasions. The minister's message for a bereaved family will be very different from her message at a wedding reception. She will not preach easy forgiveness to a congregation caught indulging in flagrant racial bigotry, any more than she will proclaim divine wrath to a community struck low by tragedy or illness. As the most contextually sensitive theologian of our epoch, Reinhold Niebuhr, used to counsel students for ministry, "Comfort the afflicted, and afflict the comfortable." The good pastor understands intuitively what the Preacher of Ecclesiastes means when in the beautiful third chapter of that treatise he recites the great variety of "times"—experience, events, spiritual states—through which human beings pass. Nearly every message can be appropriate, he says, *in its season,* but woe betide the preacher who does not know what season it is!

It's the same in the public realm, essentially, as in the personal realm. The church must forever attempt (and it can only be an attempt, ever; we will never get it entirely right) to "discern the signs of the times" (Matt 16:3). Jesus was very hard on some of his contemporary religionists because, he said, they seemed clueless about the world in which they were actually living. You can read the sky and tell whether it is going to rain or not, he told them, but you appear incapable of discerning the signs of the times—of sensing, at some profound level, the *Zeitgeist*, the spirit of the age.

This charge could be made against the church throughout the ages, and still today. For the greatest temptation of Christians is to proclaim, as gospel, messages that were hammered out in the past, in response to the perceived problems of another age, or another place, and thus to perpetuate the notion that the human condition today is no different from what it was a hundred or a thousand years ago. In this way, churches not only avoid the difficult business of discerning the signs of their own times, but they also fail to speak to those who are most affected by the spiritual malaise of their times. In the name of hardened moral conventions and theological dogma that they insist must remain always and everywhere the same, they hide the light of the *gospel* under a bushel of "tradition." For to be truly *good* news the gospel of "Jesus Christ and him crucified" (1 Cor 2:2) must address *today*, *hic et nunc*, those who are being crucified by events, attitudes, and evils that are always, as the scriptural context of this text insists, deeply concealed—concealed, often enough, beneath apparent goods! It requires enormous wisdom ("be wise as serpents"!—Matt 10:16) to delve beneath the surface of the social contexts in which we find ourselves, with a view to comprehending the underlying spiritual causes of the human dilemma. But only those who make this effort will be given the insight, now and then, to articulate in words and deeds messages deserving of the name *gospel*.

Such a one was Heinrich Grueber, the dean of the Berlin Cathedral in the 1930s, who, because he dared to expose *himself* to the evil implicit in Adolf Hitler's racial policies, openly declared: "The *gospel* for today is that Jesus Christ was a Jew."[2] This is why, to be appropriate—to be truly *good* news . . .

Gospel Must Always Be Discovered!

We are thinking about the *mystery* of the gospel, and this, I believe, is at the heart of that mystery: namely, that the good news always has to be discovered, rediscovered, received, and articulated ever anew. Gospel is not a once-for-all belief system, a full-blown and unchanging ideology,

2. See Hall, *Thinking the Faith*, 84.

permanent intellectual property of the church. To the contrary, the church is the product of the gospel. That is to say, it *becomes* the church as, and only as, it discovers gospel for itself again and again. Only through its own, often painful rediscovery of gospel is the disciple community made capable of proclaiming 'good news' in its worldly context.

And just this, I repeat, is what constitutes the gospel's essential mystery: that it does not give itself to us as something permanent, something we can possess and haul out of our ecclesiastical pockets like a VISA card whenever we need it. We come to know it only when and as we hear it for ourselves, day after day, age after age, changing context after changing context. "Pray for me, so that when I speak a message *may be given to me* to make known with boldness the mystery of the gospel" (Eph 6:19–20).

All that we can do, really, is to pray—that is, to put ourselves into the position of those who listen, who wait. The church is not an institution of those who feel that they are already *have* ultimate truth. To the contrary, when it is most *real*, the disciple community is a gathering of human beings who are united in their common longing: they are *waiting for gospel*, remembering that they heard it once, hoping against hope to hear it again. And we do this, as Christians, only as we stand together in solidarity with those who most obviously need to hear good news—the very ones Isaiah and Jesus named in that key verse: the poor, the captives, the blind, the oppressed—that is, those most nakedly exposed to the ill winds of their epochs.

To be sure, we have certain clues as to what gospel will sound like, or what it will aim to achieve in our midst. It will always have something to do with truth, compassion, justice, judgment, forgiveness, liberation, peace, hope. It will always be about "making and keeping human life [authentically] human," as Bonhoeffer's friend Paul Lehman put it—about redeeming the essential goodness of creation, about saving the human species from its worst excesses![3]

And so . . . there will always be a cross at the center of it, because none of these things can be achieved without suffering—God's suffering, human suffering, the church's suffering, *our* suffering.

But while these characteristics or "marks" will always be present in what is truly gospel, the specifics of the message—and those who proclaim gospel will always be driven to specificity!—can only be discovered as one

3. See Lehmann, *Ethics in a Christian Context*, 351.

waits and listens. And I do not mean this in a pietistic way, for this waiting and listening is not a matter of passivity; it implies not only constancy of prayer but also the discipleship of intensive study and reflection: study of the Scriptures and theological traditions that testify to remembered truth; reflection upon the texts, the arts, the sciences, and humanities that can help us to "discern the signs of the times"—that can hone the intellect to hear, beneath all the rhetoric and rumble of this noisy technique-driven society, the real questions, struggles, anxieties, longings and fears that are, collectively, the 'bad news' that this 'good news' gospel has to engage and counter.

This is not an easy calling. It will be easier for men and women who (perhaps to their own surprise) find themselves called to be witnesses to this gospel—it will be much easier for such persons to preach homilies full of *must*s and *should*s and *ought to*s, to lace their sermonettes with television-inspired one-liners, to deliver from their pulpits gently challenging admonitions to self-improvement. After all, that's what everybody has come to expect from preachers! It will be easier for them to become "professional Christians" and do all the things that people in their congregations could be doing, often better than they. It will be easier to play the role of the activist or the psychoanalyst or the spiritual court jester than to aspire to "make known with boldness the mystery of the gospel" (Eph 6:19). But their vocation—*our* vocation, as preachers and teachers of this faith—is to acquire the wisdom we need to discern what time it is, and to articulate, as best we can, a message that is worthy of this holy and precious word of our tradition, *gospel*.

And this is the vocation, not only of the priests and teaching elders of the church, but it belongs to the whole church, the whole 'denomination,' the whole ecumenical body of Christians in our much-threatened world. In these avowedly liberal or perhaps respectably moderate old churches of the Protestant mainline, we have lately gained the reputation of being deeply involved in the great causes and issues and culture-wars of our society. Many of us congratulate ourselves on being "on the right side of the issues"—meaning, usually, the leftish side! One need not be ashamed of this. It is certainly better than the kind of conventionality, moral passivity, and predictability of our establishment past.

But we also have the reputation, in these churches, of having nothing much to *say* to our world—or even to one another! We are in many ways tongue-tied churches, messengers without a message, minstrels without a song. Many of us talk a good deal—indeed, as Protestants we are notoriously a chattering folk, to the point that some who find themselves in our midst long for the quietness of Quakers or Benedictines! But it is one thing to talk and another to have something to say! The question that is being put to us in these old, established churches today is precisely whether we have anything to *say*!

Gospel and Speech

With this, I can almost hear the objections of my readers—or some of them. For in these same old churches, these once culturally established religious cults of our continent, we have learned exceptionally well the lessons of our pragmatic and activist New World history and ethos. We are *doers*, and proud of it! Or so we like to tell ourselves. Our rhetoric is full of praise for those who act: Deeds speak louder than words; handsome is as handsome does; those who can, do, whilst those who can't—teach!; Sticks and stones will break my bones, but words will never hurt me!; and so forth. To these and other such self-congratulatory conventions and homespun proverbs of an activistic culture, there has been added of late a rather gauche comparison that one can expect to hear in nearly every political or promotional address: the contrast between those who "talk the talk" and those who "walk the walk." Such simplistic slogans reinforce the existing biases against sustained thought, discussion, serious inquiry, contemplation, and speech that plague our society and make us suspect by every ancient culture (not only the European!) that has learned through bitter experience how inseparable are thought, word and act—every people that has been victimized by actions proceeding from superficial preconceptions and impulses; every tribe that has experienced the manifold ways in which words (racist words, hate literature, class and gender and sexist murmurings) not only *do* hurt us but are the very stuff out of which hurtful *actions* receive their impetus and their power.

No, gospel is not *only* words, thought, speech, ideas, intellectual-spiritual tenets, claims, and the like. Not all the verbosity in the world could form the foundation or establish the new Reality requisite to gospel. Only God's Word, which is infinitely more than words, can give substance— "flesh!"—to the living Truth on which gospel is based and to which it points. Gospel is not *only* words, but it is *also* words. And where words are *missing* acts, however obvious it may seem *to faith* that they proceed from the gospel, remain ambiguous as to their motivation and intention. Jesus not only acted, performing miracles of healing; acts of compassion; deeds of kindness; expressions of solidarity, sympathy, or (sometimes) disapproval and rejection; he also taught, interpreted, explained, reasoned. The Bible does not despise human speech, even though it knows perfectly well that speech, being human, is fallible, limited, and regularly employed for deceitful and dastardly purposes. Yet the prophetic and wisdom traditions of the Judeo-Christian faith give to human speech perhaps the highest potentiality for our imaging of God. This faith presents the Deity as such as a speaking God, *Deus loquens*; and humans make good their creation as *imago Dei* when, their hearts and minds being turned towards their Source and Ground, they speak to God and of God—and in love towards one another. As speaking creatures (*Homo loquens*), humans represent in a priestly way the whole of the less articulate creation: they put into words the gratitude and praise—and the "groaning" (Rom 8:22)—of the creation as a whole It is no wonder, then, that this same Paul, who asks his Ephesian friends to pray that he might really have some *message* capable of becoming gospel, insists that faith itself, when it is genuine, only occurs through the hearing of human language—"But how are they to call upon him in whom they have not believed? And how are they to believe in him of whom they have never heard? And how are they to hear without a preacher?" (Rom 10:14–15).

It is therefore an exceedingly serious matter when there is an impression in the public realm that the churches have nothing to say today. But precisely that impression, I contend, exists—and exists conspicuously—in the public arena today, and even among Christians themselves.

If we ask why this is so, we are thrust into the midst of a complex problem. No single reason can be given for our lack of a distinct or challenging voice, as Christians. It has to do, certainly, with our general humiliation—the decay of Christendom. It has to do too with our sense of shame over past practices, including ecclesiastical actions that are no longer secret or covered by a reputation for beneficence: the clerical sex scandals, the residential schools for native children whom we robbed of their culture and dignity, the always hypocritical homophobia Christian hierarchies have promoted, the support of unchecked capitalism and the military, and many other kinds of obvious sins that are now published abroad for everyone to see. How could we lift our heads to speak after all that! But far more damaging are the subtle and once-simply-assumed roles and relationships with which Western Christendom is inextricably associated in the minds of critics—critics who are no longer just dissatisfied and cynical minorities but major social groupings and even whole populations: compromising roles and relationships with states, economic elites, questionable racist and sexist policymakers, ideologues of Western superiority, colonizers, empires. The Holocaust alone has cast a great shadow over Christianity, not to speak of the myriad other ways in which Christendom aligned itself with the most imperialistic political powers of Western history—*as it was bound to do, so long as it wished to be Christendom, that is, an ancient but corrupt form of Christianity seeking power through proximity to power*! It is hard for Christians today to lift up their voices and speak "with boldness" when they know in their hearts that their own past betrays the wisdom and compassion of the very messages they would like sincerely to convey. And, logically enough, where in the past Christendom has been most powerful; where the church was able to insinuate itself into every nook and cranny of public and private life (as was the case, for instance, in the province of Quebec where I live, prior to about 1960), its remnants are today the most hard pressed, hesitant to speak, virtually reticent. The courage of speech requires a certain confidence, a certain clarity of conscience, a certain freedom from the past and openness to the future; and all such prerequisites are hard to come by in churches that are still this close to the contradictions of Christendom.

These negative experiences, combined with the distrust of speech and anti-intellectualism that has perhaps always been a feature of our New World mentality, is complicated further today by a new—or newly visible—reality: religious plurality. Given the imperialism, exclusivity, expansionism, and proselytism of our Christian past, augmented as it is by present-day "evangelistic" activity that is sometimes even cruder than old Christendom's, sensitive Christians find it almost impossible today to testify to their faith with conviction. In many liberal and moderate circles of Christian belief, there is an almost reverse tendency to refuse any kind of explicit Christian reference. Even in their internal dialogue, many churches manifest a kind of fearfulness lest any specifically Christian language fan the flames of religious bigotry and so contribute to the violence that the gospel of reconciliation hopes to counter. Nervous applications of political correctness have had the effect, in many liberal Protestant circles, of reducing religion to innocuous expressions of a vague spirituality that is as far as possible removed from anything that could be called *kerygma* (proclamation).

It is understandable that a religion that has been as triumphalistic as ours would have to endure a period of humiliation and even shame before it could acquire another mode of being in the world. But that other mode of being will not be achieved by mere silence or the substitution of sentimentality for thought and speech. What is needed is not wordlessness but better words, different words, corrective words—words that can point the way to an alternative way of being the church, and to other ways of comprehending the central tenets of our faith. The triumphalism of our doctrine, our *theologia gloriae*, will not be countered by retreating into silence and rhetorical modesty but only by recovering the *essential* modesty that inheres in a theology that knows that theology as such can only point to a living Truth that forever eludes it. Such is the "theology of the cross."[4] The exclusivism of Christendom's presentation of Jesus Christ will not be offset by reticence or an apologetic readiness to divest that Name of everything unique or extraordinary, but only by a Christology that is able to discern in the particularity of this person the kind of universality that opens believers to others in a manner beyond all merely human efforts to include.[5] The biblicism and biblical literalism of fundamentalism old and new will not be corrected by a modernism that denies the Bible any special pre-eminence, but only by a deeper familiarity with the Bible itself, which does not covet ultimate authority for itself but for a living Word and Spirit that it can in no way contain.[6] The easy division of humankind into saved and unsaved, sheep and goats, good and evil, will not be corrected by silence about evil any more than by a sentimentalism that sweeps all distinctions in human behavior under the rug of bourgeois niceness; it will only be changed and deepened by an anthropology that recognizes both the call to obedience and the need for forgiveness even where those ordinarily regarded as 'good' are concerned.[7]

4. See chapter 6, "The Theology of the Cross: A Usable Past."
5. See chapter 5, "The Identity of Jesus in a Pluralistic World."
6. See chapter 3, "Who Can Say It as It Is? Karl Barth on the Bible."
7. See chapter 9, "Beyond Good and Evil."

What I mean is that the question that is put to us today is whether we have—that is, whether we are earnestly *seeking*—a gospel! It's not enough to have an ethic, even a very good ethic, because an ethic, as every parent knows, always begs the question, why? It's not even enough to have a theology—though that would certainly be a very good and necessary beginning for us! What we need to be asking ourselves, as individual Christians and as a denomination, is whether we are able to proclaim and to live gospel. To our great discredit, we have allowed even the word *gospel* to be co-opted by certain groups in our midst that use and misuse that word ceaselessly, so that a great distaste for it has entered into the thought processes of most of the once mainline denominations of this continent. Well, we cannot –and we must not!—imitate the so-called, *falsely* called, evangelical deployment of that word, which cheapens gospel precisely by reducing its essential mystery to religious claims that are finally just rather trivial. But I am persuaded of this: that unless our so-called mainline Protestant denominations of North America can recover the kind of unceasing quest for *gospel* that is our chief calling as disciples of the Christ, few of these denominations will survive to participate in the *ending* ceremonies of this century that we have recently entered.

It is in particular, I believe, the task of the coming generations to set about this ongoing quest for gospel with great seriousness, and so to concentrate on it that they will be able to keep the priorities of ministry today in focus. We—we clergy, we once mainline denominations, we Protestants, we Christians altogether—are no longer a great and unchallenged force to be reckoned with in this post-Christendom society. And thank goodness! Now at long last we may learn how to exercise our discipleship in ways less diffuse, less superfluous, and merely religious, ways more focused upon our true mission: that is, the articulation and enactment of "the mystery of the gospel," for which in our ordination we are being made . . . "ambassadors in chains" (cf. Eph 6:20).

In short, most of the problems of our Christendom past that seem to stand in the way of finding our tongues in today's multicultural society positively evoke speech from us. There is no need for us as Christians and churches to be locked into a religious system that perpetuates the ills and wrong turnings of our past. It could be a matter of *gospel* (!) for us today to realize that our Scriptures and our greatest traditions of theological wisdom contain alternatives to what we have been, said, and done. Perhaps the first captive that gospel needs to release is the church itself, which for too long has been captivated by exaggerated images of its own power and false expectations for a triumphant, 'successful' future.

Whatever else Christianity has been over these twenty centuries, it has *also* been a profound, nuanced, illuminating, and engrossing tradition of wisdom—wisdom which, in the Socratic sense, knows above all that it is by no means equal to the task of comprehending reality: the reality of God, the reality of the natural order, the reality of the human spirit and human history. This wisdom cannot command therefore, it can only point. It cannot claim ultimacy, for it is inherently modest. What is, always transcends what the wisdom born of faith comprehends. Therefore 'mystery,' while never an excuse for intellectual stupor or indolence, is of its essence. "The mystery of the gospel," then, is nothing more or less than the Christian acknowledgment that even the revealed truth that is present in Jesus as the Christ remains, for all who glimpse it, concealed. Like the manna of the wilderness, it defies containment, and rots when it is bottled up. Gospel is new every morning, and must be gathered each day anew.

2

Theology and the Quest for Gospel

A church without gospel will soon be an empty church.
A church with bad theology may be a dangerous church.

The Unknown Science

A CURIOUS ASPECT OF my life as a professional theologian has been the experience that few people seem to know what such a discipline could possibly mean. Even rudimentary knowledge of the discipline appears lacking. What has been still more intriguing to me is that this deficiency is, on the whole, just as conspicuous among churchgoing Christians as in the secular realm. While exceptions may certainly be found, especially in denominations that have stressed doctrinal awareness (certain Reformed and Lutheran groups, for instance), the Christian laity in general are surprisingly vague where theology is concerned; and if it happens (as it regularly has with me) that qualifying distinctions need to be introduced into the conversation ("systematic," "dogmatic," "historical," "practical," and the like) they evoke, usually, profound and embarrassing silences. Where the silence itself did not suffice to end discussion of the matter, I have usually explained my own peculiar branch of the discipline (systematic theology) by saying that it constitutes, as it were, the attempt to understand the basic ideas or philosophy of Christian belief as a whole. Usually, this is enough to satisfy those who, in the first place, had no *great* curiosity about the subject.

What seems astonishing in all this is that a term describing the main mode of reflection in a religion that has dominated Western civilization for so long should be such an ill-understood concept—*even among that religion's own practitioners.* In a world where exotic disciplines are constantly emerging in response to new scientific discoveries, technologies, medical procedures, and so forth, it is understandable when ordinary citizens do not know precisely what (for example) *oncology* or *radiology* means, even when they themselves may be suffering from cancer. But theology has a history of centuries, and its practice in the public domain has involved not only many prominent names in Western civilization but also generations of local practitioners (clergy), who have had close contact with the rank and file in every town, village, and hamlet on those continents where the Christian religion has been dominant. No other discipline, science, art, or trade (with the possible exception of the sex trade!) has enjoyed such a lengthy and intimate association with the human community as has theology within the bounds of Christendom. Why, then, should the term *theology* occasion such signs of uncertainty, awkwardness, and noncomprehension? If someone announces, "I am a doctor," or "I am a lawyer," or "I am principal of a high school," "a violinist," "a news commentator," or what have you, no such problems present themselves; but theologians, members of a profession that was being practiced before most other occupations had been heard of, are confronted again and again by persons who are apparently bewildered by the simple declaration, "I am a theologian."

A number of superficial reasons for this confusion suggest themselves. Professionals in nearly every discipline tend to intimidate others simply because, quite apart from any personal traits, they convey an instant impression of erudition inaccessible to ordinary people. Such intimidation may even be more pronounced when theologians enter a group of persons who, as Christians and churchfolk, know that they *ought* to know more than they do, in fact, know. The theologian may evoke a twinge of guilt in these others, or at least the unwelcome recognition of ignorance. Or perhaps, on the other hand, they may occasion resentment! For theologians are loosely perceived as belonging to the authority structures of the church, and, especially in democratic Protestant churches, there exists a strong individualism that resists interference with the faith of each believer. Few if any laypersons could be found who are prone openly to question the superior wisdom of most other professionals—medics, dentists, lawyers, or even electricians or plumbers! But as every parish minister knows, six or seven years of study in theological and cognate disciplines count for little with parishioners who feel that their own religious convictions, or those of their revered progenitors, constitute an authority far more trustworthy than that of the minister—who, heaven knows, may well be a mere mouthpiece for the latest heresies of some theological school or avant garde movement! When it comes to assessing the attitude towards professional theology at work in the churches, the factor of resentment should by no means be overlooked!

The Remoteness of Theology from the Life of the Church

But beyond these and other superficial explanations of the strange reception of theology and theologians in churches and societies with two millennia's worth of proximity to this discipline, the explanation on which my argument in this chapter turns is of another order altogether. I believe that the primary cause of this strangeness lies in the remoteness of theology itself, that is, its centuries-old distance from the actual life of the church and of individual Christians. Who needed it? In the Christian church as it has existed in the Western world for fifteen or sixteen centuries, theology has been an essentially superfluous discipline so far as the vast majority of statistically designated Christians are concerned. During its early, pre-Established beginnings, the whole church was necessarily involved in theological discourse, and at every level. The letters of St. Paul, which are all essentially theological documents, are striking examples of this involvement, not only in terms of their content but in their assumption that anyone adopting this still-illicit faith would need to be able to "give a reason for the hope that was in them" (1 Pet 3:15). Paul's letters and the other epistles of the New Testament were intended to be read in the churches, and their authors assumed that even their difficult passages— passages that contemporary congregations find incomprehensible—could be understood by the very ordinary people constituting those small gatherings. The very uniqueness and newness of this faith, and the sometimes violent opposition to it, meant that theological reflection and discussion inhered in the decisions and acts of belonging to the *soma Christou,* the "body of Christ."

But after the imperial adoption of the Christian religion in the fourth century and beyond, the continuance, growth, and influence of the church was largely independent of any direct theological input. Power, and not engaged thought, kept Christianity going: the power of political status, the power of numbers, the power of possession, the power of law and convention. Generation after generation could make its way into the church without any assistance from theologians. What alternative to *Christianity* was there? For most of those officially Christian centuries in the Western world, none at all. People were Christians as a matter of course—indeed, typically, as a matter of law. Later, in more democratic times and climes, one "became Christian" (or at least did not withdraw) because of entrenched convention, custom, habit, and public expectation. It cannot of course be proven, but it seems entirely possible that over the centuries from the Constantinian establishment onwards, persons who became Christians on account of the testimony of theological-biblical-historical scholarship and through personal spiritual-intellectual struggle have been few, proportionately speaking. There were, to be sure, periods in which theological debate and conviction—sometimes fierce!—came to the fore. The Reformation of the sixteenth century was conspicuous in this respect. There were also, throughout the ages, many and often heated *internal* struggles and conflicts over specific points of doctrine, though these were usually confined to intellectual and hierarchic elites. One recognizes too that theologians (usually parish ministers or priests) played a role in what today we would called Christian education. Once Christianity became everybody's religion, a certain amount of indoctrination was needed as new generations of the baptized entered the church. Moreover, the theological scribes of the church have usually exercised a custodial role, even though they enjoyed such a function, as a rule, only at the behest of hierarchic authorities—and then, often, grudgingly. But neither indoctrination nor custodianship describe what, in essence, theology *is*, and in fact such approaches can easily detract from any profound meaning of this discipline. Of course, as we know today, in its missionizing, the church of the premodern period won more converts by the sword and the musket than by words or deeds of charity. Thus, while exceptions can certainly be found, I contend that throughout most of Christendom's sixteen- or seventeen-hundred-year history, theology has been a *superfluous* activity where the vast majority of officially designated Christians are concerned.

Theology Becomes Interesting in Itself—for an Elite

One further step is required, however, if we are to grasp the full extent of the remoteness of theology from the ordinary workings of the church. Granted that Christian Establishment made theological reflection and discourse extraneous, or at least optional, so far as the Christian majority was concerned, it remains that Christianity does entail a rich and complex theology; and, fortunately, there have always been minorities for which the exploration of these mysteries has found signal importance—often enough to the consternation of ecclesiastical authority. The majority may be more or less content to become Christian simply on the basis of external authority of cultural conditioning, but a few will insist upon trying to understand what they believe, as Anselm said: *fides quaerens intellectum* (faith seeks understanding). With these latter, the comprehension of the faith may become a veritable *raison d'être*, a lifework, a vocation. The existence of such a scholarly elite may even be thought of as a tacit demonstration of the verity of Christian truth, justifying as it were the "blind faith" of the majority, who have not the time, training, motivation, or (perhaps) intelligence to plumb the depths of a discipline that by (say) the twelfth century had become very complex and extensive indeed.

The trouble was that as theology became more and more interesting *in itself*, and more and more remote from the larger community of Christians, both the theologically sophisticated minority and the ecclesiastical majority were adversely affected. As the theologians busied themselves with the finer (sometimes, to speak honestly, the absurdly arcane!) matters of doctrine, the majority church was deprived of the kind of intellectual stimulation and criticism that could recognize and resist such ever-present temptations as superstition, idolatry, childish literalism, gross authoritarianism, and many other demons inimical to sound learning. On the other side, as the majority, including the priestly caste, was able to pursue its religious enterprise (liturgy, sacrament, feast days, the cure of souls, and the like) in rather complete isolation from the theologians and theological schools; the latter, often segregated in monastic communities, was deprived of the recurrent concerns of everyday life in a complex and demanding world, thus adding to the existing temptation of all specialists to narrow their investigations to ever more esoteric concerns.

Protestantism carried within itself the promise of undoing this unfortunate drift; and at its best Protestantism did—and here and there still does—introduce correctives to this tendency. For with its insistence on "the priesthood of all believers," its emphasis on an educated clergy and a preaching and teaching ministry, its rich production of catechisms and other resources for the laity, its development of programs of Christian education (Sunday schools, for example), Protestantism certainly attempted to introduce serious *thinking* into the core of the congregation. Its accomplishments in this regard should not be gainsaid.

Yet neither should they be exaggerated. In Protestant contexts just as in Catholic ones, most churches have been able until recently to depend for their continuance upon religious convention—in short, Christian cultural establishment. Even where lay education has been taken with seriousness, the actual character of this education has on the whole *assumed* establishment, or at last a strong public bias in favor of the Christian religion. Both rampant secularity and the felt presence of other world religions have to some extent qualified that assumption in recent decades; but these phenomena have also demonstrated how little most Christians, whether Protestant or Catholic, have absorbed of the depths of their faith traditions; rarely are they in a position to compare Christian teaching with the alternative religious or agnostic/atheistic alternatives by which, today, they are surrounded—alternatives that *are*, often, highly articulate.

The persistent division of Christianity into a simple, dependent majority and an educated, sophisticated elite may be considered by some a matter of plain realism—perhaps even a pious recognition of the differences of gifts of which the Apostle Paul spoke. Is it not completely understandable that some few persons will be impelled to dig deeply into the sacred texts and traditions of a religion whilst the majority will be content to accept on faith (as it is said) the claims of their religion?

To be sure, such an assumption may be—if not desirable—tolerable enough under the conditions of religious establishment; indeed, under such conditions it is almost inevitable. For when Christian belonging entails so little by way of volition on the part of individuals; when one is and remains a Christians without any agony of decision but in an assumptive and routine manner, it is entirely natural when the habits of *thought* concerning belief atrophy, or simply fail to develop in the first place. Neither the individual believer nor the church as a whole, under the conditions of religious establishment, is impelled to seek theological depth. The individual can have whatever benefits he or she wants from religion without any serious exercise of the mind, and the future of the church as a whole is independent of theological conviction on the part of the laity, or even of the clergy.

Theology in the Disestablished Church

The situation changes drastically, however, as soon as the conditions of establishment are reversed and a process of dis-establishment commences. When a religion is denied the political and cultural props that provide it with a certain general credibility and give it economic security, it is precisely among those whose belonging is conventional and more or less automatic that the greatest signs of disintegration are bound to occur. The great change will not happen suddenly, in most instances: conventions, especially when they involve family traditions and loyalties, die slowly. But after three or four generations, a faith that has claimed the loyalty of one's progenitors but has lacked any careful and consistent intellectual nurturing will gradually fade. Sentiment and custom will not prevent its disintegration, and since it no longer offers such fringe benefits as social acceptance or the aura of respectability, active membership in the cultus lacks both incentives and rewards. A certain degree of nostalgia may well accompany the decay of a religion, for the one-dimensional secularity that replaces it is by no means an obvious improvement! Yet ritual, pageantry, and the marking of highpoints of rites of passage in family life will not hold a laity which can no longer find even peripheral benefits in attendance upon such a cultus, and that, besides, finds itself increasingly skeptical about religious claims that, earlier, it could accept ("since everybody else does"!) without much thought.

What, in the above paragraph, I have described in a nonspecific way is precisely the religious situation in which, in these once-Christian contexts of North America and Europe, we are presently living. To be sure, the process has advanced much farther in some contexts than in others. In Canada, and especially in the province of Quebec, it has gone very far indeed. Since about 1960 (the date usually given for the beginnings of what is called *La revolution tranquille* [the Quiet Revolution]), the churches have steadily declined, as they have in most of Europe. Many, both Catholic and Protestant, have had to close altogether, their buildings transformed into condominiums, concert halls, museums, and the like. Being the heart of French Canada, the large province of Quebec was one of the last bastions in the Western world of that type of (pre–Vatican II) Roman Catholicism which could seem to have a monopoly on both public and private life. Its cities were full of impressive and immense religious structures—cathedrals, churches, monasteries, convents, seminaries, church-dominated colleges. Today, where these structures are not empty or very sparsely peopled, many of them have been transformed into other uses. There are in any case too few priests and nuns to staff them. Few, among the younger generations, feel the need for religious ceremony to seal their marriages or receive their children or bury their dead. The language, symbols, and objects of religion are frequently the subject of humor—in a manner that would certainly cause riots in Muslim societies today. One cannot say that Quebecers were denied indoctrination in Catholic faith in the past; but it was *indoctrination*, not theology. It was able to hold back the secular deluge for many decades because it was backed by both ecclesiastical and political-economic power. But that power having given way to the powers of science, technology, business, human ingenuity, and more democratic political influences, modern Quebecers are as ignorant of the doctrines and practices revered by their great-grandparents as are most secularized or nominal Protestants.

Quebec is only one of many societies in the Western world that are witnessing the disappearance of the nearly monolithic if rote and automatic Christianity that once pertained in them. The prospect of the complete or near-complete disappearance of this faith of the fathers is no longer a scenario entertained by only a few radicals; it is a prospect that colors the thinking, whether serious or casual, of nearly everyone. For some few, like Quebec's Cardinal Marc Ouellet, whom Pope Benedict XVI has recently called to Rome to become Prefect of the Congregation of Bishops, the religious situation in Quebec "is a disaster."[1] For those more casually concerned about the new situation (that is, the majority of Quebecers) the conspicuous diminution of the once-dominant Catholicism of Quebec is a matter of historical evolution—though some, more cynically, regard it

1. As quoted in Baird, "The High Ground," 50.

with indifference, or even jubilation. Some of my neighbors in the Notre-Dame-de-Grace quarter of Montreal viewed the closure of the immense Church of St Augustine of Canterbury and its possible transformation into condominiums as an affront to *notre patrimonie* ("our cultural heritage"), and thus they greet the disestablishment of the church with a degree of nostalgia; yet many believe it to be inevitable, and many even see it as a desirable development in comparison with the all-too-powerful church of the past. In Montreal, where more than fifty churches, many of them cathedral-sized, are for sale, and where the once-numerous religious orders are bereft of new recruits, citizens have grown accustomed to the idea that Christianity belonged to another epoch. But Quebec is unique only in terms of the incredible haste with which secularity has set in: it only began, at most, half a century ago. Church buildings in Copenhagen, London, Berlin, and many other cities of the "Christian" West have long since been turned into museums, theaters, and apartments. As pointed out in the introduction, the prominence of citizens who register as having "no religious preference" throughout the Western world has prompted many to believe that Christianity will become extinct in the not-distant future.

The notion of the complete extinction of Christianity seems to me farfetched and even historically naïve; but the fact that such a notion can be entertained by apparently serious observers indicates something vitally significant for the topic of this chapter. How, under such sociological conditions, can those of us who believe that Christian faith is the most indispensable source of human meaning and hope understand our new status and mission in the post-Christendom world? Cardinal Ouellet and his counterparts in both Catholic and Protestant settings (including Benedict XVI) appear to desire and work towards a renewal or renovation of Christendom. But that is to ignore the realities of history, as well as its lessons. We have already had sixteen centuries of Christendom in the West, and even where that has not meant the spread of much intolerance and violence, it has often produced such lurid distortions of biblical faith that only the most unthinking Christians would wish to repeat it.

The only worthy renewal of Christian faith and life would be one in which the most prominent teachings of the older and newer Testaments, such as Jesus's own summary of the law, would be given a serious hearing by all who wished to consider this faith a way of life. More explicitly, as I have maintained in the introduction of this book, it is only a resurgence of *the essence* of this faith that can rescue Christianity from its slow but entirely visible decline. That essence is the gospel.

Yet just here a problem arises: certain fervent elements of the Christian religion have in our time made precisely that same claim— and they are to be feared! All over the globe, there is a new outburst of Christian missionary activity on the part of those who would rush in, at the end of Christendom, and save all they could from the burning they anticipate with great eagerness. That same now-secular Quebec of which I wrote, for example, has become the happy hunting ground for any number of enthusiastic groups (the majority of them emanating in the United States of America) that are on fire with the belief that "the gospel" will save the once baptized but not twice born who have left the old churches. That same great edifice, the former church of St Augustine of Canterbury, just feet away from my residence in Montreal, is today an "evangelical" church to which people flock (or are bussed in?) every Sunday from poorer neighborhoods of the city and beyond.

This new, electronically hip evangelism is not, I think, merely to be decried. There are worse evils! Some who attend such churches may indeed find new courage for life through these services. It may even be that two or three generations from now, the most articulate and learned Christians will have emerged precisely from these enthusiastic centers of religious fervor; for, as the old churches must know, where the Scriptures are read and the sacraments celebrated, there is no telling what may happen!

But on close inspection, these evangelical versions of Christianity offer no real alternative to Christendom. They only want a better *Christendom*—a Christendom altered, chiefly, in terms of its *class* identity, its populism, its alleged rejection of clericalism and liturgical pomp, its aesthetic ordinariness, and its anti-intellectualism. Because it lacks the rigors of critical thought, it naïvely embraces big technology; because it celebrates numbers it naïvely courts power; because it rejects nuance and knows next to nothing of the dialectical and dialogical character of truth, it naïvely courts the tyranny of religious ideology and cant.

Gospel Needs and Evokes Theology

In the foregoing, as in the introduction, I have insisted that gospel alone can reform and enliven our once-established churches. But gospel, that is, the hearing of good news, is never alone—never simply the proclamation of a liberating spiritual message. Biblical faith is a *thinking* faith. The tradition of Jerusalem is just as committed to depth and rigor of thought as is the tradition of Athens. Saint Paul, essentially the first evangelist beyond the world of Jewish religion, was at the same time a learned theologian. Spiritual enthusiasm, which may indeed be engendered by the message of the cross, needs the discipline of careful thought if it is not to devolve into mindless and divisive ecstasy. "Test the spirits to see whether they are of God," warned the writer of the first epistle of St. John (4:1ff.).

In short, Gospel *needs theology; and where it is truly <u>gospel</u> and not just spiritual sound-and-fury gospel will <u>evoke</u> theology.* It was fashionable during the Liberal period to minimize the importance of the epistles of St. Paul, or even to dismiss them. But without Paul's theological acumen, which is reflected as well in the gospels, the early Christian movement would have split into millions of mutually exclusive and quarrelling cults, and we should never have heard of the Christian religion. The fundamental claims of the Christian message by their very nature, including their boldness and universality, require the most intensive, committed and sustained *thinking* that human beings can manage. This thinking is not something added to the hearing of gospel; it is inherent in that hearing—to the extent that where such thinking is *not* evoked by what is named gospel, it must be questioned whether the thing so named is what it claims to be.

When it is claimed that gospel is the lifeblood of the church, then, it is claimed simultaneously that theology—by which I do not mean dogma, doctrine, catechetical instruction, Bible reading, but rather engaged reflection and discourse on the meaning of gospel—belongs to the essence of the Christian community.

The Two Essential Prongs of Theology

What then *is* theology? Such a question cannot of course be answered in a sentence or two. Since I have written on the subject extensively elsewhere,[2]

---

2. See especially Hall, *Thinking the Faith*.

my present answer to that question will be succinct. Theological thinking—what I like to call "critical theology"—involves two essential ingredients: an historical one, and what we may call an existential one, that is, deeply engaged reflection on the realities of the here and now. Both of these ingredients are essential, and when one or the other is missing something unfortunate occurs.

The Historical Element

We do not invent Christian theology out of our own experience or entelechy. Rather, we inherit a long tradition, of which the biblical literature must be thought prominent, not only because it is more ancient that the other Christian theological sources, but because it testifies to the core events upon which Christian faith is founded. This is why classical Protestantism considered the principle, *sola Scriptura,* the chief methodological (or formal) teaching of the faith.[3] Christians are conscious of the fact that they do not, and cannot, "make up" the narrative on which their faith is based; we are told of it, learn it, study it, contemplate it, and honor it. Christianity is a historical faith, not only because it has had a relatively long history, but because the principal events on which it is grounded occurred in past history. We are not born with a knowledge of these events, or of the theological tenets flowing from them. Knowledge of these events in some way precedes all faith that is genuinely Christian, even though a full *understanding* of what they signify cannot be transmuted directly through such knowledge. Knowledge precedes understanding so far as the sheer awareness of core events is concerned; but *faith* presupposes a depth of comprehension that transcends merely knowing about these events.

Thus some knowledge of the events in question, and of the church's historic reflection upon them, is necessary for all Christians, even though it is understood, realistically, that a truly *sophisticated* knowledge of these foundations will be accessible only to a relative few. Yet even children are encouraged to learn what they can of the core events of the narrative. That is why Christian education has been stressed in all serious forms of the Christian church and especially in classical Protestantism. Without

3. The chief *content* (material) principle, for Protestants, was of course the *sola gratia, sola fide* (by grace alone, by faith alone).

study of the Scriptures and doctrinal traditions of the faith, Christianity easily devolves into a plethora of personal beliefs and preferences, unfounded opinions, and often dangerous ethical and other assumptions. It is assumed that persons of faith, in their maturity, will desire to know as much as possible about the beginnings, development, and various interpretations of what they believe. This drive to knowledge is not something extraneous but is implicit in faith as such, where it is seriously held. As Anselm of Canterbury famously stated the matter: *fides quaerens intellectum*—that is, faith is not content simply to *be*; it contains within itself an innate drive to comprehend what it believes.

It was this understanding of the relation between faith and theology that classical Protestantism tried to foster. It spurned the medieval Catholic assumption that, for the masses of Christians, the only buttress to blind faith would have to be the authority of the church. Protestants insisted that ordinary people, regardless of the limits of their native intelligence or educational experience, had a capacity for understanding that they should bring to bear upon the claims of Scripture, tradition, and the ecclesiastical authorities. Few there are who can qualify as truly learned scholars of the faith, for after two-thousand years of Christianity, and more than five thousand years of the parental faith of Israel, great scholarship is possible only for individuals who have both the calling and the leisure for study; and, given the immense body of knowledge to be considered, it has always been assumed that the theological enterprise of the Christian movement must be corporate in nature. No one individual could ever achieve fullness of comprehension.

The historical component of theology, however, is a responsibility of the whole church, and when it is missing (as it is missing, largely, in contemporary Protestantism!) its negligence shows up in such eventualities as the proliferation of the Christian movement into hundreds of opposing or mutually suspicious "churches" and sects, the substitution of opinion for true knowledge of key doctrines of the faith, and the general incapacity of many otherwise intelligent Christians to read even simple theological work—or the Scriptures themselves. This latter factor may in fact be more alarming than the break-up of post-Reformation Protestantism into 'denominations'; for a church that has lost interest in its own past, or even the ability to read, study and talk about its alleged beliefs, is certainly a church on the way to extinction.

The Existential/Contextual Component

The historical component of theology is, however, the more easily understood of the two basic ingredients of this discipline, and, given a minimal desire to learn, the more easily remedied. What requires much more by way of commitment, seriousness, and depth of thought is what one brings to the contemplation of this historical, scriptural, and doctrinal knowledge by way of awareness concerning the present realities of the human condition. History is not objective, unchanging, fixed. It is always seen through the eyes of human beings who are themselves part of history's moving edge. It is one thing for a sixteenth-century man like Luther or Calvin to contemplate and pronounce upon the significance of the core events of our faith; it is something else for a twenty-first-century person, with quite different expectations, anxieties, longings and fears, to listen to these same scriptural texts, confessional statements, records of ecumenical councils—in short the material that constitutes the "objective" side of our historical awareness. Our forebears—the writers of the Bible, the composers of our creeds and catechisms, the reformers and key figures of our denominations, the poets of our hymns and our prayerbooks—all these were moved by specific events and realities in their societies and churches. Sometimes, across the centuries, we can feel very much part of their worlds, for there are human challenges, successes and failures that apply to everyone. Yet sometimes we fail to understand both their language and their rudimentary concerns, for we live in completely different times and places, and new expressions of old problems may in fact be *so* new that not only must different words be found to speak of them, but different *feelings* must be conjured up imaginatively even to begin to grasp their significance. A Christian of the fourteenth century hearing that God created the world in six days might well believe such a claim quite literally—most did! But our knowledge of the history of the universe, meager as it still is, is almost infinitely more expansive than anything that our medieval forebears could conceive. For us, the planet Earth is a very small dot in a space so immense that it cannot even be measured, perhaps not even conceived! What does such knowledge do to our conception not only of God but of ourselves? How insignificant one little life seems when it is compared with the vastness in which, for a very short time, it is allowed to breathe the air of our biosphere?

Theology needs not only to know something about the physical character of the world in which we live; it needs to know what trends and moods and hopes and forebodings are at this moment shaping the spirits of those whom we, as bearers of gospel, wish to address. The brevity of life combined with the relative immutability of the social context in which Jesus lived helped to fashion a people who were very conscious both of their mortality and the fixed or predictable nature of their earthly sojourn. It is understandable that they, and millions of others throughout premodern history, could be excited by a gospel which assured them that their brief earthly life could be followed by a beautiful eternity. There are of course those religious bodies today that are still trying to capitalize on this "anxiety of fate and death" (Tillich) to achieve a hearing for their message. But they are seeking to apply to the present a worldview held today only in contexts that have retained a premodern outlook relatively untouched by contemporary sensibilities. The average American or Canadian still has of course to experience sickness and death and the pangs of mortality; but few among us assume a lifespan of perhaps thirty years. Though poverty or sickness or interpersonal strife may render many of the seventy or eighty years of present-day average lives less than "happy," the prospect of a relatively *long* life makes the promise of heaven (or the threat of hell!) less significant for most of our contemporaries. The "afterlife" is obviously very important for a significant segment of exceptionally religious North Americans, but for the secular majority heaven and hell are more often the material of humor than of earnest meditation.

Yet the latter—the secular majority—face problems that may be even more devastating and unnerving than the ancients' prospect of a short life with no upward mobility! We may live longer; we may be kept healthier and better fed; we may be able, even with relatively little money, to enjoy experiences that are entertaining in a manner inconceivable to our great-grandparents; but when it comes to *the purpose of it all* we are in most instances far less content than were our more physically circumscribed forebears.

The great, recurrent human anxieties were identified by Paul Tillich[4] as those of (1) fate and death, (2) guilt and condemnation, (3) emptiness and meaninglessness—with variations on the three themes. Tillich argued that these anxieties are always present in human society and conscious-

---

4. In his most popular book, *The Courage to Be*.

ness, but one of them tends to dominate in specific historical periods. It is one of the most demanding tasks of theology, since it aspires to articulate gospel for its contemporaries, to discern which of these great anxiety types is most at work in its particular social context. For Tillich himself, as for many other observers of our society and our epoch, the anxiety type most prevalent in Western cultures today is the third, the anxiety of emptiness and meaninglessness.

Of the three types of anxiety, this is surely the most difficult to discern, and it is even more difficult to respond to this anxiety from the perspective of faith. Comparatively speaking, the fear of death and the sense of inescapability from one's station or class (an anxiety that is still observable in societies where severe economic and other conditions place strict limits on human potentiality) can be "answered," in some measure, by a gospel that emphasizes the freedom of the *spirit* or the life hereafter. Similarly, the anxiety of guilt and condemnation (which is actually *cultivated* by some forms of Christianity and other religions) can find satisfaction in the assurance of divine forgiveness, obedience to moral law, faithful observance of religious rites, and the like. But a society in the grips of an anxiety that suspects there is no purpose in life and so moves from one diversion to another, or is tempted to despair—such a society is, in the first place, very difficult to analyze, and it is even more taxing to know how to *address* it. For, as Kierkegaard (perhaps the first spiritual cartographer of this peculiarly modern social anxiety) noted, real despair is the despair that will not and cannot admit itself to itself. Countless of our contemporaries, who seem to live very normal lives, perhaps even attending their churches with regularity, are in fact in the silence of their hearts skeptical of any great purpose in living. The extreme manifestation of such purposelessness is of course self-destruction, and one cannot ignore the high incidence of suicide—including suicide among the very young—in our society. But one may effectively "kill" the self in ways far less conspicuous (and perhaps even more effective!) than suicide. The frantic quest of North Americans for entertainment; our fascination with the gadgetry of 'communication' (though we may have little or nothing of consequence to communicate!); our excessive interest in food, sex, tourism, or in anything allegedly new: all such realities may be seen as substitutes for any profound or lasting sense of purpose and vocation. There is no need to discredit every interest in these and similar pursuits—they are often genuine enough. But when an entire society is caught up in pursuits that are patently trivial and diversionary, it would be short-sighted not to suspect that such pursuits were being used repressively. Pascal once quipped that the trouble of the world is caused by the inability of individuals to sit quietly in a room for fifteen minutes! But when an entire people go to enormous lengths to avoid introspection and quiet cogitation one must wonder what sort of future is being prepared.

The question confronting Christians who seriously wish to engage their contemporaries today is how to perceive and interpret this third and most hidden type of human anxiety, and how to address it from the perspective of faith. The truth is, Christianity as a whole has little experience of this anxiety. The very fact of one's being Christian implies that one has embraced a sense of meaning and vocation. It is hard for those who feel that life is indeed full of purpose to comprehend, let alone to feel profound compassion for, those who are burdened, openly or covertly, with the sense of life's futility. At the same time, a *profound* awareness of the emptiness at the core of this anxiety type can be personally debilitating and fearful—*even for those who do profess belief in God!* It is indeed the form that *tentatio* (temptation) takes for many of the most sincere and learned persons of faith in our time.[5]

It is perhaps the difficulty and the spiritual threat involved in the attempt to comprehend "the anxiety of emptiness and meaninglessness" that prevents many Christian ministers and laypersons from delving into the roots and symptoms of this anxiety. Many prefer to continue speaking to the older, more readily understood anxieties of "fate and death" and "guilt and condemnation." Particularly the latter type has left an indelible mark on Christianity because of its long history. It is built into our liturgies, our hymns and prayers, and our expectations of the worship and services of the church. Few, in my experience, are the preachers who consistently speak from a perspective of compassionate participation to those who wonder whether life can be said to be purposeful. The arts, including film, have been much better at recognizing "the despair that will not name itself" than have the churches.

But theology will not and cannot be—in the fullest sense—*theology* until the *two* prongs of its concentration meet and engage one another. The historical prong—doctrine (to use that particular shorthand)—re-

5. Consider such novels as Bernanos, *The Diary of a Country Priest.*

mains archaic and largely irrelevant until it is confronted by the questions and doubts that are contained in the regnant anxiety of the age. It will not do to address the human anxiety of fate and death when the truly active and perhaps even demonic anxiety at work in a society is a dearth of purpose—when the question being asked by most people is not, why do we die? but, why do we live? It is in fact a repression and betrayal of Christian truth when the church continuously speaks to the well-rehearsed anxiety of guilt and condemnation, which truly did belong to the medieval and early modern periods; for this more 'traditional'—one could almost say more cultivated—anxiety, put forward as if it were the dominant anxiety-type today, only serves to distract attention from our real, existing *tentatio*. To fall into the nets of the demons who specialize in despondency, despair, and futility is probably the worst fate human beings can know; it is not accidental that Dante pictured the gates of hell standing under a sign, "Abandon hope, all ye who enter here."

But if this *is* the dominant (not the only, but the dominant) anxiety of our age, then Christians who desire to proclaim *gospel* have got to enter *far enough* into that dread gloom to feel compassion for all who live there—and to bear witness to a Christ who shares that compassion: the Christ who cried, "My God, my God, why have you forsaken me?" the Christ who "descended into hell."

The only Christians who can address the anxiety of meaninglessness and emptiness are those who allow themselves to know that they themselves—with a doubting and perhaps deeply repressed part of their own being—are also participants in the anxiety of the age. If a Christian refuses to know the doubter that he is in part, he should question the depths of his faith; and if he or she is a minister, the question will extend to the authenticity of his or her vocation. People may ask after a minister's *faith*, because they are conditioned to do so; but what they really want to know is how the minister copes with his or her own doubt. And so they should! Because as Miguel Unamuno truly said, "Faith without doubt is dead faith." Thus, along with large numbers of my contemporaries, I will go *gladly* to hear any preacher who seems to understand something of my own doubt concerning the purpose of my life, however haltingly he or she may attempt to assuage that doubt. I do not need sermons that want to demonstrate once more that God really exists, the new atheism notwithstanding; I need sermons that know how frequently I doubt the purpose of *my own existence*! Gospel today, I think, must speak to *that* kind of doubt; and the only preachers who can do that, however hesitantly and 'unprofessionally', are those who know and live with the consequences of their own anxious doubt. There are no experts here. There are only wounded and needy human beings who can pray, "Lord, I believe, help thou mine unbelief" (Mark 9:24).

3

Who Can Say It as It Is?

Karl Barth on the Bible[1]

IN THE TITLE ESSAY of a well-known book, Paul Tillich asks whether "the Protestant era" has already ended or is coming to an end. The essay is in the form of a question ("The End of the Protestant Era?"), but in it Tillich comes very close to answering that question in the affirmative—yes, perhaps the Protestant era is over, alas.

Now we should be clear that the Protestantism Tillich had in mind here is not empirical or sociological Protestantism. In the USA, where he spent the last third of his life, the great German theologian could hardly think that something calling itself Protestantism had nearly petered out! Tillich was referring, rather, to what should be called historical or classical Protestantism. Classical Protestantism is Protestantism defined by its historical roots in the mainstream of the sixteenth-century Reformation, with its fifteenth-century background in pre-Reformation figures like John Wyclif and Jan Huss. Tillich defines the *essence* of classical Protestantism by what he calls "the Protestant principle."

The Protestant principle, in a word, is the consciousness that God, who is the living subject of Christian faith, must not be equated with anything less than God. So Protestants—Pro*test*ants—protest the identifi-

1. See Barth, "The Strange New World within the Bible."

cation of the ultimate with anything provisional, of the absolute with anything relative, of the infinite with anything finite, and so forth. Protestants do this, not because of an inherent cantankerousness, as some might suggest, but because of their determination to preserve the sole sovereignty of God against every human desire to have another sovereignty alongside God. If God is sovereign, nothing else must be regarded as sovereign, *including our ideas about God.* As I have sometimes put it, the great advantage of believing in God is that you are then liberated from believing in a lot of other things that incessantly try to set themselves up as god—like nations, and governments, and ideologies, and dictators, and presidents, and (yes!) religions, and churches, and priestly hierarchies, or even (in democracies) majority opinion!

But this protest against things that are less than God seeking power and authority for themselves immediately raises a question: what about the Bible? Does not classical Protestantism uphold the ultimacy of the Bible? Is not the chief methodological teaching of the Reformation, its so-called formal principle—*sola scriptura* (by Scripture alone)—in fact the great exception to this Protestant principle? While popes and councils and majority church opinion are put aside by the unconditional sovereignty of God, does not the Reformation regard the Bible as the very Word of God, and thus as the one authority that in effect *qualifies* the Protestant principle? Does not this Protestant elevation of Scripture even, in effect, *nullify* the insistence that God *alone* is ultimate, confining as it does our conception of God to the biblical testimony to God?

If we want to answer this question strictly through reference to the main Reformers, I think we would have to say no: the theology of Scripture that informs the thought of Luther, Zwingli, and Calvin—to mention only the three primary figures of the Reformation's mainstream—does *not* allow for the creation of a "paper pope" out of the biblical canon. Whatever may have become of Calvin*ism*, Calvin himself was not about to jeopardize his primary affirmation, *soli Deo gloria* (his very motto!) by flirting with bibliolatry! Like Zwingli before him, Calvin was trained in the humanist school. *Ad fontes!*—back to the sources. This humanist cry was also the cry of the French and Swiss Reformers. Knowledge of the original sources is paramount for the cleansing of the movements that claim to be based upon them. As for Luther, who was not humanistically trained, his treatment of the Bible seems almost sacriligious to the true-believing Bible-

Belter. He was fond of quoting the popular saying of the time, "The Bible has a wax nose"; you can twist it to whatever may be your preference in . . . noses! Not the letter, but only the divine Spirit, acting upon the letter of Scripture, can establish the practical authority of the Bible in the church.

But it is just this refusal of the Reformers to let even their adored and indispensable Bible usurp the sole authority and glory of God that seems to me to have been all but lost in contemporary Protestantism, and more particularly in North America and some of the newer churches in the developing world (some African situations, for instance). In fact, if Paul Tillich were to return and rewrite his essay on "The End of the Protestant Era?" (question-mark), he would at least incorporate a new section that would begin in this way: "The most convincing evidence we have of the near disappearance of classical Protestantism in present-day Christianity is the near disappearance of the classical Protestant understanding of the nature and authority of Scripture." He would then go on (as I have heard him go on in other contexts) to explain that the biblicist/fundamentalist conception of Holy Scripture was not only a *hardening* of the Reformation's *sola Scriptura* but a complete misappropriation of it, explicable only by the fact that it was worked out in the nineteenth and early twentieth centuries in opposition to Liberalism and Modernism—indeed that biblical literalism is incomprehensible except as a reaction to the perceived relativization of Scripture on the part of Christian liberals. But then Tillich would say (what I did *not* hear him say in his time, because it was not yet quite true in his time)—he would say, he would in fact *exclaim* that what he had not foreseen was how easily the old mainline guardians of a *more or less classical* Protestant attitude to Scripture would capitulate. How, with too few exceptions, they would gradually, tacitly, allow themselves to believe that the biblicists were indeed the rightful heirs of the Reformation—that if you were going to retain an effective, working conception of the Bible's authority for the church's faith and life you would pretty well have to go that route. On that assumption, Tillich would note, some once-mainline Christians have actually gone over to a more or less biblicist point of view, whilst others, spurning such antiquarianism, have joined the various camps of neoliberalism. And so, he would conclude with a frown well known to his students, the whole discussion of the Bible's role in the church has been reduced to the usual polarized simplism so beloved of the media, with one element championing an absurd literalism foreign to the

Reformers, and the other element courting the kind of supposed religious freedom that, when it does not mean pick and choose your texts, means (in practical terms), forget about the text altogether. And, as a last word, the revived Tillich would sigh and say, "Alas, the latter element attributes its enlightened ways partly to *my* teaching!"

But this is where Karl Barth comes in! And were I to continue in this dramatic mode of using my teachers, revived and au courant, to carry my own ideas, I would of course have Karl Barth say to the lamenting Tillich, "Well, *I told you so!* I knew you'd regret all that remythologizing and ontologizing of yours! You should have kept closer to the Bible yourself!"

But I am not really capable of sustaining such a dramatic approach to the subject, so I shall revert to straightforward assertion, in the manner of true theology!

And what I want to assert, to put it in a nutshell, is that Karl Barth is *not* the friend of biblical literalism that he is too often made out to be, both by his critics and (even more damagingly) by his avowed admirers. *Nor* is he the friend of those who assume laissez faire liberal attitudes to Scripture—though he is less critical of such than is often supposed. Or, to state this negative thesis in positive terms, what I want to show is that Barth, among the great theologians of our immediate past, was the truest representative of classical Protestantism's approach to the Bible. And beyond that, I will suggest that those who are satisfied with neither biblicistic religion nor a Christianity that has nearly lost track of the Bible could do no better than to read and reconsider Barth. In particular, those who encounter biblical literalism on a regular basis and find it, as I do, appalling, will be better advised to look into Barth than any other modern interpreter of Protestant thought on the subject; for no one can contend that Karl Barth does not pay attention to the Bible, and yet precisely as one who pays extraordinary attention to the Bible, he does not come out where the vast majority of North American Bible-defending Christians come out.

But with this, let us try to see where Barth does come out.

The Bible as Word of God

The first thing that has to be said, of course, is that for Karl Barth the Bible, namely, the canonical writings of the older and newer testaments, *is* indispensable to faith, to the church. He would certainly have agreed with Luther who said, "Abandon Scripture, and you abandon yourself to the lies of men." And he does embrace, wholeheartedly, the Reformation's identification of the Bible as Word of God. But we have to pay close attention to how he develops that theme.

God's Word, he says, is addressed to us in "a threefold form." It is the word preached, the word written, and the word revealed or incarnate. All three forms of the divine Word are required if anyone is really to "hear"— as the Hebrew might put it, "hearingly to hear"—the gospel that brings faith into being and sustains it. Each of the three forms of the Word needs the other—in almost a way that parallels the doctrine of the Trinity. We do not meet the incarnate Word, the *Logos* of God in Jesus Christ, apart from hearing the written word as it is made present to us through the preached word. Nor have we really heard the biblical word or the word of proclamation until they have become the means through which we are encountered by the living Word. Apart from that encounter, the biblical word and the preached word remain mere words, even though they are themselves indispensable to the encounter. Something almost comparable to a transubstantiation must take place if these scriptural words are to become for us God's word to us.

And yet this does not and should not mean a belittling of the biblical testimony in itself and as such. Like the preached Word, the biblical Word exists to serve the living Word, the Christ, who for Barth is at the center of everything. Yet the Bible—and preaching too, when it is authentic—participates in the mystery and meaning of the living Word. Like the three *personae* of the Trinity, each of the three forms of the divine Word has its specific character: the preached word is speech, the written word deed, and the revealed word the mystery of personhood. But speech, deed, and mystery are involved in all three forms, just as all three modes of being in the Trinity interpenetrate one another—as in the concept of *perichoresis*.

Reading Barth on the Bible, one is made conscious of what Whitehead might have called the "livingness" of the Bible for him. Though he usually uses the neutral pronoun *it* when he refers to this collection of writings, one thinks often that he might have said "Thou," in some Buberian sense. As I shall say in the second part of this, that thought must not be carried too far—there is no hint of bibliolatry here. But the quality of encounter is never far from Barth's mind, I think, when he refers to Scripture. That is why one must conclude that his rather stylized and even awkward development of the so-called threefold form of the Word is not a merely theological-academic device. The Bible has this "thou-dimension," not in and of itself but because, when it really comes into our focus, it is already participating in the livingness and the mystery of the Incarnate Word that it serves.

But this encounter, far from being all fuzzy and warm, as it has been for so much Christian pietism, is for Barth (as it was for the Reformers) more nearly a rude awakening, full of surprise and even shock. Especially in Barth's earliest writings, reaching their pinnacle in his *Römerbrief*, the Bible contains for him an almost Kafkaesque kind of judgment of human and religious assumptions—*judgment* in Greek is *krisis*. What was first called Barth's "theology of crisis" has its origins in precisely this. As a preacher (and it should not be forgotten that Barth, and not only Barth but Tillich, Reinhold Niebuhr, Dietrich Bonhoeffer, and most of the other prominent theologians of the first part of the twentieth century, unlike most academic theologians since, were first preachers!)—as a preacher, the young Barth, trained in the highest traditions of theological liberalism, felt personally judged and summoned by the Scriptures that were still, even in European liberal circles, the basis of sermons.

Thus, in a stirring essay, written in 1916 when Europe was in the throes of the Great War, Barth writes about "The Strange New World within the Bible." We go to the Bible, he says, expecting all our religious and human values to be confirmed—and of course we usually find what we are looking for (because like Luther, Barth also knew that the Bible has a wax nose!); but if we actually let ourselves be taken into these writings we shall be in for a jolt—what Nietzsche called a "transvaluation of values." "There is a river in the Bible," Barth writes, "that carries us away, once we have entrusted our destiny to it—away from ourselves to the sea."[2] We look in it for history, but it is not our kind of history. We look in it for morality, but it is more shocking than any allegedly new morality: "At certain crucial points the Bible amazes us by its remarkable indifference to our conception of good and evil":[3]

> not industry, honesty, and helpfulness as we may practice them
> in our old ordinary world, but the establishment and growth of a

2. Barth, "The Strange New World," 34.
3. Ibid., 38.

> new world, the world in which God and [God's] morality reign. In
> the light of this coming world a David is a great man in spite of his
> adultery and bloody sword; . . . Into this world the publicans and
> the harlots will go before your impeccably elegant and righteous
> folk of good society. In this world the true hero is the lost son,
> who is absolutely lost and feeding swine—and not his moral elder
> brother.[4]

Even our typical religious questions find no immediate correlate
with the biblical witness:

> It is not the right human thoughts about God which form the
> content of the Bible, but the right divine thoughts about men. The
> Bible tells us not how we should talk with God but what he says
> to us; not how we find the way to him, but how he has sought
> and found the way to us; not the right relation in which we must
> place ourselves to him, but the covenant which he has made with
> all who are Abraham's spiritual children and which he has sealed
> once and for all in Jesus Christ. It is this which is within the Bible.[5]

We see from this kind of Barthian concreteness that for Karl Barth
the Bible cannot be reduced to theory, theory *about* the Bible. If it remains
a closed book, or a book whose contents seem to us old hat, or a book that
we revere without really knowing what is in it, the Bible can never become
what it is meant to become, the primary concrete witness to a Word that
confronts us and questions us, and only out of *that* kind of confrontation
also comforts and consoles us.

But I have used the term "witness to the Word," and this leads me
to introduce, on Barth's behalf, an important nuance into this discussion
of the Bible as God's Word. Of the threefold forms of the Word, only one
can be called Word of God without any qualification, and that is the Word
made flesh, Jesus the Christ. Insofar as faith sees in Jesus (in the words
of the Barmen Declaration) "the one Word of God that we must trust in
life and in death," all other forms of God's Word are relativized. For Jesus
Christ cannot be translated into sentences and paragraphs and books—
into words. Here is where Barth adopts quite unabashedly what Tillich has
named the Protestant principle. God precludes definition. If God's Word
could be translated into words, those words would themselves become

---

4. Ibid., 40.
5. Ibid., 43.

our god, our ultimate. Barth is by no means ready to travel that road. If we want to state the matter straightforwardly, then we must say that the Bible is the primary and indispensable *witness* to God's living Word, and therefore not to be treated as though it *were* the reality to which it bore witness. What the Bible itself wants of us, says Barth, is certainly not that we should give our full attention to it! "What it wants from the church, what it impels the church toward—and it is the Holy Spirit moving in it who does this—is agreement with the direction in which it looks itself. And the direction in which it looks is to the living Jesus Christ."[6]

But let us not think that for Barth this constitutes a diminution of Scripture and of its authority for the church. If the Bible is denied the status of absolute truth, it is only in relation to what is truly absolute: God as such, not in relation to other sources and authorities. Only the Bible, of all the empirical authorities upon which the church calls, including tradition and church authorities—only the Bible has primary authority. The test of Christian and ecclesiastical authenticity is first and foremost Scripture.

> If the Reformation of the 16th century means the decision for Holy Scripture, conversely we must also say that for every age of the Church the decision for Holy Scripture means the decision for the reformation of the Church: for its reformation by its Lord Himself through the prophetic-apostolic witness which He established and the force of which is revealed and effective because it is written. Let the church go away from Scripture as such. Let it replace it by its traditions, its own indefinite consciousness of its origins and nature, its own pretended direct faith in Jesus Christ and the Holy Ghost, its own exposition and application of the word of the prophets and apostles. In the proportion in which it does this, it will prevent that entry upon which its whole life and salvation rests, and therefore at bottom *refuse to be reformed.*[7]

These are strong words. They do not sit lightly with the Catholic, Anglican, or other declaration that "the Bible is the church's book." No, the church exists under the authority of the Book, not vice versa. The church's real life and witness, to which it is called anew in each age, requires that it be continuously reformed—re-formed—(*semper reformanda*) by the same biblical Word that is the source of its message to humankind, its gospel. Jesus Christ alone is Lord of the church. Yes, but apart from the

6. Gollwitzer, *Karl Barth, Church Dogmatics*, 73.
7. Ibid., 75.

continuously renewed hearing of the Bible the church makes of Jesus Christ whatever it wishes to make of him; and therefore the Bible must remain something like the medium through which the sovereignty of the Christ is communicated to the body of Christ.

So (to conclude this first section) Barth's theology of Scripture is indeed a ringing endorsement of the Reformation's *sola Scriptura*. The Bible is for the church 'the Word of God.'

The Bible As Human Words

But it is also of course the words of human beings.

In 1925–1926, when he began to teach in the Protestant Faculty of Theology at the university in that very Catholic city, Münster, Westphalia, Karl Barth gave a series of lectures on the Prologue to the Gospel of St. John, a chapter of the New Testament that has been pivotal for so much Christian theology. In the introduction to these lectures, Barth quotes Augustine, who had written a famous series of tractates on John's gospel. How, asks Augustine, can mere humans (and the writer of John's gospel was certainly human!) understand the things of the Spirit of God? And the bishop of Hippo answers (in Barth's paraphrase), "They must all understand what they can, [and say what they can]. *For who can say it as it is?*" And then Barth quotes Augustine directly:

> I dare to say, brethren, that perhaps not even John himself has said it as it is, but only as he could, for *a man* has here spoken about God, a man enlightened by God, but still a man . . . Because enlightened, he has said something; if he had not been enlightened, he could have said nothing; but because he is an enlightened *man*, *he has not said it at all as it is, but only said it as a man can say it.*[8]

This is both Augustine and Karl Barth speaking, and it is a pure case of the Protestant principle—applied directly to the Bible. What the Bible wants to say and tries to say cannot be said, not even by this highest authority concretely accessible to humankind. And it is perhaps precisely because this highest concrete authority knows that "it" cannot be said as "it" is, and constantly acknowledges this and refuses our human and especially our religious efforts to turn it, the Bible, into the "it" that cannot be said: it is perhaps just for this reason that it is the highest authority for the

8. Barth, *Witness to the Word*, 1.

church. For it denies us the very status that we long to lay claim to, namely, the status of Truth's *possessors*, the status of becoming *ourselves and as such—as the church, as the Christian religion, as Christendom*—what is ultimate and absolute, in relation to whom all others, with their claims and beliefs, are set aside or rendered inferior. The Bible denies us, in short, the quintessential religious temptation and quest, the quest at the heart of the biblical story of *corporate* fall, Babel: the quest, namely, for mastery through proximity to, or even control over, the master of the universe.

I have never forgotten some words that I heard from the pulpit of James Chapel in Union Seminary fifty years ago. In those halcyon days, when mainstream (if not exactly classical) Protestantism still had a strong voice on this continent, Union Seminary had invited the rising star of fringe Christianity (yes, it was fringe Christianity then, and in Union Seminary we often referred to it, snidely as "the *lunatic* fringe")—the Seminary invited one Billy Graham to speak from its main pulpit. Billy Graham, who today, in the light of subsequent evangelicalism, seems a veritable elder statesman of the church universal, was evidently in that bygone context very conscious of being in the enemy's camp, and so he gave it to us with both barrels: "I've got it right here in the Bible," he shouted from the pulpit. And as a young and avid reader of Karl Barth I said to myself, "Aha! And I know what the most important words are in that sentence of yours, Billy. They are the first three words, '*I've got it*' (with the clear implication, "And you don't, you godforsaken liberals!"). But, Billy, if you really knew what that Book is all about, you'd never use that kind of language; because that Book that you think you've got would not even make such a claim *for itself*. What it would tell you, if you listened to it and not your own religious predispositions and temptations, is that it can't be got. That Book at every point utters a polemic against the entire human project of possession—the possession of property, the possession of things, the possession of health and vigor, the possession of other people, and (this above all!) the possession of Truth, with a capital T. For the Truth to which this book is pointing to infinitely transcends its own words. Like the figure of John the Baptist in Gruenewald's Isenheim Altarpiece, who is pointing to the crucified Christ (Barth's favorite piece of art), the Bible in all of its testimony is saying, "He must increase, I must decrease." The Truth that God is revealed to be in Jesus Christ cannot be said "as it *is*" because it is a living Truth, it is Person, it is Thou and not it.

45

It cannot be reduced to words, propositions, doctrines, stories; it cannot even be *understood*, as we normally use that word; it can only be stood under (which is of course the etymological background of the English word *understood*.) It is this *living* Truth, this Word that became and becomes flesh, to which the words of the Bible, human words, point; and we only honor the Bible (as we have already heard from Barth) when we actually "look in the direction to which it is pointing."

Differently put, in itself the Bible is only a sign. "Indeed," says Barth, "it is [only] the sign of a sign." The "primary sign" is Jesus Christ himself. Not even he, the living Word, points to himself; he points to the God whom he represents in our midst. The Bible is a sign whose function is to point to this living sign, Jesus, whose life, death, and resurrection point us to the God by whom he is sent.

On Having It Both Ways

So, to sum up, Karl Barth seems to be saying two things about the Bible: that it is God's Word; and that it is a compilation of human words. But how can these two things be said at the same time? Isn't that a contradiction? Doesn't Barth want to have his cake and eat it too?

Certainly that is the way popular religion is bound to see it. This religion thinks in either/or terms: either the Bible is the Word of God or it is not. Is it or is it not God's own word? We cannot have it both ways.

But unlike the popular or so-called evangelical Protestantism that has come to be in North American and elsewhere, the classical Protestantism of the Reformation, which Barth faithfully represents, insists that the church must and does have it both ways; that Christians must live in the dialectical tension between the yes and the no; and that when, instead of living in this tension, the church opts for either Yes or No in answer to the question whether the Bible is the Word of God, some very bad consequences—quite predictable on the basis of church history—occur. To those who say, "Yes, the Bible is unqualifiedly *God's* Word," it inevitably happens that they fall into idolatry, by the Bible's own standards: the idolatry of Bible worship, bibliolatry. And to those who say, "No, the Bible is really only a compilation of human words, documents, letters and the like," it happens that they fall into a vacuum of authority, where anything and everything goes, and, eventually, where other authorities that are less helpful and less merciful than the Bible easily take over. We do not need to speculate about these dangers; they have dogged the steps of Christendom since its inception, and they are with us in abundance still today.

So Barth's and the Reformation's conception of the role of Scripture is at least *pragmatically* important. It guards against these very characteristic dangers, on the one side bibliolatry, on the other confusion and fragmentation. But is it not also more than a merely pragmatic teaching? Is it not the attempt of thoughtful human and Christian minds to describe what is finally not reducible to an either/or. Life is full of realities that cannot be defined in straightforward, 1, 2, 3 thinking; realities that we have to walk around, and examine from many different angles; realities about which, to describe them with any kind of adequacy, or at least not to dishonor them, we must say things that seem (to the strictly logical mind) contradictory. And are not such realities in fact most of what we experience most deeply, like love and death and fear and friendship and every living person who enters closely into the sphere of our existing?

Clearly, a Book that has been and is so significant for the whole Christian sojourn as the Bible has been and is cannot be dispensed with or rendered optional without very serious consequences for the community that does this. Guardians of the Bible in our context are in this respect quite right in warning liberal Christian bodies that they will lose touch with their own foundations and *raison d'être* if they do not become better students of the Scriptures.

On the other hand, no thinking person or community today can approach the Scriptures as though they had fallen straight from heaven—a possibility that the Scriptures themselves consistently reject. The Bible is to be taken with great seriousness, and studied, and made the basis of our preaching, and the guide to the church's ongoing reformation of itself; but in the knowledge that it is a human book, however transcendent the message that it wants to convey to us.

Is there a way of stating this duality—this both/and—about the nature and authority of the Bible without contradiction: can one at the same time affirm its unique spiritual authority for us *and* its character as an historical collection of writings, humanly produced and therefore, like fall human productions, fallible?

Yes, I think there is. And Karl Barth himself puts it admirably in the following statement from his *Church Dogmatics*, with which I shall end:

We cannot regard the presence of God's Word in the Bible as an attribute inhering once for all in this book as such and what we see before us of books and chapters and verses. Of the book as we have it, we can only say: 'We recollect that we have heard in this book the Word of God; we recollect, in and with the Church, that the Word of God has been heard in all this book and in all parts of it; therefore we expect that we shall hear the Word of God in this book again, and hear it even in those places where we ourselves have not heard it before. Yet the presence of the Word of God itself, the real and present speaking and hearing of it, is not identical with the existence of the book as such. But in this presence something takes place in and with the book, for which the book as such does not indeed give the possibility, but the reality of which cannot be anticipated or replaced by the existence of the book. A free decision is made. It then comes about that the Bible, the Bible *in concreto*, this or that biblical context, i.e. the Bible as it comes to us in this or that specific measure, is taken and used as an instrument in the hand of God, i.e., it speaks to and is heard by us as the authentic witness to divine revelation and is therefore present as the Word of God.[9]

9. Barth, *Church Dogmatics* I/2, 530.

4

Where in the World Are We?[1]

Introduction

CHRISTIANITY THROUGHOUT THE WESTERN world today finds itself in a
state of unprecedented confusion. It would even appear that the more secure the churches have been in the past, the more confused they are now
about their situation, their status within their host cultures, their message
and their mission. Whether we are Anglicans, Presbyterians, Lutherans,
Methodists, United Church of Canada, Roman Catholics, or members of
other denominations that once, not long ago, enjoyed a privileged status
in our societies, the sensitive among us feel ourselves to be living today
on the cusp not only of change but of an ill-defined crisis of survival.
While some denominations are more self-assured than others, we all face
losses—losses of material resources, of membership, of social prestige and
influence, of confidence and enthusiasm—losses that only the unthinking
can ignore. A century ago, when the nineteenth century after Christ was
giving way to the twentieth, the hopes of the churches for a rather glorious future were running very high: the new century, it was said, would
be in fact, the *Christian* century, and a journal so named was launched to
attest to that happy prospect. Today, while that kind of optimism may be
entertained in certain newly prominent religious circles in this country

1. An earlier version was presented as the first of two lectures for the Youth Forum at
Princeton Theological Seminary in the spring of 2006.

and elsewhere, there is among the older, once most *established* denominations of the West a kind of religious future shock. We had become so accustomed to being here—a permanent and prominent feature of the cultural landscape, like schools and banks and government offices; we were so certain of our continuation, with generation after generation filing into the pews of their forebears, that the prospect of diminution and decrease—possibly even of extinction—shocks us profoundly.

Our alarm manifests itself in two ways that are neither of them helpful: one response to our changed status (I suppose it could be called the Chicken-Little or Henny-Penny syndrome) rushes about excitedly crying that something terrible is happening and that we must act straightaway to stop it. The other response, which in my opinion is a great deal more problematic, is some version of that well-practiced human habit universally referred to as the ostrich approach to reality: in the face of any kind of trouble, thrust your head into the sand and believe that the trouble is illusory or will vanish if it is ignored long enough. Sometimes, as I move about in the churches of this continent I fear we are being held captive by these two strange birds—manic chickens on the one hand, and repressive ostriches on the other!

Over against the panic of those who cry that the sky is falling, and the forced and unconvincing calm of those who believe the storm will blow over, those of us who are seriously searching for a way into the future feel that we must begin with an honest assessment of the Christian past and present. What is wanted is *perspective*, and the only way of gaining a perspective on what is happening here and now is by reflecting on the how we got to the here and the now. Historical reflection is of the essence of Christian responsibility. How, as a religious faith, did we arrive at this point in our sojourn? What were our expectations? Were they legitimate expectations in the first place—given the beliefs and assumptions with which our movement began? To what extent is our present dilemma the consequence of false hopes or misleading conceptions of our mission? And so on.

These are the kinds of questions that have occupied my thinking for many years now, and they have led me to develop a broad historical generalization that I want to share with you in this lecture. We may call this an historical overview or simply . . .

The Big Picture

Christianity in our time, I believe, is passing through one of the two really immense and far-reaching transitions in its two-thousand-year history. To exist in time is of course, by definition, to exist in transition; and there have been many highly significant changes in the life of the Christian movement since its inception—including such momentous events as the split or schism between Eastern and Western Christendom, the Reformation of the sixteenth century, and the subsequent and ongoing division of the church into countless and often mutually suspicious churches, denominations, sects. But, particularly when we consider the relation between Christianity and the world or social context in which it exists, there seem to me to have been only two truly imposing and far-reaching changes. I call them *metamorphoses*, for they are quite literally changes in the shape or form (*morphe*) of the church.

The first of these two great changes began to occur in the fourth century, as Christians measure time. Ostensibly as a result of his victory over his rivals for the imperial throne in the year 312 (the Battle of the Milvian Bridge), the young emperor, Constantine (he was then only twenty-five), issued, in the following year, the so-called Edict of Milan. This pronouncement of religious tolerance was particularly important for the Christians, who, prior to it, were an illicit and often (as you know) a persecuted minority, but who now began to be the favored religion of the empire. James Carroll, in his book *Constantine's Sword*, writes of Constantine's apparent conversion to Christianity, his mother's faith, thus: "In a way, this is the second-greatest story ever told, at least concerning what we think of as Western civilization. After the death and Resurrection of Jesus, the conversion of Constantine may have been the most implication-laden event in Western history."[2] For it was the effective beginning of Christendom, namely, of that particular *form* of the Christian religion that consists of a strong alliance of Christianity with political and social power, sometimes amounting to the practical *identification* of Christianity and with the dominant forces of the society in which it finds itself.

By the end of the fourth century, what had begun under Constantine as official recognition of the Christian religion had become, under the Emperor Theodosius the Great, a matter of Christian establishment.

2. Carroll, *Constantine's Sword*, 171.

Theodosius not only made Christianity (as practiced by the imperial court) mandatory for Roman citizens, but effectively outlawed all other faiths, calling them in some documents simply "insane." Thus, within the space of about seven decades (one lifetime, today) the Christian religion went from being a countercultural, minority faith—a religion, chiefly, of lower classes and a few intellectuals—to being the only *licit* religion of the greatest empire to date.

And after that, as I do not have to tell you, Christianity in its most powerful Western expressions continued to be the religion of empire, one empire after another—the so-called Holy Roman Empire, the Dutch, Portuguese, Spanish, British, and other European peoples who either were or aspired to be preeminent. And then last, but by no means least, the American Empire, which in many ways is the last bastion of Christendom in the Western world. (I know that Americans are usually loath to regard their republic as empire, but that is how America is perceived by the rest of the world today, and the way in which the Christian religion is represented by this only remaining superpower must be the concern of every serious Christian—especially those who are themselves Americans.)

This first great metamorphosis in the history of our faith, then, was (as we may phrase it) its adoption by empire—its recognition and promotion by the most influential elements of its host society. The process begun by Constantine resulted in the association of the Christian faith with the richest and most powerful peoples of the planet. In short, the transmutation of Christianity into Christendom.

Christendom has never been without its critics. The monastic movement grew in the post-Constantinian centuries partly as a result of the absorption and domestication of Christianity by the majority culture: *If Christianity is now everybody's religion, officially*, thought many serious Christians, *those of us for whom this faith is something all embracing and life changing must find another way of living it.* Or again, at the time of the Reformation, the radical reformers (Anabaptists and others) struggled to avoid the co-optation of the faith by political power, which, rightly or wrongly, they felt was the fate of the main stream of the Reformation.

So there have always been minorities that protested against the identification of Christian faith with the ways of the dominant culture and the policymaking classes; but something new has taken place during the past half century or so. Apart from Søren Kierkegaard in the nineteenth century and a few like-minded souls, it is really only recently that, within Western Christendom itself, significant minorities in all of the mainline Christian traditions have begun to explore at depth what the birth of Christendom in the fourth century and beyond has really entailed.

These minorities (and I would like to be thought one of their number) believe that the alteration in the shape or form of the church (its *morphe*) that began with the Edict of Milan is to be seen at the level, not only of ecclesiastical polity and property and social status, but also at the level of Christian theology. We remember that the great decisions of the early church concerning the Trinitarian nature of the Godhead and of the dual identity of the Christ (the councils of Nicaea and Chalcedon) were taken by the church *after* its establishment. At very least, the post-Constantinian social status of the Christian faith elicited from its sources and representatives a general tone or mode or complexion quite different from the way in which the early church presented itself and its message to the world. Clearly, the new political and cultural functioning of Christianity after Constantine made it necessary for Christians to emphasize some aspects of their foundational story and to de-emphasize others.

Constantine and his imperial successors throughout the ages have not been fools! They have all known the power of religion to keep their always-fragile empires from falling apart. Christianity, with its strong emphasis on unity under one God (an emphasis that it shares with Islam) can seem an almost natural ally of empire—*unless*, of course, the prophetic-critical dimension of the biblical tradition, which the Jesus of the Synoptic Gospels certainly represented, is allowed a hearing. But as the history of Christology in the West easily demonstrates, after the establishment of Christianity, the *prophetic* office of the Christ, based not only on Jesus's teaching but (even more so) on his *suffering* at the hands of power, was definitely subdued in favor of his priestly and kingly offices. Triumphant peoples, successful peoples, possessing people—empires!—do not want crucified criminals as their chief cultic symbol—especially not when they themselves are the crucifiers . . . as they regularly are! Empires want eagles and other symbols of power—risen, glorious, heroic figures, for instance, ensconced at the right hand of *heavenly* power and so (it can appear) in a position to undergird and legitimize the *earthly* powers that be. The *crucified* Christ has never been a popular symbol for imperial forms of the Christian faith—unless the cross is presented as a kind of necessary prelude to the great triumph of Easter. Historically, Christianity has shown itself very adaptable when it comes to making alliances and working arrangements with powerful societies.

But Christianity paid—and, wherever this applies, still pays—a high price for its covenant with imperial peoples. For the limited and largely superficial power that it is reluctantly granted by its imperial host, the church pays dearly in credibility. Its working arrangement (*modus vivendi*) with worldly power contradicts—and often contradicts flagrantly—its gospel of the suffering love of a God who has compassion for the weak, and vigilance for the *victims* of power; a God who, as the liberationists remind us, manifests "a preferential option for the poor." And this contradiction is by no means hidden from the world. It is especially visible to those who are made to suffer on account of the alliance of the Christian religion with powerful civilizations, races, or classes, or genders. Listen, for instance, to this illuminating statement of a Jewish scholar Leon Wieseltier in the *New Republic*: Against many of his own people who said they found the Christian symbol of Jesus on the cross as such "repugnant," Wieseltier, with greater sensitivity to the prophetic traditions of Israel that is the background of Jesus's cross, wrote, "'No, Jesus on the cross is not a repugnant symbol to me.'" But then he added the yet more damning critique, not of the crucified Christ but of *Christendom*: while the cross is not repugnant, he said, yet "the sight of it does not warm my heart either. It is the symbol of a great faith and a great culture *whose affiliation with power almost destroyed my family and my people.*"[3]

As the Latin American theologian Gustavo Gutiérrez and many others remind us, this first great metamorphosis of the Christian religion (its morphing into Christendom) has by no means spent itself. To this day, the way of a power-seeking, success-oriented, numbers-conscience Christianity has its advocates, its lobbies, and its worldwide missions. In the United States it has become particularly noisy in the past two or three decades. Having captured, almost, the religious communications industry, militant, world-conquering Christianity of the most unabashed variety can seem to many Americans and Canadians normative Christianity. If Christendom is in its death throes, as it seems to me to be, it is following the pattern of many dying institutions that, precisely in their decline,

3. Ibid., 15.

make extraordinary efforts to appear alive and vibrant. These efforts may well continue for a century or more.

All the same, the *second* great change—the second metamorphosis—has long since entered the scene of history. It is nothing less than a *reversal* of the process of Christian establishment begun in the fourth century: that is, it is a process of *dis*establishment. This effective disestablishment or (as some call it) de-Constantinianization of Christendom has been washing over us in the West, like a great tidal wave, for at least two centuries. Indeed, it may have had its genesis in the breakdown between faith and reason that effectively ended the Christian Middle Ages. Certainly by the eighteenth century it was conspicuous, and for those who were unable to appreciate the Enlightenment's dismissal of biblical religion, the French Revolution (and in a more subtle sense the American Revolution) made the twilight of Christendom plain to even the nonreflective, at least among perceptive Europeans.

Of course, the great change of which we are speaking is a process: it does not happen quickly, and it has not happened evenly all over the formerly Christendom territories. Even Christianity's establishment, begun with Constantine, required centuries to be brought to fruition; and it was ordered (so to speak) from the top down. So it is not surprising that our *dis*establishment, which is largely a movement of the grassroots, implies an even longer period. The long process of what has been called the sidelining of Christianity may, as I said, require another century or so; but the axe has long been chopping away at the roots of this tree—also for us in North America.

In our case, to be sure, this second great transformation in the shape of the Christian movement is complicated. For in the first place our *establishment* was never a legal one. In the earlier days of the European settlement of this continent, legal establishment was desired by some in both Canada and the United States—for instance, in my birth province of Ontario (or Upper Canada as it was then called), certain influential Anglicans attempted to make their church the established church. But this kind of arrangement was not conducive to the spirit of the new world. For many Christians among our pioneer forebears (including my own) had fled to these shores precisely to escape Catholic, Lutheran, Anglican, and other forms of European religious establishment. So apart from certain privileges granted to recognized churches (such as nontaxation of ecclesiastical properties), the legal establishment of the Christian religion in the United States and Canada did take root on this soil.

Instead, what occurred was what has been termed cultural establishment, that is, the close association of Christianity with the predominant mores, values, and goals of our culture as a whole—our way of life. That is to say, Christianity has been established in the United States and Canada in a nonlegal, informal sense. Traditionally, we have thought ourselves Christian countries, not only because the majority of us were in some way associated with Christian institutions, but because it was felt that our way of organizing ourselves and of conducting our life both privately and publicly was Christian.

Perhaps ironically, this de facto or cultural establishment of Christianity in North American has conspicuously outlasted the legal establishments that still pertain, to some extent, in several European countries. It seems that legal arrangements—as we note in the case of marriage on this continent today—are more easily undone than informal liaisons, like friendship. At any rate, the close association of Christianity with our way of life has persisted well beyond the breakdown of legal establishments in Britain and the European continent, especially in the United States. Particularly since the end of the Civil War, according to Sydney Mead, whom many regard as the dean of American church historians, Christianity and Americanism have been nearly inseparable concepts.

I experienced the entrenched character of this identification of Christianity and American culture in certain US contexts rather dramatically a few years ago. At the end of some lectures on the theology of stewardship that I was giving at a public forum in Idaho, a gentleman arose, obviously irate, and declared that he had never heard such "un-American stuff" in all his life. I said to him, "Sir, as a Canadian, I am unsure how to respond. Can you explain what you mean by 'un-American' in this charge?" "Easy," he quipped, "it just means unchristian." American equals Christian; so un-American means un-Christian.

I do not have to tell you that this kind of equation of Christianity and America is one that is still being exploited by powerful segments of the population of this country. And by comparison with both European and Canadian statistics, Christianity in the United States is indeed still very popular. But this does not alter the fact that the second great metamorphosis—the disestablishment of Christianity in the Western world—has been occurring also in the United States. As I hinted earlier, it is particularly visible in those denominations which, prior to about 1950, were clearly the most established—culturally established—forms of the church in this country. All of these once dominant denominations have been touched by the general humiliation of Christendom, as the Dutch theologian Albert van den Heuvel has called this process. All—some more than others—suffer losses in membership and church attendance, in finances, and above all in influence in high places or even popular respect. Nearly all are plagued by big or little scandals, by divisions over hotly debated moral questions, or by a great uncertainty about the role and mission of the church in a world that is not only secular but, increasingly, militantly multicultural and religiously pluralistic.

Today, since these older, once clearly established denominations no longer represent the religious majority, or at least the most vociferous form of Christianity, they are not often called upon to perform the priestly offices of the state. When the Church Center (the so-called God-Box on Riverside Drive in New York City) was opened in the early 1960s, the president of the USA himself came to do the honors. When, after September 11, 2001, Washington needed a preacher for its highly and even militantly Christianized memorial service, it did not knock at the door of the old, once-established denominations to find a preacher. Ironically, the biblicist and fundamentalist groupings that constitute the Christian Right—elements frequently referred to in my student days in New York City as the lunatic fringe—have taken over the function formerly performed by the old historical denominations: that of chaplain to political power. And the growth and power of those elements is obviously related to their strange readiness to assume just such a function—a "strange" readiness, I mean, in view of their earlier reputation for strictly distinguishing themselves from the dominant culture.

To sum up, though the process is uneven and varies in intensity from place to place, yet in one way or another, to one degree or another, Christians of the mainstream of historical Christianity in the Western world today find themselves being edged out towards the periphery of their host cultures. Our whole history from Constantine onwards has conditioned us to assume and expect that we would and should play the role of the official cult of the official culture—that Christianity and culture, the dominant culture, would always exist in tandem. With few exceptions, nothing in our past has prepared us for life *on the edges* of the majority culture and of political power—on the edges of empire. Yet our world seems no longer ready to allow the Christian religion to occupy, all by itself, the center stage, religiously speaking, in its unfolding drama; and we ourselves, most of us, know by now that attempts at forcing ourselves on our world, where they are not futile, are fraught with potentiality for conflict and violence. We seem, then, to be caught between two conflicting visions of our faith: on the one hand, that of a victorious and world-conquering religion, fifteen and more centuries in the making; on the other hand, a religion that must share the spiritual nurture of the world with many other faith traditions, and must learn to live without social props and political favors. This, or something like this, is the source of our great confusion.

The Choices

It seems to me that until we have realized that we are caught up in some such dilemma as this, however it may be spelled out concretely, all of our plans and visions and actions will be hampered by a basic confusion about our identity and our mission. I suspect that nothing will offset the crisis of confidence that characterizes especially these old Protestant denominations of ours until we have achieved a greater and more *reflective* level of historical, biblical, and theological understanding than—*as churches*—we have managed to date.

The fact of our effective disestablishment after fifteen or sixteen centuries of being, in the Western world, the established religion, confronts us, it seems to me, with four basic alternatives, with variations on the four themes.

The *first* response to the challenge posed by our effective disestablishment draws heavily on the ostrich syndrome: deny it, or just look the other way, as long as possible. This is a very popular alternative, especially where a church's economic circumstances and reserves of personnel permit a period of inaction and business as usual. But most of our denominations are clearly running out of time. Especially in rural and inner-city areas, many congregations experience such losses that they have grave difficulty surviving. I know that the Canadian situation is more dramatic than the American in this regard, but in my city of Montreal, once the center of a huge and powerful Roman Catholic-majority culture, over fifty large church buildings, many of them cathedral-size, are for sale. The repression or suppression of reality only works as long as reality is held at bay for a little while by factors extraneous to the actual problem—like a financial nest-egg on which, in its extremity, the church may draw.

The *second* approach to the great change through which we are passing could be described in this way: blame the decline of the church on lukewarm—perhaps liberal—leadership, and set out to reverse the trend. This is the approach chosen by many self-styled evangelical bodies, and by most megachurchianity whether liberal or conservative. People inspired by this vision do not appear to notice that the way of quantitative success and world-conquering mission was tried for about 1500 years; and particularly they do not notice that it could only be carried on now, in our religiously pluralistic society and planet, by expecting and tacitly approving an exponential increase in the *violence* that militant forms of Christendom perpetuated throughout most of past history.

A *third* approach that has become newly interesting to some people lately is to look for the continuation of Christendom elsewhere. The Christianity of the West, it is argued, has been watered down, corrupted, secularized, and in other ways rendered ineffectual. Perhaps it is simply part of the general decline of the West that Oswald Spengler heralded in 1918. But meanwhile, it is said, Christendom has moved elsewhere to hang its hat. In Africa, Asia, and Latin America, Christianity is strong and growing. By 2025 or so, argues Philip Jenkins in a book with the revealing title *The Next Christendom*,[4] "50 percent of the Christian population will be in Africa and Latin America, and another 17 percent will be in Asia. Those proportions will grow steadily." This kind of statistic, combined with the knowledge that much of this non-Western or "new" Christianity is theologically and morally very conservative, is oddly comforting to the minds of some North American Christian conservatives, who, disillusioned with *our* prospects, turn to the so-called developing world for evidence that Christendom is still viable and seemingly victorious. As Jenkins writes, "The moral and sexual conservativism of Southern [hemisphere] believers is music to the ears of North Americans or Europeans who find themselves at odds with the progressive leaderships of their churches. When they suffer an ideological defeat at home—when, for in-

4. Jenkins, *The Next Christendom*, 202.

stance, a denomination approves of same-sex marriages—conservatives are tempted to look South and to say, in effect, 'Just you wait!'"

But even recognizing the vibrancy of much Christianity in the southern hemisphere, it is hard to see how the increase of Christendom in that part of the world can resolve any of the theological, moral, and ecclesiastical problems in the West. We cannot ignore our own history and development—for instance, we cannot go back behind the Enlightenment of the eighteenth century to embrace a worldview that people in our culture could only experience as pre-scientific and retrogressive. As Principal John Simons of the Diocesan College in Montreal has argued in an excellent review of Jenkins's book, "Many of the practices that constitute modern western society are hard won, and perhaps even gracious, achievements. The liberal democratic state, for example, though a bastion of secularity, might well be viewed as a Christian invention."[5] Looking for Christendom's continuation elsewhere seems to me a very inappropriate way of dealing with the end of Christendom in the West! Even the phrase "The Next Christendom" seems historically naïve and theologically unsound. To all who think that another Christendom could or should be pursued elsewhere, I am tempted as a Western Christian to say, "Been there, done that!" Western Christendom has failed, not because of bad secular people who ceased believing in God, but because of certain flaws in the Christendom form (*morphē*) of the church from the outset—flaws that have become visible at this point in time, when Christendom is challenged by other religious, quasi-religious and non-religious alternatives to itself.

This leaves a *fourth*—and to my mind the only Christianly authentic—way of meeting the challenge of this second great metamorphosis in the form of the Christian movement. I would characterize this approach as follows: (1) Frankly and openly admit the reality of the humiliation of Christendom; (2) resist the temptation to regard this great change in purely negative terms, as though the failure of a *form* of Christianity meant the failure of Christianity itself; and (3) try to give the process of our disestablishment some positive and meaningful direction, rather than simply allowing it to happen to us.

The essence of that meaningful direction is identified in a paragraph from a recent book by an Anglican bishop, Richard Holloway, retired

5. Simons, "The Next Christendom: Prospect and Challenge."

bishop of Edinburgh, with which I shall conclude. Commenting on the Council of Nicaea, which was convened by the Emperor Constantine himself in 325 AD, Bishop Holloway writes—

> Historians have traditionally seen this event as the final triumph of the Church and the beginning of its long dominance of European history. It established dogmatic Christianity in a long partnership with the world of political power that became known as Christendom, and only in our day is it in its final stages of dissolution. So glorious and powerful was the institution of Christendom that it was almost impossible to see through it to the man who stood behind it, the peasant from Galilee who had refused to cringe before the very powers that crucified him and was later, officially, to deify him. *The fascinating thing about our own day is that, as the political and theological structures of Christendom crash down before our eyes, we can see once again, through the rubble and dust of the centuries, a clearer picture of the prophet of Nazareth.*[6]

6. Holloway, *Doubts and Loves*, 172.

PART 2

The Basics of Gospel

5

The Identity of Jesus
in a Pluralistic World

Those who are turned towards the truth that Jesus is will be able to recognize and honor others who look beyond themselves for what is ultimate, even when these others are not looking towards Jesus.

The Challenge of Religious Plurality

PERHAPS THE GREATEST CHALLENGE facing Christianity in the formerly almost monolithically Christian West is the presence among us now of large numbers of persons who pursue a variety of other religious traditions. This situation, religious plurality, by all accounts, will not decrease; to the contrary, it will greatly increase in the decades and centuries ahead—both globally and locally. This raises a great many questions for us Christians, but in particular it challenges our Christology. In this chapter I would aim to speak to that challenge.

Christianity is Christocentric

Christianity is centered in the confession of Jesus as the Christ, the illuminator of the divine, the exemplar of the human, and the "costly" (Bonhoeffer) response of God to the human predicament. And therefore I do not see how any theory of religious plurality can be embraced by Christians that circumvents or minimizes this christological center. We are not talking about being nice, or being democratic, or being cooperative; we are talking about being Christians in a world where many other people—good, earnest, intelligent, morally authentic people—are Islamic, Hindu, Buddhist, Bahai, Jewish, and so forth. We shall not arrive at a *Christian* way of being with all these others by ignoring or silently looking past this central confession of Christian faith.

I always like to quote Paul Tillich at this point, since no one could accuse Tillich of being either a rabid liberal or a rabid conservative. In his *Systematic Theology*, volume 2, on the doctrine of the Christ, Tillich writes:

> Christianity is what it is through the affirmation that Jesus of Nazareth, who has been called "the Christ," is actually the Christ, namely, he who brings the new state of things, the New Being. Wherever the assertion that Jesus is the Christ is maintained, there is the Christian message; wherever this assertion is denied, the Christian message is not affirmed. Christianity was born, not with the birth of the man who is called "Jesus", but in the moment in which one of his followers was driven to say to him, "Thou art the Christ." And Christianity will live as long as there are people who repeat this assertion.[1]

In short, Christianity is a *christocentric* faith. I would like to be quite clear about that. I see no reason at all for something called Christianity that is not centered in this Person, this Event, this name.

The Temptation to Christomonism

Yet precisely this centrality of Jesus as the Christ has become again and again the locus of a narrowness, an insularity, a contempt for otherness that, both in theoretical and practical terms makes it impossible to entertain dialogue with other faith traditions. For under certain conditions,

---

1. Tillich, *Existence and the Christ*, 97.

by no means all of them religious, this concentration on Jesus Christ devolves into a stultifying fixation—a fixation that is neither biblically nor doctrinally justified, but a fixation that nonetheless (again *under certain conditions*) becomes particularly *tempting*.

The conditions to which I refer usually involve the felt need on the part of the religious community to distinguish itself sharply and decisively from all alternatives to itself, and therefore to achieve an inordinate degree of certitude about its own beliefs. Since Jesus as the Christ *is* the pivotal aspect of Christian belief, when Christianity believes itself threatened, whether from within or from without, this paramount teaching of the faith becomes hardened into dogma, and the mystery of the *Person* is exchanged for doctrinal data *about* the Person of the Christ. So that, for example, when certain Christians bring out that favorite Johanine verse, which declares, "I am the way, the truth and the life; no one comes to the Father but by me" (John 14:6), they do not really mean that *I* (namely, the irreducible and ineffable Person who allegedly spoke these words) "am the way. . .", etc.; they mean rather that their dogmatic conception of this Person, their Christology, whether sophisticated or simplistic, constitutes the only truth, ergo the only way to salvation.

What happens to the christocentric confession under these conditions is that christo*centrism* becomes christo*monism*—and christomonism of a very rationalized and sloganized character. The incarnate Word is again reduced to words! Sometimes I think that Christian history should be characterized in this way: *The Word became flesh and dwelt among us, and we couldn't stand that, so we quickly retranslated the living Word back into words and this enabled us to feel we were again in control.*

Christomonism is what happens when the Christ is made the sole principle and object of faith's "ultimate concern" (to use a Tillichianism). For christomonistic faith, the Christ is no longer the *revealer* of God but (as I once heard J. A. T. Robinson put it—nicely, I thought) "all the God of God there is."

At least in theory (and sometimes in practice) that kind of christomonism can be undertaken by Christian liberals as well as Christian conservatives; for there is a liberal way of speaking about the humanity of Jesus that is just as monopolistic and intolerant of difference as is the conservative overemphasis on the divinity principle. Nevertheless, the greater temptation here lies with conservatives; for if the humanity of Jesus is paid strict attention to—that is, if the gospels' testimony to his personhood is followed closely—there is an inherent corrective to the temptation of the theorist to turn the Christ into a Word that can readily be retranslated into words. It is not accidental therefore that the most common form of the christomonistic temptation comes form the side of dogmatic conservativism, which tends to confess the humanity of Jesus in a purely *formal* sense and to accentuate the divinity principle—indeed, in its most portable and simplistic form, simply to declare, "Jesus is God"—a declaration that you can hear on American radio and television every hour of the day, seven days a week.

Correctives to Christomonism

I will suggest several correctives to this practice: Perhaps the most important corrective to the christomonistic temptation is simply to keep ever before us the real and concrete humanity of this One who stands at the center of our faith. Had the church done this with any kind of consistency, the entire phenomenon of anti-Judaism (to mention only one consequence) could not have evolved in the way—the tragic way!—that it did; for to confess Jesus's humanity is to confess his Jewishness. And here I would like to quote Karl Barth (who is not always so good on this particular subject!):

> there is one thing which we must emphasize especially. It is often overlooked . . . It is not taken seriously or seriously enough. Yet from this one thing everything else . . . acquires its contour and colour, its definiteness and necessity. The Word did not simply become any "flesh", any man humbled and suffering. It became Jewish flesh. The Church's whole doctrine of the incarnation and atonement becomes abstract and valueless and meaningless to the extent that this comes to be regarded as something accidental and incidental. The New Testament witness to Jesus the Christ, the Son of God, stands on the soil of the Old Testament, and cannot be separated from it. The pronouncements of the New Testament Christology may have been shaped by a very non-Jewish environment. But they relate always to a man who is seen to be not a man in general, a neutral man, but the conclusion and sum of the history of God with the people of Israel, the One who fulfils the covenant made by God with this people. And it is such that He is

the obedient Son and servant of God, and therefore the One who essentially and *necessarily* suffers.[2]

Despite the line regularly taken by Christian fundamentalism, it is not the divinity but the humanity of Jesus Christ that has been perennially neglected by the church of the ages, and is still neglected today. And the greatest testimony to the wrongheadedness of Christendom's allegedly high (that is, overdivinized) Christology is Christendom's almost unrelieved anti-Judaism. As the late Dorothee Soelle often observed about much American fundamentalism, Christomonism easily translates into Christofascism; violence is never far away from militant Christomonism. The best way of guarding against this propensity of so-called true-believing religion is continuously to remind ourselves in the church that Jesus was a human being, a Jewish human being—a human being, to be sure, whose very way of being human made it necessary for his first-century witnesses to look beyond his humanity for its source, but yet "truly human."

Now, by the time of Chalcedon (451 CE), the language of Christian theology had gone over to the world of the Greeks, and this quintessentially *Jewish* sense of Jesus's particularity was lost in favor of a generalized, substantialized, abstract humanity—"perfect" humanity, indeed so perfect as to be quite incredible to ordinary mortals. Even so, the Formula of Chalcedon *does* at least insist upon the genuine humanity (*vere homo*) of the Christ—and the fact that it does so represents a huge victory of biblical faith; for the temptation simply to *divinize* or *apotheosize* Jesus must have been enormously powerful in that heady Hellenistic air.

Thus, not only Scripture, but also historic doctrine can be brought to bear against the christomonistic temptation. Chalcedon not only did *not* declare, "Jesus is God," plain and simple; but in the debates around Chalcedon and the other early councils of the church those who *were* led in that direction (docetists, Sabellians, monarchians, and others) were ruled out of order—in a word, were declared heretical. I like to remember that when I hear the electronic preachers, in the line of Billy Sunday and many other evangelists of this continent, assuring us that "Jesus is God."

The other chief *doctrinal* guard against christomonism is of course the doctrine of the Trinity. This is often overlooked, for the tendency among conservative Christians (who, alas, are the ones most likely to up-

---

2. Barth, *Church Dogmatics* 4/1, 166.

hold Trinitarian theology today) is to accentuate that side of the Trinity that affirms the unity principle: the Father is God, the Son is God, and the Spirit is God. But that, after all, is only one of the two paradoxical principles involved in Trinitarian thought, and indeed without the other principle, namely, that of differentiation, there would have been no need for a concept of the holy Trinity in the first place. It is true, on the one hand, that the thought behind this unbiblical conception of divine trinity has to do with the church's need to emphasize the ultimacy of the Christ event: Jesus is "from the Father," and not a second theistic element to be added by Christians to their parental religion's monotheism. There could be no point in paying such attention to Jesus, his teaching, his life, his death and resurrection, unless this could be linked inseparably to the person and will of God.

But on the other side, the doctrine of the Trinity evolved in response to the tendency in some quarters (and especially in the Western church) simply to *equate* Jesus with God. The Trinity is perhaps the most awkward of all Christian doctrines, but behind it there is an absolutely vital need of Christian faith to be christocentric whilst remaining monotheistic—or in other words, to pay the closest attention to Jesus Christ without, in the process, displacing or replacing the transcendent God.

This is not just a matter of the history of dogma. We must rehearse—we must "profess"—our historic faith because we shall only *con*fess it rightly when we have experienced for ourselves the rationale behind its evolution, and especially the dangers it intended to avoid. Today, on this continent in particular, there is a rather desperate need to recover the doctrinal history both of christological and Trinitarian theology. H. Richard Niebuhr, perhaps more than any other theologian of our immediate past, felt that American Protestantism had erred very seriously in appropriating—that is, misappropriating—Trinitarian theology. In the name of keeping the Christ at the center, we had, he felt, substituted for real Trinitarian thought what he called a "unitarianism of the second person of the Trinity"—"Jesus is God"; "Jesus is all the God of God there is."

To summarize thus far—if we are not to end with a christomonism that excludes, a priori, any real discourse with other religious faiths—discourse at the level of serious thought, and not just pleasant concourse at the level of human decency—we shall have to work constantly, as preachers and teachers, at pointing to the *Person, the Thou-ness* of the Christ who is at the center of our faith; and we may do this by continuing to study and contemplate the true *humanity*, the *true* humanity, of this Person as he is testified to in Scripture, and by revisiting and reflecting upon the evolution of the christological and Trinitarian doctrines in the slow unfolding of Christian theological history.

Particularity as "Scandal" and as Entrée to the Universal

But we must go a little deeper. For even when we recognize that Jesus Christ is *Person*, is a center of consciousness and of mystery whom we cannot understand but only "stand under"; even when our Christology has been able to resist this awful religious temptation of trying to *have* this living Truth to whom we can only point—even then, and perhaps especially then, we nevertheless realize that we are, as Christians, believers in God through a *particular* point of revelation, a particular window of discernment. This, in the earlier decades of the twentieth century, came to be known as the scandal of particularity. Why this *particular* person?, it was asked. Why Jesus? Why not Socrates? Moses? Or (some asked) Albert Schweitzer? Gandhi?

The language of "scandal"—*skandalon*—comes of course from Paul; and the real scandal, in Paul's understanding (especially in 1 Corinthians 1 and 2) is not just that Christians concentrate on Jesus, but that Jesus is the crucified one: a "crucified God"! (Luther)—a stumbling block to the religious, and a scandal to the worldly wise. Against all triumphalistic expectations and assumptions and desires both of the philosophers and of the theologians, God makes Godself known in this scandalous, foolish, and "weak" way.

But of course the *skandalon* is also the sheer fact of singling out, as it were, from among all the possibilities, this one person, this one constellation of events centered around this one person. Is it not an indication of childishness, or at least of a serious lack of sophistication, when a religion does this kind of thing?

But in fact, surely, all religions do it! Islam, for all its attempts to be a pure monotheism, presents the divine as envisaged by a particular prophet, Mohammed, and as testified to by a particular book, the Qur'an, which is even more literally definitive for Muslim faith than is the Jewish and Christian Bible for Jews and Christians. Judaism, the parental faith, has its particular core events, especially the exodus, and its particular Torah. Certainly neither Hinduism nor Buddhism escapes the "scandal of particularity"; and a modern religion like Baha'i, despite its syncretism and universalism of intent, names the nineteenth-century Baha Ullah as having particular significance for its unfolding.

All religion does this, and for a very good reason: namely, because there is no grasping of the ultimate that does not pass through the sieve of some proximate or penultimate reality; there is no experience of the absolute that is not conditioned by something relative; there is no sense of the universal that is not mediated by some particularity. We are human beings, ourselves entirely particular, and our feeling for that which transcends our own quite limited if unique lives depends upon our being grasped by particular experiences, events, persons, or whatever that, for indeterminate reasons, point beyond themselves to a reality and a mystery they cannot themselves fully contain.

Whatever our philosophic predisposition, whether we are platonists or aristotelians or nominalists, we none of us meet universals head on! I have never met childhood or womanhood or manhood or truth or goodness or beauty. We only form our understanding of universals through our meetings with particulars, or our sense of what is ultimate or infinite through encounter with relative and finite realities.

How Does *Your* "Particular" Function For You?

The key question—always!—with respect to particulars is how they function for us. We know from everyday experience that particulars may function in radically different ways. Intimate knowledge of a particular woman or man may function to exclude every other. And I suppose there are purists who would say that that is just how it should be: "forsaking all others, you cleave only to her—or him." But most of us would say, I think, that marriages that actually turn intensely inward either don't last very long or become clinical cases of co-dependency. My own experience of marriage, for what it is worth (it has endured for half a century by now), is that because of that one woman I learned, male-chauvinist that I undoubtedly am, to feel a certain sympathy, even sometimes genuine empathy, for women in general. I would not claim that for *every* particular woman, including a few that I *might* in my folly have married long ago; but this *particular* particular did and does that very splendid thing for me.

Something similar could be said for children. A child may (often does) become the excuse for parents who can't abide children collectively and want to have nothing to do with any other children than their own. But on the other hand a child may become a veritable entrée to the mysterious world of childhood that we all once knew but quickly left behind— an entrée to the world of childhood, and thus to the future. Children, for the enlightened, are the future with faces. (And so much theology has been done by bachelors, hasn't it! At least 'til Luther, most of it in fact!)

So at this point the key question must be: **And how does the particular called Jesus, the Christ, function for Christians?** Clearly, for a large number of people calling themselves Christians on this North American continent Jesus functions in the same way that a jealous husband functions in certain marriages, or a pampered child in certain families. That is, he functions to confine, to restrain, to exclude. He is "my" Jesus, or "our" Jesus. He allows his followers to associate only with others of the same ilk, and even with them (as the constant splits in such ecclesiastical communities regularly demonstrates) there needs to be a certain carefulness, a certain suspicious vigilance. Combined with the reductionism of dogma that usually accompanies this kind of alleged interest in Jesus, such religion quite naturally begets the sort of exclusivity that can be found everywhere on this continent today—exclusivity in relation to other faiths, in relation to other races, in relation to other political agendas, in relation to other lifestyles, and so on. We are not thinking here about sociological or religious theory: we are in the vicinity of real life. We who still want to claim a biblical faith and a classical Protestant heritage should be shocked and dismayed at the manner in which the name of Jesus stands in our society today for the most exclusivistic, self-righteous, and intolerant styles of life on our cultural horizon.

To some, it will sound predictably liberal if I say that the function of Jesus Christ biblically and "protestantly" understood is to include and not to exclude. Actually, I don't much care if that sounds liberal; but I do want it understood that the kind of inclusivity I am talking about is not inclusivity in principle: the kind of inclusivity that includes without asking what it is including or whom, or without bothering to determine whether the included ones want to be included! The inclusivity into which the divine Spirit introduces us, by faith, is always a matter of grace: grace towards ourselves, because for the most part our nature is to exclude; grace towards and in the other, who for the most part is suspicious of being included. In some ways I do not like the language games of inclusivity and exclusivity (personally, where religious plurality is concerned, I prefer the language of hospitality). But however else we speak of this, what is important for the present argument is only this: that the Jesus to whom both Scripture and the best doctrine of the church always testifies is—yes, a *skandalon*, both in his particularity and in the specificity of his particular life, in his *suffering*; but a particular revealer of a merciful ultimacy whose function for those who meet him is to enlarge their horizon, broaden their vision, and (both figuratively and literally) open their eyes to others—*all* the others. Particulars, we said—particular women and men, particular children, particular teachers and so on—*may* indeed function to exclude, and many (one may well suspect) do so function. But this *particular* particular—Jesus, called by faith the Christ—would only be profoundly—*profoundly*—misunderstood and misused were he to be perceived as such a one. Given the hoary and mostly bloody history of religion, including of the Christian religion, we should all be properly astonished when we encounter, in the gospels and in the lives of those most formed by the gospels, a Christ who is so full of compassion, so open to diversity and difference, so merciful, so forgiving, so ready to reason with opposition, so committed to practical justice, so accessible to ordinary mortals—men, women, children, servants, masters, rich people, poor people—and above all so thoroughly identified with the human condition in his voluntary suffering with us—his being truly Emmanuel: we should (I say) be so astonished at this Person that we would never be ashamed of the *skandalon* of his particularity in every and all senses of that term.

Conclusion

Thus, I conclude that we Christians open ourselves to other communities of faith (with whom, from now on, we must try to live both peaceably and with extraordinary respect), not by *abandoning* our specifically Christ-centered focus but by looking more steadfastly and more *deeply* into the mystery of Jesus's being, teaching, and living, and following where *he* leads. God, in Jesus Christ, does not give us Christians the Truth; God only allows the Truth, the *living* Truth, ineffable and uncontainable, to live among us. And I believe that those who are turned towards the truth that Jesus *is*, will be able to recognize *and to honor* others who look beyond themselves for what is ultimate, even when these others are not looking specifically towards Jesus.

6

The Theology of the Cross

A Usable Past

Two Preliminary Observations

The Term *Theology of the Cross*

"THE NAMING OF CATS," wrote T. S. Eliot in the introductory poem of his *Book of Practical Cats*, "is a difficult matter." Not everyone is able to *name* things (whether that means cats or matters of religion) accurately and insightfully. It was part of the genius of Martin Luther that he detected, quite brilliantly, the difference between the biblically based theology appropriate to our faith, and the culturally and philosophically based Christianity that has colored most of the history of Christendom, which Luther designated *theologia gloriae* ("theology of glory"), that is, religious triumphalism. Luther gave a nomenclature to this distinction, and did so in such a way that it clarifies for all subsequent theological reflection the great struggle in which the church is perennially engaged: namely, a struggle between religion and faith. Religion in all of its historical manifestations strives for preeminence, certitude, and finality; faith seeks the Source of compassion, confidence, and the courage to live under the changing conditions of history. The church, in its daily life, of course vacillates between these two, religion and faith; and it seems fairly obvious that the church is still sorely tempted to settle for religion, though in the present and impending future it is and will increasingly be hard pressed to discover any hard evidence for the religious triumphs its past conditioned it to believe worthy. The church has not, and still on the whole does not, find the theology of the cross very attractive; nevertheless, ever since Martin Luther named these two quite different ways, serious Christians have had to contend with their divergence, and some (no doubt a minority) have been helped to make their way through the maze of Christendom's Babel discourse by their recall of this quite basic distinction.

The correct naming of things is of vital importance for the corporate thinking of the church, and Christians should be eternally grateful for Luther's permanently significant designation of this theology. But of course he did not *invent* the theology of the cross. He himself depended, as we must, upon a much more ancient tradition: the tradition particularly of Paul, but behind that the tradition of the Hebraic prophets and poets, who understood the highest consciousness of Hebrew faith to consist in the awareness of the "pathos of God," as Abraham Heschel insisted.[1]

But when we ourselves want to *draw upon* the tradition named *theology of the cross* we—if we go deeply enough—will find ourselves drawing not only on this *biblical* and classical past but, in addition to Luther himself, on a modern host of exemplars of this tradition that is both numerous and impressive. It includes, certainly, Kierkegaard, the early Karl Barth, Paul Tillich, Reinhold Niebuhr, Dietrich Bonhoeffer, Kazuo Kitamori, Kornelius Miskotte, Hans-Joachim Iwand, Helmut Gollwitzer, Jürgen Moltmann, Kosuke Koyama, Dorothee Soelle, Elisabeth Moltmann-Wendel, Mary Solberg, Marit Trelstad, and many others—persons who, in their particular times and places, have grasped essential aspects of this theological tradition and applied them to their analyses of and messages to their social and ecclesiastical contexts. Luther in many ways stood alone when he first introduced this term and this distinction, though the German mystics Tauler and Nicholas of Cusa and others were certainly there in the background, along with Augustine of Hippo; but Luther has not been alone in the exemplification of this tradition in subsequent centuries, and I will draw upon some of these in what follows.

1. Heschel, *The Prophets*.

Two Ways of Being Lutherans

The *second* preliminary observation concerns Luther himself, or rather our appropriation of his thought—though it could be applied to any great thinker of the past (for instance, Karl Rahner applied something like this same observation to St. Thomas Aquinas).[2] When as Christians in the here and now we turn to the great figures of our faith's past, there are two attitudes that can be taken: one is a strictly historical attitude that asks, what did this thinker actually say and do? The other is an attitude that, whilst wishing to take history seriously, is asking for something more than history alone can give. Standing in the present and wanting to be a faithful witness in that present, this second attitude asks what would this thinker say and do if he or she were here with us?—here, therefore, as one conscious not only of the problems and possibilities of the past to which he or she belonged, but conscious also of our present-day context in all its specificity.

My interest in Luther is *chiefly* of this second type. In fact, I have found Luther as interesting as I have (for decades now) *because* from the first I sensed, in what I learned from and of him, that this was indeed a figure from our common Christian heritage who *could* understand something of our present situation, and who *could* be shown to have some very important things to say to us. In short, his life and work was such that it *could* constitute for us "a *usable* past." Not all that makes up the past of the Christian sojourn through history is usable today. In fact a great deal of it, when not simply use*less*, is positively misleading for us, and a hindrance. For instance (to consider a recent period) nineteenth-century utopian liberalism is at least misleading today, and the nineteenth-century fundamentalist *reaction* to that liberalism and modernism is more than misleading, it is dangerous—a fact that is illustrated for us on this continent daily, and (as one says) "in spades." The need for a past, which is an *essential* need for Christians (for we do not invent our message arbitrarily as we go along!) cannot be satisfied with any and every testimony from the past. Theological judiciousness is nowhere more vital than in our choice of pasts on which to meditate in our search for foundations. I have found Luther a trustworthy guide in most things; but my interest in him is not that of a historian, who only wants to know what Luther did and

2. See Rahner, *The Spirit in the World*, especially the Author's Introduction, xlix–l.

said *then*; I want him to help me know what to do and say *now*. I *hope* to have grasped his own person and thought with something like a reasonable intuition, but my purpose is quite clearly not that of the historian or Luther scholar, but that of the theologian; and (linking this with the first observation), *as* a theologian I am bound to hear his theology of the cross (which is a term I would apply to his theology as a whole) in tandem with those later and earlier witnesses to this tradition, who tried in their own times and places to comprehend and apply this tradition, even when they did not designate it *theologia crucis*.

A Spirit and Method

This being said by way of presupposition, I turn now to the main part of this essay. If our purpose is to find in the theology of the cross such a 'usable past,' it is essential that we attempt to achieve some grasp of this theology that can be shared by as wide a spectrum of Christians as possible. It is certainly not a theology that lends itself to popularity—as Jürgen Moltmann said of it, "There is a good deal of support in the tradition for the theology of the cross, but it was never much loved."[3] But while it will likely never be a theology with wide popular appeal, neither ought we who feel its power and relevance imagine, in our false pride of seeming ownership, that it is so far above the ordinary grasp of churchfolk that it is unprofitable to make the attempt. The truth, as I have experienced it, is that minorities within all the once mainline churches of this continent, disillusioned with the pompous Christian triumphalism of popular religion and sickened by the religious and cultural imperialism that that triumphalism inevitably begets, are *extraordinarily* open to the alternative that this submerged theological strain represents. But of course, as with any theology, it needs to be cast in language that can be grasped by persons without a great deal of theological and historical background, and above all it needs really to *engage* the real problems and possibilities of the present.

What *is* the theology of the cross? I have tried on many occasions, in both sustained argument and more metaphoric ways to *describe* this "thin tradition"—as I called it in my first book on the subject, *Lighten Our Darkness*. I know that I will never do justice to it because, to begin with,

3. Moltmann, *The Crucified God*, 3.

the theology of the cross is not an it—not a specific and objectifiable set of teachings or dogmas; not a theology, as for example liberation theology or secular theology or the theology of hope are theologies. The theology of the cross, rather, refers to a *spirit and method* that one brings to all one's reflections on all the various areas and facets of Christian faith and life. I have never been able to improve on Moltmann's metaphor when he says that the theology of the cross is "not a single chapter in theology, but *the key signature* for all Christian theology."[4] This is a theological approach that is not easy to pin down, as one can (with care) pin down terms like *orthodoxy* or *neo-orthodoxy* or *liberalism* or *fundamentalism*. But as a spirit and method of theological thought *theologia crucis* cannot be stated in a formula. It may, however, be *recognized* when it is heard or experienced, whether in sermon, serious theological writing, or artistic expression. With regard to the latter, I have found it interesting that some of the best expressions of this very classical Protestant approach to the Christian message are found in plays and novels by Roman Catholics—like Shusaku Endo's *Silence*, Graham Greene's *The Power and the Glory*, or George Bernanos's *The Diary of a Country Priest*. It is also representable in art, and some works of art are marvelously illuminating in their presentation of this theology—though most us need the help of art critics and historians of art to appreciate this. The great figure of modern Protestant ecumenism, W. A. Visser 't Hooft, wrote a beautiful book about his countryman, Rembrandt, in which he presents Rembrandt as an "artist *of the cross*,"[5] and in letters to me he reinforced this connection between Rembrandt's paintings and sketches and the theology of the cross. I think one could make a similar observation about Georges Roualt, Kaethe Kollwitz, Ernst Barlach, and many other artists. In music, too, the dialectic of light and darkness, affirmation and negation, hope and despair, life and death, fulfillment and longing—i.e. the coincidence of opposites (Nicholas of Cusa) that is at the heart of this theology is audible in many works—for instance, the requiems of both Mozart and Brahms,[6] for those whose ears are trained to hear them.

4. Ibid., 72.

5. Visser 't Hooft, *Rembrandt and the Gospel*.

6. Brahms's requiem is usually called *A German Requiem*, but Brahms himself wanted it to be called a *human* requiem. Significantly, he used only scriptural texts for the entire work.

If one cannot exactly *codify* the theology of the cross, what one *can* perhaps do is to identify certain informing or overarching *principles* that inform this "thin" tradition. And in what remains of my presentation I should like to attempt just that.[7]

Informing Principles of This Theology

The Compassion and Solidarity of God

This must be thought the first principle of this theology. The *christological* basis of the theology of the cross is at the same time its *theological* basis (and I am using *theology* here in the more restrictive sense, meaning our understanding of the nature of the Deity). For this theological approach, the cross of the Christ is not only Jesus's cross, it is also and simultaneously God's cross. As Jon Sobrino writes: "Our theology of the cross becomes radical only when we consider the presence (or absence) of God on the cross of Jesus. It is at this point that we face the alternative posed by Moltmann: Either the cross of Jesus is the end of all Christian theo-logy [by which he means the end of speculation concerning the being and acting of God] or else it is the beginning of a truly Christian theology."[8]

This is indeed a radical affirmation in the light of the entire theological background of the church triumphant, especially from the time of its establishment in the fourth century. The need of all self-declared "high" religion, particularly when it is politically and culturally established (to keep God absolute in power and transcendence, and therefore free of contamination by earthly involvements and passions) is so strong in the whole history of Christian theology—also today!—that it is astonishing and unacceptable to many Christians whenever God is too closely associated with his crucified son. Curiously, especially in the Christian West, we characteristically accentuate the second person of the Trinity—to the point, as H. Richard Niebuhr complained, of ending with a "unitarianism of the second person of the Trinity"; and yet when it comes to assumptions about God the Father, we fail to apply this same christomonistic tendency and so accentuate attributes of magnificence, especially of power,

---

7. I have attempted something similar in chapter 10, "Dietrich Bonhoeffer and the Ethics of Participation."

8. Sobrino, *Christology at the Crossroads*, 182.

that scarcely reflect either the God of Israel, who is so deeply *involved* with his people, or the God and Father of Jesus, the Christ.

Luther (and in this I think he has been followed by all who took up the theology of the cross subsequently) dared to break with this hold of classical philosophic theology, as it was held especially by the school of Alexandria, and in the spirit of the school of Antioch accentuated the themes of compassion and solidarity. One could say, using other terms, that he christologized the deity, even going so far as to speak of "the crucified *God.*" As Moltmann characterizes this, "Christian faith stands and falls with the knowledge of the crucified Christ, that is, with the knowledge of God *in* the crucified Christ, or, to use Luther's even bolder phrase, with the knowledge of the 'crucified God.'"[9]

The implications of this radical identification of God with the crucified Christ are manifold, for it means not only that the famous distinctions between the persons of the Trinity are radically qualified and their tendency to devolve into tritheism checked; it means also that theories of the *work* of Christ (soteriology) that depend upon these distinctions, as does that of Anselm of Canterbury, are implicitly called in question. And in that connection I think that Gustaf Aulen was entirely justified when—in his famous little study, *Christus Victor*, he affirmed that Luther did not follow the grand tendency of the Christian West in picturing Christ's work as satisfaction offered to a holy, remote, and implacably righteous God for the sins of the many. Such a conception of the atonement depends upon keeping God strictly differentiated from the substitutionary victim, Jesus; and it is one of the anomalies of Western Protestantism that most of it has nevertheless clung to an Anselmian soteriology indistinguishable in essentials from the very Catholic ("Latin") Theology (doctrine of God) that Luther questioned. Calvin, I will just whisper, did not help very much in this process.

The Cross as World Commitment

If the cross of Jesus is first of all a statement about the nature of the Deity, it is in the second place—yet not even as a second step, but implicitly and necessarily—a statement about the world and God's abiding love for the world and all its creatures. It is not strange to faith, however astonish-

9. Moltmann, *The Crucified God*, 65.

ing or incredible it may seem to unbelief (which is always at base cynicism about the worthwhileness of the world), that when the author of the Fourth Gospel, allegedly the most Hellenistic of the four gospels, wished to state in a sentence *the whole intention of God in the incarnation,* he expressed the most *worldly* orientation of the gospel ever conceived: "God so loved the world [*cosmos*] that he gave his only Son, so that everyone who believes in him may not perish but may have eternal life." (John 3:16, NRSV). Nor is it surprising that this same verse of Scripture is the best-remembered New Testament sentence of them all; for despite the rhetoric and the activity of Christians and churches, which often betray precisely such an affirmation of the creational grounding of redemption, that which is best in all of us remembers that at the center of this faith there is an extraordinary affirmation of creation. Doctrine must never become so drunk on redemption, or rather on its own superlatives and exaggerations of the redeemed estate, that it ends by denigrating the actual, existing "world" that God "so loved" and loves.

The cross is at once, for Christians, the ultimate statement of humankind's movement away from God and of God's gracious movement towards fallen humankind. I think of the cross of Golgotha as the divine determination to *claim* this world, however wretched its history and however costly its redemption. On Golgotha it is still the God of Israel who speaks—the God who found everything that he had made "very good," and who insists "I will be *your* God and you will be *my* people!" Against the clear tendency of the creature to degrade itself and abuse its environs, God in Christ reinstates the divine ownership of creation and commits Godself to creation's fulfillment, its flourishing.

It was this sense of the divine commitment to the world that made the young prisoner, Dietrich Bonhoeffer, perhaps the best advocate of the theology of the cross in our epoch, call in question the interpretation of Christianity as a religion of redemption. "The redemption myths," he writes,

> try unhistorically to find an eternity after death . . . [For them] redemption . . . means redemption from cares, distress, fears, and longings, from sin and death, in a better world beyond the grave. But is this really the essential character of the proclamation of Christ in the gospels and by Paul. I should say it is not. The difference between the Christian hope of resurrection and the mythological hope is that the former sends [a person] back into . . . life on

earth in a wholly new way . . . The Christian, unlike the devotees of the redemption myths, has no last line of escape available from earthly tasks and difficulties into the eternal, but, like Christ himself . . . he must drink the earthly cup to the dregs, and only in his doing so is the crucified and risen Lord with him, and he crucified and risen with Christ. This world must not be prematurely written off; in this the Old and New Testaments are at one.[10]

Honesty about Experience (Christian Realism)

As a third principle at work in the theology of the cross I would name an extraordinary commitment to truth telling, a rare determination to be honest in one's faith claims—rare, I mean, in the whole realm of religion. For me at least, the twenty-first thesis of the Heidelberg Disputation has been vital:

> Der Theologe der Gottes unverborgene Herrlichkeith sucht, nennt das Übel gut und Guttes übel; der Theologe des Kreuzes nennt die Dinge beim rechten Namen.

> [The theologian who seeks God's unconcealed glory names evil good and good evil; the theologian of the cross calls things by their proper name.]

This is in some ways an enigmatic statement, but only if we fail to grasp the critique of religious triumphalism that is being contrasted with the theology whose character Luther is attempting to depict. A theology that seeks to show the *obviousness* of the divine power and glory has to end in exaggeration and untruth. Why? Because in order to uphold its exaggerated positive it must downplay or neglect everything by which that positive is negated or called in question—which is to say, the evil, sin, demonic, and death that manifest themselves unmistakably in everyday life. By contrast, he says, the *theologia crucis* names the negating realities openly, beginning with the cross of Christ itself: the cross and all that it stands for by way of human degradation and suffering is not good, not *in se*—in itself! We are not called to laud and embrace this symbol of violence and torture and death as though it were something splendid! What is good lies hidden underneath or behind this dreadful reality: namely, God's concealed presence and determination to mend the creation from

---

10. Bonhoeffer, *Letters and Papers from Prison*, 336–37.

within. The theology of the cross is thus not only allowed but commanded to draw the attention of church and world to that, in both, which contradicts and demeans the glory of God. The theologian of the cross is not (as is childishly alleged by some) a pessimist, but he or she is also not the congenital optimist who must repress every thought of doubt, despair, the demonic, and death. The theology of the cross therefore leads to a *prophetic* stance on the part of the church, a boldness that "calls a spade a spade." It is here that Reinhold Niebuhr's Christian realism has its foundations.

But thesis 21 has another connotation that is easily overlooked. It means not only that faith is called upon to be *honest* about the reality of historical experience, but that it must be *modest* about its own claims. For if God's triumph is indeed hidden beneath its apparent opposite, we dare not imagine that we have captured the truth of God in our theology! That is precisely the error of the theology of glory! We rather, who live under the cross, are able only to point to the mystery of the divine *agape* that is manifested in this strange, paradoxical manner. As Walter von Loewenich writes in his biography of Luther, "Luther's view appears to be complex, but basically it is quite simple. The apparent paradoxes prove to be true in experience. It is a question of honesty whether we acknowledge the reality of this experience or whether we reject it. Luther calls this honesty *humility*."[11]

This humility has *always* been mandatory for those who have grasped the fact that God is *Person*, "Thou" (in Buber's terms), and who contemplated in all seriousness the *mystery* of God's compassion and solidarity with us *en Christo*. But today it is of the very essence of Christianity, for like all religion our religion too, as religion, is sorely tempted to make grandiose claims for itself, and in that direction—in our pluralistic world—lies violence and death. Whatever else may be said of the monumental theology of Karl Barth, his ties with Luther's *theologia crucis* are no more clearly in evidence than when, in his *Evangelical Theology*, his Chicago lectures, he insists, "evangelical theology is *modest* theology, because it is determined to be so by its object, that is, by him who is its subject."[12]

In this aspect of the theology of the cross we may also glimpse what is seldom noticed, namely, this theology's compatibility with the *apophatic* traditions of Eastern Orthodoxy; in fact, I would say that the theology of

11. Von Loewenich, *Martin Luther*, 123.
12. Barth, *Evangelical Theology*, 7.

the cross can be seen as a *type* of apophatic theology. In its recognition of the *mystery* of divine revelation, its insistence on the importance of the *via negativa*, and its essential modesty the theology of the cross creates bridges to the East just as, on the other hand, it raises serious questions about the altogether too affirmative (*kataphatic*) theologies of the Christian West. It is not accidental that Søren Kierkegaard, one of the great examplars of the theology of the cross,[13] is thought by some the most consistent *apophatic* theologian in Western Christendom.

The Contextual Character of This Theology

In my book *The Cross in Our Context*,[14] I argue that the theology of the cross is inherently and fundamentally a *contextual* theology. I suppose such a claim could be interpreted as an attempt, on my part, to justify by reference to an authority figure whom I respect, a predilection of my own for contextuality in theology. I am a sinner, also intellectually, and therefore I shall not seek to argue for the purity of my motives. Yet I do not see how one can immerse oneself in this theological tradition, not only Luther but the whole tradition, without coming to that kind of conclusion. As for Luther himself, it is of course perfectly obvious that he did not think of his work in modern contextual terms. Contextuality in theology is a byproduct—rather late in time, actually!—of historical consciousness, which is a modern mindset. Nevertheless Luther *acted* in a contextual manner, as one intensely aware of the fact that he was—for instance, a German; an Augustinian; and a critic of Aristotelianism and its ascendency in the official theology, and so on. That Aristotlianism, as James M. Kittelson notes in his biography of Luther, assumed as its primary methodological presupposition, that "all important truths . . . were universal. Circumstances of time and place made no difference to the truth of propositions that could be developed by the exercise of right reason."[15] Precisely that assumption, which in the hands of religious authority was no innocent teaching but a potent tool for the suppression of difference, was what Luther had to challenge—and not only because he had been influenced by the so-called *via moderna*, but because as a German con-

13. See Hall, *Lighten Our Darkness.*
14. See Hall, *The Cross in Our Context*, 35ff.
15. Kittelson, *Luther the Reformer*, 47.

scious of his own and his people's particularity he simply could not accept as binding truths that were "made in Rome," a quite different context from his own. One could argue, surely, that the whole Reformation was steeped in a place consciousness that could not be fitted easily into the religious ideology of external authority.

But in addition to such *historical* reasons for concluding that this theological approach is inevitably contextual, there are (in my estimation at least) solid *theological* grounds for such a conclusion. It follows irrevocably from all three of the previous principles: (1) A conception of God as one having compassion for, and desiring solidarity with, the creature would be an empty sentiment unless the creatures for whom such love is intended were seen in all their particularity—which only represents, in fact, a return to the tradition of Jerusalem, with *its* historical consciousness, and away from the kind of abstractionism belonging to that side of the tradition of Athens that loves universals at the expense of particulars. (2) To speak of the cross of Christ in terms of God's world-orientation and commitment could only be an empty claim if "the world" remains at the level of an intellectual construct and does not become explicit. The "world" that God loves is not a construct but a reality, constantly in flux, rich in variety, old in sin but redolent of potentiality. Love itself, whether divine or human, is never love for generalities but for specifics; and it becomes an absurdity and a pretense if it indulges in generalities that defy specificity—which unfortunately happens all too often in religion ("I love the world; it's only these wretched people I can't stand"). (3) A theology that is committed to truth telling, realism about evil, modesty about itself, can only be a contextual theology. Its honesty (*Wahrheitsorientierung*—its orientation towards truth) is nothing but a determination to pay "attention" (in Simone Weil's sense) to what is actually there in front of it—"on the ground," in the modern idiom. It is not permitted to contemplate an ideal that is wholly unrelated to the here and now. It entertains change, certainly, and even strives for change with every fiber of its being, but it wishes to change *what actually is*, and (as in the famous serenity prayer of Reinhold Niebuhr) "*can* be changed."

To translate all this into other terms, the theology of the cross is at base a *practical* theology. It is not interested in pure theory. It is inherently critical of ideology. It drives always towards incarnation, towards enactment. This at least it has in common with liberation theology, that it is never satisfied with being theology but must become an ethic. Yet never an ethic separable from its own theological base and point of departure. Bonhoeffer, the Lutheran, complained about the Lutheranism that nurtured the theology of justification because it did not find its inherent goal in just action but rested in the security of a doctrinalized grace. One could complain just as appropriately of the Christian activism that never ponders the why of the act and therefore, perennially complicates the very problems it would address.

The Refusal of Finality

It would be difficult to grasp the character of this theological tradition without paying a good deal of attention to the eschatological dimension that runs through its length and breadth. One could even say that the *chief* difference between the theology of the cross and the antithesis that Luther uses as his contrast, the *theologia gloriae*, is their eschatology. The theology of glory depends on an eschatology that is fully "realized"—namely, realized in the church, realized in theology as true and irrefutable doctrine. Hence a theology *of glory!* Now, there is a realized *dimension* in the theology of the cross, too; but it is not a realization to which the church and its theology can lay claim. The purposes of God are realized *in Christ*, and faith looks to God in trust and hope. But the faithful live without finality, without "closure," without certitude. All our ancestors were "under the cloud," says Paul. "Nevertheless with most of them God was not pleased; for they were overthrown in the wilderness . . . Therefore let any one who thinks that he stands take heed lest he fall" (1 Cor 10:1ff.) In confidence (*con fide*) we may feel that we are on the right road, but woe to any who imagine they have arrived.

The following statement seems to me typical of Luther: "Christian living does not mean to *be* good but to *become* good; not to *be* well, but to get well; not *being* but *becoming*; not rest but training. We are *not yet*, but we shall be. It has *not yet* happened, but it is the way. Not everything shines and sparkles as yet, but everything is getting better."[16] This kind of statement does not deny a pilgrim's progress or betterment, but neither does it affirm the kind of perfectionism that John Wesley courted. We are living, it is true, after the victory of God in the risen Christ; but while the

16. Luther, *WA* 7:336; *LW* 7:336, trans. Edward Furcha.

Christ is risen we ourselves live in hope and not fulfillment—we live, as the late Alan Lewis put it so beautifully, in holy Saturday, between cross and resurrection.[17]

And this is perhaps the best place to address the question, what is the relationship of the resurrection to the theology of the cross? Contrary to many critics say about the theology of the cross, this theology does not overlook or downplay the victory of the third day; what it critiques is the use, or rather the misuse, of the resurrection to render the cross null and void—*passé*! And that misuse is by no means a minor thing. Especially in North American popular Christianity, the resurrection—or what I call resurrection-*ism*—functions to turn the religious *away* from the cross as a thing well and truly overcome. And that means not only the cross of Jesus, but the cross of reality; so that the religion thus mythically bolstered becomes a primary factor in the deadening of otherwise relatively sensitive people to the pain of God in the world. I suspect there is no greater theological task in North America today than to refuse and redirect this false and dangerous functioning of Easter in this society. Rightly to grasp the meaning of Christ's resurrection is to be turned *towards* the cross, with understanding and gratitude, not away from it. Moltmann puts it this way: Easter "does not overcome the story of Christ's passion so that we no longer remember it. Rather, it establishes Christ's cross as a saving event. The one who goes before us into the glorious and liberated future of God's resurrected is also the one who died for us on the cross. We come face to face with the glory of the coming God beholding the features of the crucified and not through infinite demands or flights of fancy."[18]

Being turned by resurrection faith and hope towards the cross of Jesus is not merely an act of piety; it is also an act of human and ethical solidarity with all who suffer. For Jesus is never alone, never just Jesus. He is this representative of the suffering God and of suffering creation and creatures. A religion that in the name of faithfulness to Jesus turns away from or becomes smug and indifferent in relation to the world is a blasphemy in the service of false religion, the religion of glory without the cross (and perhaps "religion" is always precisely *without the cross*). We are living in a society that walks very close to this blasphemy.

---

17. See Lewis, *Between Cross and Resurrection.*
18. Moltmann, *Theology of Play,* 30.

Conclusion

I must bring this essay to an end, and I can only do so reluctantly, for I could have wished to cover all the aspects and facets of this theological tradition in a persuasive and final way. But that too indicates the temptation of theology always to covet glory for itself. If it is the theology of the cross that we are treating, there can be no final statement. Final statements in Christian theology are invariably to be mistrusted. That is the frustration of this discipline whenever it wishes to be a theology of the cross.

In concluding, I will leave you once again—as I did in *The Cross in Our Context*—with a kind of meditation on the three Pauline virtues, faith, love, and hope. The best way that I have found of conveying what *I* think this theological method and spirit is all about is by considering these so-called virtues in the light of what they are each negating. Unless the negation of each is understood, the positive statement (the virtue) of each is cheapened and made into a cliché. We do not have to speculate about what these virtues negate, for in each case the negation is clearly present in the collected works of Paul; and as the New Testament's chief exemplar of this "thin tradition," Paul speaks, I believe, not only for Luther but for all who have been grasped by the principles of this tradition.

Faith

What does this term negate? The metaphor that crops up time and again in Paul's writings is sight. Faith, which "comes by hearing" and is precisely a *not*-seeing. "Now faith is the assurance of things hoped for, the conviction of things *not seen*,"—one of Luther's favorite texts. The eschatological element—especially the *not-yet* side of Christian eschatology—is here strongly present. The theology of the cross is a theology of *faith*, and while faith is certainly a positive term for Luther, it must not be elevated beyond its proper limit. In the act of *trusting*, the One trusted is glimpsed—as through a glass darkly—but not seen. Faith that is not sight is thus a faith warned against presumption. It is also a faith that is able to live with its antithesis, doubt, and that is in fact dead faith (as Unamuno said) when doubt is no longer allowed a hearing.

Hope

Hope is at once an orientation to the future and a recognition that the present is still lacking its promised fulfillment. Hope *realized* is no longer hope. The stance that we call hope is one constantly made conscious of the fact that the present, the *hic et nunc*, is a falling short of what is most to be desired. So the hope that is faith's future dimension is always "hope against hope" (Rom 4:18). As faith must live with doubt, so hope must live with its antithesis, hopelessness, despair. What is hoped for must not be taken for granted, as though it were already experienced reality, already seen—for here too Paul resorts to the metaphor of sight: "For in hope we were saved. Now hope that is seen is not hope. For who hopes for what is seen? But if we hope for what we do not see, we wait for it with patience" (Rom 8:24–25, NRSV).

Love

Love negates many things, as Paul makes plain in the famous hymn to love in 1 Corinthians 13. But I think that what must receive priority where this discussion is concerned is power. "Love does not insist on its own way" (13:5). "The crux of the cross," wrote Reinhold Niebuhr, "is its revelation of the fact that the final power of God over man is derived from the self-imposed weakness of his love."[19] This, I think, is of the essence of this theology, and it is hard for all to accept who think of deity chiefly in terms of power—*omnipotence*, almightiness. But if God is love, then the divine power must accommodate itself to divine love, and not vice versa. And that, for the theology of the cross, is basic. Paul Tillich writes (and I will quote the entire thought because I think it is wonderfully illuminating):

> One of Luther's most profound insights was that God made himself small for us in Christ. In doing so, He left us our freedom and our humanity. He showed us His heart, so that our hearts could be won.
>
> When we look at the misery of our world, its evil and its sin, especially in these days which seem to mark the end of a world period, we long for divine interference, so that the world and its daemonic rulers might be overcome. We long for a king of peace within history, or for a king of glory above history. We long for a

19. Brown, *The Essential Reinhold Niebuhr*, 22.

Christ of power. Yet if *He* were to come and transform us and our world, we should have to pay the *one* price we could not pay: we would have to lose our freedom, our humanity, and our spiritual dignity. Perhaps we would be happier; but we should also be lower beings, our present misery, struggle and despair notwithstanding. We should be more like blessed animals than men made in the image of God. Those who dream of a better life and try to avoid the Cross as a way, and those who hope for a Christ and attempt to exclude the Crucified, have no knowledge of the mystery of God and of man.[20]

To summarize: the theology of the cross is a theology of faith (not sight), a theology of hope (not consummation), and a theology of love (not power). And if you want to understand what the theology of glory is you just have to turn this ordering of the virtues around: it is a theology of sight (not faith), of consummation (not hope), and of power (not love).

The one aspect of the theology of the cross that I have omitted from this characterization concerns its consequence as an *ecclesiology*. This is a serious omission, because the *theologia crucis* is only a viable theology as and when it expresses itself in an *ecclesia crucis*. To make up for this omission, besides referring you to part 3 of my book *The Cross in Our Context*, I want to quote the final paragraph of Paul Tillich's best-read book, *The Courage to Be:*

A church which raises itself in its message and its devotion to the God above the God of theism without sacrificing its concrete symbols can mediate a courage which takes doubt and meaninglessness into itself. It is the Church under the Cross which alone can do this, the Church which preaches the Crucified who cried to God who remained after the God of confidence had led him in the darkness of doubt and meaninglessness. To be as a part in such a church is to receive the courage to be in which one cannot lose one's self and in which one receives one's world.[21]

---

20. Tillich, "He Who Is the Christ," 148.
21. Tillich, *The Courage to Be*, 178.

7

The Identity and Meaning of the Self

DIETRICH BONHOEFFER IN HIS brief life bequeathed to the world not only enough seminal theological thought to keep an entire industry of scholarship occupied ever since; he also left us some memorable poetry. His best-known poem is called simply, "Who Am I?" I shall use it as a kind of background text for what I wish to say about the self in this essay. The poem was written in his prison cell not long before, at the age of thirty-nine, Bonhoeffer was executed by the Nazis, his mad, deluded countrymen.

> Who am I? They often tell me
> I stepped from my cell's confinement
> Calmly, cheerfully, firmly,
> Like a Squire from his country house.
>
> Who am I? They often tell me
> I used to speak to my warders
> freely and friendly and clearly,
> as though it were mine to command.
>
> Who am I? They also tell me
> I bore the days of misfortune
> equably, smilingly, proudly,
> like one accustomed to win.

Am I then really that which other men tell of?
Or am I only what I myself know of myself?
Restless and longing and sick, like a bird in a cage,
Struggling for breath, as though hands were compressing
My throat, yearning for colours, for flowers, for the voices of birds,
thirsting for words of kindness, for neighbourliness,
tossing in expectation of great events,
powerlessly trembling for friends at an infinite distance,
weary and empty at praying , at thinking, at making,
faint, and ready to say farewell to it all.

Who am I? This or the Other?
Am I one person to-day and to-morrow another?
Am I both at once? A hypocrite before others,
And before myself a contemptible woebegone weakling?
Or is something within me like a beaten army
Fleeing in disorder from victory already achieved?

Who am I? They mock me, these lonely questions of mine.
Whoever I am, Thou knowest, O God, I am thine.[1]

The poem considers three possible responses to the question contained in its title. They correspond to what Reinhold Niebuhr called the three dialogues of the self: its dialogue with others, with itself, and with God.[2] I shall group my reflections around these three. For purposes of clarity we may call them, *first*, Other-Determined Selfhood (or, employing the terminology of another of my teachers, Paul Tillich, "Heteronomous Selfhood"); *second*, Self-Determined (or "Autonomous") selfhood; and *third*, Responsive (or "Theonomous") Selfhood—that is, the self responding to its transcendent Source of identity and meaning.

Other-Determined (Heteronomous) Selfhood

Significantly, the first thought that came to prisoner Bonhoeffer's mind as he contemplated the question of his own identity was what others seemed

1. Translated by J. B. Leishman, and reproduced in G. Leibholz's 'Memoir' of Bonhoeffer, in Bonhoeffer, *The Cost of Discipleship*, 15.

2. In *The Self and the Dramas of History*.

to believe of him. "They tell me . . . / They often tell me . . . ." That he should have begun there is probably the most natural thing in the world. Do we not all tend to place a great deal of weight upon the opinions that others have of us? Sadly, many human beings seem never to get beyond this source of self-identity and meaning. They spend their lives in a never-ending attempt to ascertain how they are perceived by others, seeking to accommodate themselves to—or perhaps to escape from, or refute—the images that others have to them, images that are nearly always, in the biblical sense, *graven* images. Whether these images are negative or positive ones, or, as they usually are, admixtures of both, they can play havoc with one's life. Excessive attention to the opinions of others probably accounts for a good deal of the mental illness within our society. The problem does not lie so much with the ones who formulate the images as with ourselves, the recipients, who grant these opinions too much significance. Human beings must, of course, form conceptions of one another. We cannot live from day to day without some preunderstanding of each other's ways, preferences, and foibles. But to be *dependent* upon others for one's sense of identity and purpose is surely one of the most demeaning personal forms of human oppression. And the flattering images are in the end no less oppressive than are those less complimentary, for they too blur the truth; they too exchange the complexity and mystery of the self for simplistic and one-sided assessments. Bonhoeffer's fellow prisoners entertained images of him that he, like most of us, could only regard as adulatory—courage in the face of adversity, cheerfulness, calm self-confidence, and so forth. But finally he could not find satisfaction in these kinds of answers to his anxious question, who am I? For he knew within himself an entirely different sort of *I*.

The heteronomous determination of the self is by no means limited, however, to the interplay between individuals. At least where individual persons are concerned, there is usually sufficient *variety* of imagine-making that few of us are left to the mercy of a single opinion. We may set the opinions of one group of our acquaintances against those of another, and so escape captivation by narrow definitions of ourselves. By far the greater danger, where other-determined selfhood is concerned, is the sociopolitical molding of the self.

In our society, we are all subjected on a daily—even hourly!—basis to image-making of the most insidious and subtle sort, most of it determined by crass commercial interests. Modern communications have made it possible for the ever changing but ever similar modes and patterns of the consumer society to be imposed upon us, quietly but very effectively, from the cradle to the grave. Only the strong or the doggedly eccentric are able to withstand these pressures consistently; and on the other hand those who have not been able to develop lively *alternative* resources of identity and self-worth (and this applies especially to the young) are often pathetically misled or even ruined by the bogus standards of acceptability conveyed to them at every turn. In recent years a term hitherto largely unheard-of has entered nearly everyone's vocabulary: *anorexia nervosa.* In a society that values physical attractiveness as much as ours does, perhaps because we are secretly ashamed of our bodies, the messages that are communicated to young women and men in every television commercial can be devastating. Who can measure up to the "perfect" bodies, faces, hairstyles, complexions, muscularity, and the like, that the advertisers thrust upon a fascinated public?

The other-directedness that stems from the public realm is far more extensive, however, than such extremities might convey. The truth is, surely, that it is very, very difficult to be (let us say, in Kierkegaard's sense) an "individual" within this society. We are victims of a promotional in-dividual*ism* that smothers individuality in the name of preserving it. It is one of the abiding ironies of recent world history that a society which tried to *impose* conformity on its citizens (the former USSR) was in con-siderable measure undone, at last, by critical individuals who refused to conform; meanwhile, a society that noisily celebrates individual freedom, our own, has produced four generations of jeans wearers!

Obviously enough, the opinions and demands of others (including the community as a whole) on the self cannot be ignored or dismissed as having no validity. The object (at least where the Judeo-Christian tradi-tion is concerned) is not to turn out a world full of adamant and aloof individuals, stubbornly determined to be "true to themselves alone," a la Shakespeare's Polonius. Yet nothing seems more needful to human whole-ness (and especially in our present sociohistorical context) than that a person should be able in some calm but decisive way to say with St. Paul, "To me it is a very little thing that I am judged of men" (1 Cor 4:3, KJV) At very least, the heteronomous determination of the self must be held in tension with a certain critical, perhaps even stubborn, sense of the uniqueness and inviolability of the *I*. But here we are led to the second "dialogue" of the self.

Self-Determined (Autonomous) Selfhood

Dietrich Bonhoeffer's poem, beginning with the third stanza, follows the movement of the self in its quest for self-knowledge with great accuracy. Having considered the opinions that others hold of him, he turns to conscious reflection upon his own usually half-repressed assumptions about himself. The unsatisfactory or inconclusive nature of the other-determination of the self evokes the need for a more intentional, and more honest, *self*-determination.

Both historically and ontologically speaking, it is the awareness of oppressive or inauthentic heteronomy that causes persons, and peoples, to turn to this second source of self-identity and meaning: the self itself, as the bearer of memory and hope. Autonomy is the logical polarity of heteronomy. As individuals, we spend a good deal of our time and psychic energy fluctuating between these two poles. Conscious of being overly determined by others round about us, we flee to the secret chambers of the self to find solace and liberation. Yet often (sometimes to our sorrow!) we discover within those inner spaces of the soul a self-knowledge that is too deep for our conscious minds or too deviant for our consciences; and then we return to the others and ask them to deliver us from ourselves. So we move back and forth, from *Tell me who I am* to *I will tell you who I am*, in a vicious circle of frustrated evaluation.

But this pattern is not only observable in personal life; it is also a rather obvious dialectic of Western history. Classical civilization, including not only that of ancient Greece and Rome but also the Christian Middle Ages, was dominantly heteronomous in its approach to the question of the self. One was given one's identity and one's meaning by society, with its hierarchic and class structures, its religious and moral presuppositions, its predictable distribution of wealth and work. From the emperor to the slave, one received one's being and purposing from beyond the resources of individual imagination, ambition and choice.

What we call modernity, beginning with the Renaissance and reaching its apex in the Enlightenment of the eighteenth century, has been above all a refutation of heteronomous self-determination and an insistence upon autonomy—species autonomy and individual autonomy. Indeed, the idea of the "self-made man" (and here we must use masculine language if we want to be accurate) encapsulates in the most graphic way the *imago hominis* promoted by modernity—*especially*, it seems to me, in our North American appropriation of the modern vision. It is not accidental that so many of the heroic and symbolic figures of our mythology are individuals who, in the face of great challenges and drawbacks, *made themselves*. Their greatness lay precisely in the assertion of their own triumphant will-to-succeed. From literary heroes like Horatio Alger to real life personages such as Thomas Jefferson, Henry Ford, Thomas Edison, and the great captains of industry and money (including Rockefeller, Vanderbilt, Frick, Mellon, and the founder of my university, James McGill), we encounter individuals who themselves establish their very decisive identity and determine the direction and meaning of their own lives.

This approach to the self, which undoubtedly constitutes the philosophic as well as the general cultural background of North American individualism, is nevertheless inseparable from the larger, sociohistorical picture. There is a curious if frequently overlooked connection between private hopes and societal expectancy. It should not be forgotten that the nineteenth century, which saw the emergence of so many heroes of apparently autonomous achievement, was a time of high social vision. Political idealists (including Karl Marx!) dreamt of establishing perfect societies; Christian idealists dreamt of "the kingdom of God in our time"; and in London it was possible to rent a box in Albert Hall for 999 years—and many wealthy patrons of the arts did so! The much-lauded autonomous man of the modern epoch, with human reason elevated to ultimacy, and individuals courting the status of gods, needs to be seen within this larger context of societal expectancy.

But in the twentieth century, beginning with what Barbara Tuchman called "the guns of August" (1914) another sort of worldview began to take hold of the collective spirit of the West, expressing itself eventually in what has been termed "future shock" (Toffler) or "radical futurelessness" (Lifton and Falk) and the like. If the twentieth century was not a century of heroes (and it was not), it is surely because, by comparison with the two previous centuries, it could not entertain so promethean a view of the human species. Prometheus had given way to Sisyphus, Horatio Alger to Willy Loman. In North America we still try desperately to keep the optimistic individualism of our whole experiment alive, and therefore *attempts* at self-determination are continuously advanced. But the social confidence necessary to these personal formulae for self-improvement is conspicuously lacking.

Dietrich Bonhoeffer was a man of his times. In fact, for him as for other sensitive Germans of his era, the "malaise of modernity" could not be camouflaged, for, from the Treaty of Versailles onwards, the demise of the modern world view and what Spengler called "The Decline of the West" had been visited upon them in dramatic and unmistakable ways. It is not surprising therefore that the fourth long stanza of Bonhoeffer's poem, where he looks inward for an answer to his question, who am I? reflects more than anything else the angst of late modern humankind. The restlessness, longing, and powerlessness of which the stanza speaks is of a piece with the literature of existentialism and the theatre of the absurd.

Yet, unlike the existentialists (or at least the most prominent among them), Bonhoeffer does not seem surprised by his discoveries about the predicament of the self; for his thinking has roots that are older than those of modernity. As a Christian, he knows something already of what his contemporary and countryman, Paul Tillich, called "the shock of non-being" and "the anxiety of meaninglessness and despair." For that consciousness of negation has always been part of the deeper, if neglected, wisdom of the tradition of Jerusalem. That tradition, both in its older and newer Testamental expressions, understands that when the self attempts to achieve its own identity and sense of meaning it exposes itself, eventually, to the vulnerability that is a necessary if painful dimension of its finitude. In contrast to modernity, both Athens and Jerusalem—though in differing ways—know (in Reinhold Niebuhr's phrase) that "Man's story is not a success story." The Wisdom literature of Israel, especially Job and Ecclesiastes, was familiar with the prospect of human absurdity long before that possibility was self-consciously publicized by Sartre, Becket and Ionesco! And at the centre of the specifically *Christian* dimension of this tradition there is One who, remember, cries out in abandonment—who *must* do so, because his destiny is to unite himself to 'fallen' humanity in order, from within, to lift from it its wilful yet tragic degradation.

This tradition therefore mistrusts self-determined selfhood as much as it mistrusts selfhood heteronomously imposed; in fact, it may mistrust the former even more than the latter, for heroic humanity, suffering as it does under the burden of an illusion in relation to which it is doomed to fall short, is finally more pitiable than humanity humiliated and oppressed by others. Thus, from the third chapter of Genesis onwards, the quest for human self-sufficiency is shown to be the most pathetic of human quests: starting out to make ourselves great, we end by being smaller than ever. Seeking, like the pair in the Garden, to be "like gods," we regularly end by being less than authentically human—and by knowing that we are . . . "naked."

This does not mean that the Judeo-Christian tradition despises humanity's collective and individual struggle for species- and self-fulfilment. Overagainst every sort of other-directedness, every fatalism, every form of passivity, this tradition assumes that humankind, collectively and individually speaking, has a high potentiality for understanding and for responsible stewardship within the sphere of creation. But the Judeo-Christian tradition refuses voluntaristic self-determination as consistently as it refuses determination by others; and it finds in the persistent attempts of human beings to control their own lives and destinies the greatest source of disintegrative suffering. Without denying the partial validity of both heteronomous and autonomous selfhood, then, this faith tradition turns to a third possibility—namely, to a relationship in which the destructive propensities of the first two sources of the self may be, if not eliminated, at least held in check.

Responsive ("Theonomous") Selfhood

It is this third possibility to which, in the last line (yes, just a single line!) of his poem, Dietrich Bonhoeffer gratefully turns: *gratefully*, because as he shows us in the fifth and penultimate stanza, the dilemma posed by his anxious question about himself, far from being resolved by his reflections on the answers provided by others and by himself, has only been aggravated by these reflections. In fact, a terrible impasse has been created by the contraposition of the two sources: Who then am I, he asks: the one whom others believe me to be, or the one I meet when I turn inward? Am I finally just a confused and amorphous bundle of impulses—one day this, another that? Given the grave circumstances under which the poem was written, it is not surprising that the level of frustration present in the fifth stanza—a frustration familiar in one degree or another to all thinking persons!—here approaches anguish. It reminds one of St Paul's agonized outburst, in the seventh chapter of Romans, to what he calls "the war" going on within his own person: "The good that I would, I do not, and the evil that I would not, that I do . . . Wretched man that I am! Who will deliver me from this body of death?" (Rom 7:15, 24). In such dramatic circumstances as Paul's obvious need to authenticate his witness to an unknown readership or Bonhoeffer's lonely questioning of the drastic turn his life has taken, the self-doubt that is always present under the surface of life rises to accuse and taunt us. Torn between the identity laid upon us by others and the self that we feel (or perhaps fear) ourselves to be, we lack both integration and direction.

And this dialectic applies also to social contexts, which can and do aggravate the personal quest for identity and meaning. Our own period—this "time between the times" that some call postmodern—is conspicuously fraught with a widespread public confusion, often a repressed anguish, affecting private life at every turn. Unless we are obsessively committed to the modern vision, we know that we cannot any longer simply "make ourselves," any more than we can "make history" or bend nature to our collective will. Yet, apart from very artificial and contrived endeavour, neither do we have immediate access to premodern systems of meaning that can give us our identity and purpose ready-made. Neither heteronomous nor autonomous selfhood works for us. The resultant frustration as persons move between these two horizontal and now seriously non-functional sources of the self is well-expressed in Bonhoeffer's fifth stanza (it is perhaps his anticipation of postmodernity!).

> Who am I? This or the Other?
> Am I one person to-day, and to-morrow another?
> Am I both at once? A hypocrite before others,
> And before myself a contemptible woebegone weakling?
> Or is something within me still like a beaten army
> Fleeing in disorder from victory already achieved?
>
> Who am I? They mock me, these lonely questions of mine.

And yet—*and yet* . . . it is precisely this terrible loss of certainty about the self that constitutes the spiritual matrix for the response that the poet is finally able to hear—the only satisfying response to his "lonely questions." And such a recognition ought to be regarded by us all as a matter of hope, for it affirms the importance—even the potentially redemptive significance—precisely of periods such as ours, periods of confusion and spiritual doubt. Not all is lost in such historical moments. Perhaps in these gray, twilight times real *thought*, as distinct from ideology and mere convention, is possible—and real *faith*, too, as distinct from rote religious habit and mere credulity! As Hegel said, "The owl of Minerva [goddess of Wisdom] takes its flight at evening." In the midst of his bleak prison, his time almost run out, his great question still unanswered, Dietrich Bonhoeffer was caused to be open to a new and lively recall of what he had known all along, and to fashion out of that remembrance the very stuff of an authentic hope: "Whoever I am, Thou knowest, O God, I am thine!"

There are two dimensions of this third dialogue of the self upon which, in conclusion, I should like to dwell briefly, and they are both wonderfully demonstrated by this little poem of the martyr-theologian. The first is that this last and only satisfying response to the question of personal identity and meaning is a *response . . . without being an answer*. I consider it a matter of utmost wisdom that Bonhoeffer devoted only one line of his poem to this ultimate source of the self. To be sure, he was a Christian minister and theologian—one of the most perceptive of our epoch. But unlike the self-consciously and professionally religious, who feel it is their duty and right to speak authoritatively and vociferously for God, Bonhoeffer's reference to the divine is the essence of modesty; for it emerges, not from certitude, but from faith—from *trust* in God, not from theological omniscience! There is nothing in it of the doctrinaire, or of finality, only a certain humble gratitude for the relief from the debilitating dimensions of the struggle for self-knowledge in which the poet has been spiritually immersed.

In fact, given the great weight of the *question* (who am I?), this is no answer at all, in the usual sense, and if we turn it into an answer we shall do the poet-theologian a great injustice. As in the voice out of the whirlwind in the poem of Job, there is more question than answer in this final line of Bonhoeffer's poem. What we have here, as also in Job, is not an answer but a new and different orientation to the question. As for the question, who, really, am I?, it remains. But the sting of it has been re-moved—at least for the time being. It remains, but it remains as a question set within a context that has been missing in the two previous dialogues of the self: namely, the context of a relationship that is both primal and decisive, the relationship that Martin Buber called I–Thou. The *Eternal*

Thou, whom Bonhoeffer—radically altering the whole grammar of his poem—now actually *addresses*, is a Presence providing the anxious self with a new courage, whilst denying it presumption; a new confidence, whilst withholding certitude, a new freedom, whilst sustaining radical obedience and (what for Bonhoeffer remained a very important word) "discipleship." The response from a source transcendent of others *and* the self, unlike the two previous dialogues which only intensify the anxiety of the question, librates the self from its preoccupation with itself and frees it for the service of others: for discipleship.

Not an answer, then, but the presence of the Answerer: that is the response that Bonhoeffer receives, at last, to his, who am I? And it does not matter that the Answerer, as in Job, shows up with still more and still greater questions than the questions that we, in our existential need, are driven to ask. This is where faith and religion must part company. Religion wants to have answers—preferably in very explicit, propositional form: This is who you are—this and this and this! Faith, which is to say trust in the Eternal Other, is content to know that *it is known*: "Whoever I am, *Thou* knowest . . ."

And this leads to the second observation concerning this third dialogue of the self: Because it refuses to claim finality *for itself*, because the Source of its confidence lies in a trust that transcends the self, faith is free to open itself to all the answers to the identity and meaning of the self that the human mind and spirit devises; it is free to discourse with reason; it is free to discourse even with doubt—perhaps even especially with doubt, including self-doubt. Authentic faith is not threatened by rationality, even in its most radical forms—as for instance in the agnostic refusal to know anything about the human condition; or the atheistic denial of ultimate meaning for humans, individually or as a species. Religion, and particularly in its most fervent exponents, always excludes or sets strict limits to human questioning and speculation. It wants to displace human autonomy in favor of religious authority: sometimes, ironically enough, the authority of a collection of literature, the Bible, that contains such books as Job and such human cries as Jesus's cry of dereliction from the cross! But what is this kind of religion but the substitution of one sort of heteronomy for another? Its god, whatever his name (and it is usually a very masculine sort of god!) desires to tell us who we are, have been, and shall be—and so silence forever all our questions.

But the God of Dietrich Bonhoeffer (and of Jesus of Nazareth!) will not so thoughtlessly violate the mystery of our being, our identity, our vocation, our destiny. For this God wills to have vis a vis himself/herself, a real *other*, a person, a living, growing, changing being—a genuine *thou*: one who is able now and then, here and there, to say to God, "*Thou knowest*," and to be content to be known, and as such accepted as one profoundly affirmed by this Eternal Other.

To be sure, the Judeo-Christian understanding of the self is not all sheer mystery. There is an anthropology as there is a theology and a Christology and an ecclesiology and all the rest. I would be a naïve and shiftless representative of my profession were I not to say so. One does not despise the countless works of those who have tried, in their time, to define, in Christian or other religious perspective, the nature and destiny of humankind—including the seventeen or so volumes that now constitute the collected works of Dietrich Bonhoeffer!

But through the best of all these works, beginning with the Bible itself, there runs a theme that the faithful must certainly honor, and that is the theme of the *livingness* and so of the mystery of all life, above all of life as it rises to consciousness of itself in the human spirit and mind. The world is full of answers to the question, who am I? History moves jerkily, even frantically, from one set of answers to another, one ideology to another, one trend or fashion or image of the human to another. Humankind as a whole seems incapable of living with its own deepest questions, and will resolve them superficially—even knowing its answers to be superficial!—rather than living with trust in our creaturehood and in its Creator.

Biblical faith clings to the mystery of life and of the self, not because it is just another mysticism but because it believes that the ultimate source and ground of our existence is a transcendence of whom it may be said that it is *love*. The self that knows a little—even a little—of this undergirding love does not request, and will not put its confidence in, any of the "answers" that are given to the question of its identity and its meaning, as if they were absolute. Whenever that self (as it does, being human) finds itself once again thrust naked into the burning questions of its being, meaning, and destiny, it must again discover the only satisfying answer, the answer that is beyond all the answers: "Whoever I am, thou knowest, O God, I am thine."

8

What Are People For?

Stewardship as Human Vocation

Introduction

The 10,000-year experiment of the settled life will stand or fall by what
we do, and don't do, now ... The great advantage we have, our best chance
for avoiding the fate of past societies, is that we know about those past
societies. We can see how and why they went wrong. Homo sapiens has the
information to know itself for what it is: an Ice Age hunter only half-evolved
towards intelligence; clever but seldom wise.[1]

LET ME LAY MY cards on the table right away: I think there is probably no
more immediately important theological and ethical task for Christians
today than that of developing a worldly theology of human stewardship.
I wrote these words at the height of this past summer's sustained heat
wave. Temperatures in my home city of Montreal, which people falsely
imagine is a very cold place (well, it sometimes is—in midwinter) soared
into the high 90s and sometimes over 100 Fahrenheit, and stayed that way

1. Wright, *A Short History of Progress*, 131.

for days. They were accompanied often by serious smog conditions, and by dangerous ultraviolet indexes. Yet the patterns of human behavior in the city continued without a change. Though Montreal has one of the best public transit systems in the world, the North American preference for the automobile continued unabated. Every morning, often as I stood at the bus stop nearest my home, I watched as car after car went past on its way into the inner city, which is congested beyond belief—almost always with one person only, the driver. I wanted to paint a big sign and hold it up as I stood there: "Take the bus, dammit!" But my wife cautioned me against this: she felt I didn't need the publicity that such an act would bring—in addition to the cancer with which I had recently been diagnosed. Meanwhile, ads in the local papers continued to praise us for our love affair with cars. "Buy one of these new cars," cried one blatantly smug ad in a local newspaper, "and throw your bus pass away!"

Standing in all that heat, and breathing in the noxious fumes that were contributing to the smog that had engulfed us, I had very bleak apocalyptic thoughts—though I am not, on the whole, an advocate of apocalyptic religion. Are we at the beginning of a really dangerous period in the history of our planet? Is the global warming of which so many have warned us quite literally real, and not just the rantings of gloomy environmentalists, as status quo politicians and industrialists keep telling us? Is this maybe the onset of planetary catastrophe?—How do you know when you are already into a catastrophic period? When is the point of no return? Is it already too late to alter the tragic course of a planet in the throes of repression, self-deception and the delusions of ideological progress-theory?

I begin in this perhaps alarmist way because—frankly—I *am* alarmed. Environmental degradation is not the only crisis by which our civilization is threatened—there are dozens more. But the radical deteriorization of the environment is both the most ubiquitously threatening (since without a habitable environment all the other problems are "resolved," along with life itself) and the most difficult for the possessing peoples of the planet to grasp and admit. Moreover, as the citizens of such an apparently favored society we are deterred from coming to terms with this condition by the fact that we are both the greatest benefactors of the technological society we have created and the greatest polluters. We may be creating the conditions that will make earth uninhabitable, but in the meantime—in this little "time between"—we seem to "have it very good," all things considered; and the fact that we have it so at the expense of the majority of the rest of earth's creatures, human and extra-human, clearly does not disturb our conscience; it apparently doesn't even stir us to know (what we must surely know, deeply) that we are robbing our grandchildren and great-grandchildren of their birthright!

One feels desperate, thinking such thoughts. But we must think them—we must think them in all seriousness!—if we are ever going to act to offset the catastrophe we are courting. It is not just action that we need, however; it is a change at the level of self-understanding, of the imaging of ourselves, the human species.

And that is where the theology of stewardship comes in. It comes in, first, not as an ethic or moral imperative; but first as theology—or as Karl Barth would have said, theo-anthropology: a conception of God that is at the same time a conception of human creaturehood. We should perhaps alter the traditional answer to the old Westminster catechism's famous question, "What is the chief end of man?"—the traditional answer being, as perhaps even Lutherans know, "The chief end of man is to glorify God and enjoy him forever." I would like to rewrite this answer in order to make it fit the reality of our present context: "The chief end of the human being is to be God's faithful steward in a profoundly threatened creation."

That would be putting stewardship right out front and center, where it should be. It would also be "glorifying God" in a real, not merely a rhetorical, way. We Christians have been hiding this biblical metaphor under a bushel, the bushel of religion. We've talked endlessly about stewardship, to be sure, but in a truncated, unworldly manner: that is, we've associated it too narrowly with support for our churches, which, unlike the old European version of Christian establishment, have had in this new world to fend for themselves. Well and good; but in doing this we have prevented this potent symbol from entering the mainstream of Christian, human, and worldly consciousness. Sometimes churchfolk have actually criticized me for wanting to open the theology of stewardship to its worldly application. They fear it will take away from support of the church! Nonsense! What is needed is a transformation of human beings, churched and unchurched, in their way of regarding themselves in their total intercourse with the world. Churchfolk who feel themselves to be a stewards in this larger sense will be far more likely to support the church too than if they confine their notion of stewardship to a restrictive ecclesiastical deployment.

What Are People For?

But having begun by sounding this alarm, let me start all over again, in a more reflective way. And, since I have mentioned the famous question of the Westminster Catechism, let me begin by reworking that question in contemporary terms. The old Westminster divines stated the primary anthropological question of our faith in admirable doctrinal language: "What is the chief end of man? [read, of the human being]?" And as we have seen they not only stated the question in a fine doctrinal manner, but they also provided a wonderfully nuanced religious answer: "The chief end of the human being is to glorify God and enjoy him forever." Splendid! But this question and this answer belong to a calmer and more pious age than ours—an age that, for all the calamitous nature of daily life, was decidedly more ordered and spiritually sure than ours. If we want to discover the Christian anthropology appropriate to our own age, we shall have to begin by rewording *the question itself*, not only the answer.

And how shall we state that question in a manner that has sufficient urgency to capture the crisis of our times? There are of course many ways of stating it, but none, in my experience, is so contextually perceptive as wording proposed by one of the truly prophetic minds at work in these United States. I refer to Wendell Berry, and specifically to his book *What Are People For?* That's it! That's how we should state the primary anthropological question of Christians today. *What are people for?*[2]

There are now more than seven billion of us on this planet (the world population has tripled in my lifetime), and the rate of population increase, which many expected to show signs of lessening, is in fact continuing apace. The US Bureau of Statistics estimates that by the year 2050 the population of planet Earth will be nine and a half billion. In the two-thirds world, abysmal poverty, disease, starvation, and interracial and religious hatred prevent most human beings from entertaining even the most modest expectations and purposes. In our own society, even with its relative affluence and the high expectations of individuals, many of our people still feel unwanted, some—especially among the old, the young, and the

2. Berry, *What Are People For?*, 123ff.

poor—feel quite superfluous. The suicide rate among the indigenous peoples of North America is the highest in the world. Surrounded as we are by complex machinery and whole technocratic systems in relation to which we feel very small indeed, human beings ask as perhaps never before in history what reason could be found under the sun for their existence.

Not only that; we are the recipients, daily, of messages about our species that can only render us still more confused and depressed about our *raison d'être*. Indeed, a great deal of what we hear suggests that humankind is not only the most problematic species of all (a bit of news that would not surprise readers of Augustine and Calvin, though it is still shocking to middle-America), but that we are a species whose very existence *impedes* creation and its promised flowering. The great Harvard scientist E. O. Wilson notes, for instance, that if the human species were suddenly to disappear, the earth would flourish; whereas, if the *ant* species disappeared there would be catastrophe. Such a statement is hardly calculated to make us humans feel wanted, let alone needed!

What *Are* Human Beings For?

Do we have any positive purpose at all? Are we destined from the outset to self-destruct?—and perhaps to take down the whole ecosystem along with us? Christians would do well not to underestimate the power of this attitude in the general populous. If people develop indifference toward such ultimate questions as purpose and meaning, life and death, it is generally because they sense that no answers are trustworthy—or perhaps that none but negative answers can be given. The cynicism and nihilism that are just underneath the surface of our culture—cynicism and nihilism that can be heard in the popular music, most of which sounds to me like one gigantic, noisy cry for help!—should be taken with great seriousness. It may sound blasé, "cool," when it comes from the affluent young; but it is really, I suspect, the most deadly form of despair, which (as noted elsewhere) Kierkegaard rightly said is the despair that does not and will not know that it is despair.

What then is the Christian response to this question? What *are* people for?—according to this faith?

Biblical tradition gives many answers to that question, because it believes that where *purpose* is concerned no one answer suffices. Each epoch has to revisit this question in the light of the exigencies, the problems and the possibilities of the here and now. In tranquil times (and there have been a few such in history) it may be enough to say, "The chief end of the human creature is to glorify God and enjoy God forever." Ours is not a tranquil time. Stronger medicine is needed. And none of the ways in which the biblical tradition answers this question is more potent, more evocative, under the circumstances of today, than is just this metaphor of stewardship. Not only so, but quite apart from us Christians, the world itself, in many voices, has discovered this metaphor and made better use of it than we have. If you listen, you can hear this term being used today in many quarters (political, economic, scientific, certainly ecological) that are strictly secular. Stewardship is a term that has achieved coinage in our time. It is (as I said in the title of my first book on the subject) an ancient symbol "come of age." Symbols are not arbitrarily imposed on society. As Tillich said, they come to be, and they fade away—unlike signs, which are deliberately adopted. Symbols come to be when they are existentially needed. If many of the most concerned earthlings have turned to this symbol; if even in foreign settings (like the German) where there is no good word for the concept, the English term *stewardship* has been adopted, it is simply because there is, in our society, a linguistic and vocational vacuum that needs to be filled. And, thank God, our religion has kept this term alive, albeit in truncated versions, so that now it can be picked up and used by many who do not darken the doors of our churches.

Yet the churches—or at least those within them who still are given to serious thought—have something very important to contribute to this rediscovery of the symbol of the steward. For, like all symbols, this one too can be misused and misleading.

One of its perennial misconceptions is its confusion with *managerial* conceptions of the human. Many ecologists and environmentalists, and several theologians as well, positively dislike this term because it suggests to them that the human, differentiated from and highly superior to all the other creatures and processes of the planet, is called upon to direct and interfere with nature. And this is a very serious charge. For precisely human technocratic interference with the processes of nature is responsible for the greater share of the problematic that now confronts us. Again and again, our vaunted image of ourselves in terms of an almost divine rationality, combined all too often with a *religious* sense of our destiny as "lords and masters" of the earth, has introduced chaos and catastrophe into the very systems we thought to fix. It is in fact precisely our image of ourselves as earth's 'managers' that, in the view of the most responsible ecologists, must be changed.

I regard it as one of the greatest blunders of Christian scholarship in the last century that the translators of the New Revised Standard Version of the Bible saw fit to replace the ancient world *steward*, in several places, with the word *manager*. However linguistically acceptable that change might be, it was theologically and apologetically stupid beyond belief. Whatever the Bible and the best traditions of the Christian faith may have to say about the grandeur of the human (and they have a lot to say on that subject) they *never* entertain the ludicrous notion that the human being is equipped to be the CEO of creation! Not only the doctrine of sin, but already the doctrine of creation, militates against just such a conception of human nature and destiny.

The Two Poles of Stewardship

Accountability

For biblical faith, two polar—that is opposing yet mutually informing—conceptions characterize the metaphor of the steward: we may call them *accountability* and *responsibility*. And each of these poles not only tells us something positive about human vocation in the midst of creation, but they also warn us against two distortions—distortions that are not only theoretical but very practical and common.

First, consider accountability. The steward in biblical usage (for instance in the Old Testament saga of Joseph, and in the parables of Jesus) is *not* the owner. Decidedly not! The very word *steward* bespeaks the steward's accountability to another. The "other," in the biblical story, may be an unnamed householder or a monarch (Pharaoh, for instance) or God. But the accountability factor is paramount in all instances. Stewards who do not act with a view to their superior's wishes are severely chastised. And when the metaphor is applied to the human creature generally, in relation to his or her "Lord," the accountability factor is at the very heart of the symbol. For "the earth is *the Lord's* and the fullness thereof." It is not ours to do with as we please. Not only are there obvious *limits* to the human steward's activity—limits symbolized, for instance, by the injunction against touching the fruit at the center of the garden in the Genesis creation narrative; but there are also rights and privileges of the other, nonhuman creatures, who "have their seed within them"—that is, who develop and prosper according to their own inherent properties and needs, and who must not, therefore, be thoughtlessly tampered with by the human.

This accountability factor in stewardship is not incidental to the symbol, it is of its essence. Moreover, the emphasis here is by no means on *status*, as if the human were separable from or superior in relation to the other creatures; the emphasis rather is on calling—vocation. The term *manager*, at least in our society, is clearly a status symbol. ("My son, you know, is the *manager* of that department." "The management cannot agree with the union on the subject of working hours, etc.") Stewardship, biblically understood, is not a status symbol. Even when it applies to servants, like Joseph, who are highly placed and revered by others, they are still servants; and if they start behaving like managers, they will be chastised by the highest authority—if Jesus's parables have anything to say about it!

Stewardship, therefore, militates against all those conceptions of the human that elevate our species above all the others, and interpret the *dominion* granted to the human creature by the Creator in the second story of creation as though it clearly meant mastery. In fact, as I argued in my book *Imaging God*, the "dominion" that the human creature is to exercise, according to biblical faith, is the dominion of service, not mastery. The sovereignty, the deity, that we are to "image" when we are being true to our calling as creatures made in God's image is not the sovereignty of a Caesar or a Louis XIV but the sovereignty of the Christ. It is *his* dominion, the dominion of the one we call Lord (*Dominus*), and not the dominion of a tyrant or potentate, that we are to represent in our life vis-à-vis all the others. And *Christ's* dominion is the dominion of the one who *suffers* in behalf of others, not of one who reduces others to servitude.

Responsibility

The other side of this dialectic of stewardship is *responsibility*. The steward is accountable, but the steward is also responsible. Stewards, in the biblical literature, are not just people who take orders from others. They have to think for themselves, to make decisions, to manage the households over which they have been given responsibility. Joseph, as the chief steward of Egypt during a critical period in its history, made momentous decisions that affected the whole land and its neighboring countries—including the land of Joseph's brothers. He has to think carefully, plan wisely, consider the future, and act with foresight in the present. And the Bible assumes that Joseph, a human being, has these possibilities—is capable of such responsible behavior.

This is of course a very different image of the human from all those anthropologies, whether secular or religious, which assume that human beings as such are wholly untrustworthy or incapable of responsible behavior. The Hebraic-Christian tradition has a high anthropology: it expects much of the human—not only in the realm of deeds, but also in the realm of understanding. Even in its fallen estate, the human being can pursue this stewardly vocation—never perfectly, but with enough sense and insight to preserve life in the face of many threats.

And here is where the theology of human stewardship takes on all those conceptions of human nature and destiny that depict humankind as being so weak, so inept, or so thoroughly at the mercy of fate that nothing much can be expected of humans. The biblical teaching of stewardly accountability counters every exaggeratedly *high* conception of the human; the biblical teaching of stewardly responsibility also counters every excessively *low* estimate of human capability.

There is, for instance, among some of the so-called deep ecologists a feeling—sometimes openly expressed, sometimes just under the surface of analysis—that since the human species is both the great troublemaking element in planetary existence and virtually incapable of effecting any kind of change, the best thing would indeed be the disappearance of this species, or at least that it should refrain from any kind of interference in the natural order.

I had my first encounter with this attitude some forty years ago, when I was part of a large interdisciplinary course in the big secular university to which I then belonged. The course was called "Man and the Biosphere" (I hasten to say that this occurred prior to our new consciousness of oppressive language!), and it was heavily represented by the sciences—especially the so-called life sciences. One after another, my scientific and social-scientific colleagues stood at the lectern in the great amphitheater and told the students how devastatingly the human population of earth had acted. Then one evening, when the whole teaching staff was assembled before the class to address questions, a young woman stood up and put the following question to the panel: "If Man is the problem, wouldn't the world be . . . better off . . . without him?"

The panel of professors was totally stumped—I think they grasped for the first time, at that point, the pessimistic nature of the message they had been giving to this audience of young people, and I think (and hope) that the realization shocked them. Then I noticed that all my colleagues were looking at me! I was the theologian in this study—a rare thing, in fact, in our very secular university; but apparently I was also to be the defender of "Man," and not only God. I was glad to do so—and the experience made me realize more than ever how right Karl Barth was in calling our discipline *theo-anthropology,* or *the-anthropology.*

All the same, it was a scary moment; for the entire thrust of the class until now had been precisely what the young woman student rightly identified: Human beings are the problem; and we intellectuals are here as problem-solvers; so let us rid ourselves of this problem and then the world will be . . . better off.

Somehow I found words—and I am sure they were less coherent, in the heat of the situation then, than what I shall report to you now. But I had found myself immediately intrigued by that term, "better off"; and so I said to the young woman (while my scientific friends listened with great curiosity), Now, I wonder what it would mean, after the disappearance of humans, to employ this language, "better off." Would the elephants, do you suppose, hold a symposium in which they would assure one another that the absence of the human element represented an immense improvement over the past? Or would the rabbits, notorious for fecundity, gather en masse and sing a great *Te Deum,* the planet having been left to them to repopulate? And would creatures big and small, along with "all things bright and beautiful," assemble in some amphitheater similar to this, with representatives from all parts of the globe, and produce papers on the subject of the beneficial elimination of the human element?

The point is, I said, that so far as we know *homo sapiens* is the only creature that indulges in valuation—that is, in thinking in terms like "better off" and "worse off" and so on; and *homo sapiens* can do this because of the complex character of its brain, the sensitivity of its feelings, the capacity of its spirit for compassion and sacrifice and so on. And the question that we all have to ask ourselves is whether there is any need, any place, any role for such a creature in the universe—that is, for ourselves; for we are not speaking here about abstract things, but about ourselves and our own place in the scheme of things. Are we *only* problematic creatures? Or do we, *could* we, make a difference—not only for our own species, but for all?"

Conclusion

I have no idea whether this message penetrated or changed anyone who heard it, but I, for one, have never forgotten the incident. For I think that Christians must indeed be and become, in this skeptical and often despairing world, the defenders of humanity. Without waxing romantic about the "piece of work" called Man or Humankind, we must also be prepared to stand up for the capacity of human beings *qua human beings to understand, to care, and to try to effect change.* Fatalism about humankind is the surest way to hasten catastrophe. Nothing at all will be accomplished in the struggle to avert ecological disaster, or enhance justice, or create the conditions of peace, unless, collectively, we humans have some real belief in our own capacity for *responsibility.*

It belongs to our tradition—to our Protestant heritage—to remind our fellow humans that we are accountable to Another. As Calvin kept saying, "We are not our own." It also belongs to this tradition to keep before the world of people and nations the many ways in which we *fail* in this calling to be accountable stewards of God's good creation. We cannot join the ultra-liberal, ultra-romantic chorus that has nothing but good to say about human nature and destiny.

But neither can we join the chorus of those who denigrate the human and fatalize it and consign it to oblivion. Humans are stewards—servants; and often we are "unworthy servants" and presumptuous stewards. There is much to be said against us. But we are not superfluous, we are not *only* problematic, and we are not as dispensable as some of our fierce critics think. Would the world *really* flourish if we disappeared? And what would that mean—*flourish*? Who would notice that? Who would appreciate that? Who would write poems and make films and write music about it? E. O. Wilson's *bon mot* is finally as absurd as was the student's question in our class of long ago. "Man"—corporately, individually—is accountable, and if and when we are all called to account, we shall have much to confess! But we are also capable of an astonishing kind of responsibility. We are all, to one degree or another, capable of *thought*. We are all, to one degree or another, capable of *understanding*. We are all, to one degree or another, capable of *articulation*, of *finding words*. We are all, to one degree or another, capable of *acting*. We are even (no doubt some of us more than others, but all of us in our differing ways) capable of compassion, empathy, solidarity, suffering with and for others. One may certainly agree with Ronald Wright (in the opening quotation of this address) that human being "seldom" achieve "wisdom"—*yet sometimes they do.*

In other words, the *stewardship* to which we are called is not an idle or merely idealistic vocation; it is a real possibility. God our Maker made us to be keepers of a garden; and when the garden became a wilderness God did not see fit to alter our vocation. No, we are to be stewards now in the wilderness. It's a difficult calling, and none of us ever fully succeeds at it. At the end of the day we have to confess that we are . . . "unprofitable servants." And yet . . . it can be done!

PART 3

The Law within Gospel

9

Beyond Good and Evil

The good that I would, that I do not; and the evil that I would not that I do
... Wretched man that I am, who shall deliver me from this body of death?
—ROMANS 7:15, 24

THE MYSTERY OF GOOD and evil may be approached in two related but
distinct ways. One way concentrates on good and evil as impersonal and
even cosmic realities affecting all life (natural catastrophes, diseases and
death, geological and geographic conditions beneficial or detrimental to
life, and so on). The other approach asks more directly about good and evil
as they manifest themselves in human individual and social life, that is, as
a moral inquiry. We are not only passive recipients of the consequences
of good and evil influences at work in the natural order; we are ourselves
agents of good and evil, and the confluence of these opposing tendencies
in both persons and societies constitutes a large part of the "mystery" of
this whole subject. It is, however, the second, moral or ethical aspect of the
subject on which I intend to concentrate here.

To set the tone for what I hope to argue in this essay, let me comment
briefly on the title I have given it: "Beyond Good and Evil." Readers will
recall that they have heard this title before. It was the title of a book published in 1886 by one of the great "mis-evangelists" (as Rosenstock-Heusey

called them) produced by the intellectual fevers of the late nineteenth century, namely, Friedrich Nietzsche. In his *Beyond Good and Evil*, Nietzsche, an offspring of generations of Lutheran theologians, who renounced the Christian religion as the West's great concession to human weakness and cowardice, insisted that all persons aspiring to the brave new humanity he heralded must rise above petty concerns of good and evil and grasp, with boldness, the natural and laudable craving for *power* with which humans, freed from the bonds of religion, are endowed. Ordinary morality, Nietzsche announced, is for those incapable of originality, fit only for following. Such "herd-morality" must be surpassed if the human species is ever to achieve its high goal, the goal of mastery. That goal demands of the few who are capable of attaining to it that they embrace a new, "*heroic morality*" that dares to establish its own "*values*"—a morality in which everything is permitted if it advances the cause of human autonomy and dominion: a morality that is *beyond good and evil*.

It is not difficult to see how such a philosophy could seem attractive to Adolf Hitler and his followers, though Nietzsche scholars argue persuasively that Nietzsche himself would have been horrified at such a misappropriation of his ideas. What is less obvious is how correctly Nietzsche perceived the ethical consequences of the secularization of the West—what he called, symbolically, "the death of God." If God is no longer a lively factor to be reckoned with in our consideration of good and evil, he asks in effect, then is it not precisely our human responsibility to *invent* ethical priorities ("values")[1] that foster our own ascendancy?

Just that, it seems to me, is what we have been doing in our society, largely without either realizing or naming it. But there are consequences of such "value engineering," and our present moral confusion cannot be separated from them. We cannot, I think, return to old moral codes that depend upon the hegemony of the Judeo-Christian tradition; but neither can we abandon transcendent sources of the good without compounding our moral confusion.

Accordingly, the *thesis* I want to advance here is strictly anti-Nietzschean. It may be stated in this way: *Over against the contemporary drift towards ethical relativism and moral chaos, good and evil are permanently*

---

1. The language of values has become almost universal; but few who employ it know its origin. If they did, they might think twice before giving it the moral weight and respectability they intend!

legitimate distinctions, the contemplation of which is necessary to the survival of civilization. At the same time, contrary to every type of moral absolutism, good and evil are inextricably interwoven into the fabric of our actual living. Human <u>authenticity</u> therefore depends upon a grace that is indeed (but not in Nietzsche's sense) beyond good and evil. These three sentences, in that order, designate the three sections of what follows.

Not Everything Is Permitted

What I shall argue here, then, is that *over against the contemporary drift towards ethical relativism, good and evil are permanently legitimate distinctions, the steady <u>contemplation</u> of which is necessary to the survival of civilization.*

How, I wonder, can one defend a claim like this today without seeming to be an old-fashioned moralist? To begin with, let me assure readers that I am not one of those who hanker after an old morality that made it perfectly clear what good and evil quite specifically and permanently are. I am old enough to have had firsthand experience of the remnants of Victorian morality, and I have no wish to revive it. At the same time, can anyone doubt that the many-faceted dilemma of our present society manifests itself most conspicuously in our moral confusion? Indeed, we shall not have become quite serious about a theme like the mystery of good and evil until we have faced the difficulty even of using these terms today, especially as they apply to the ethical side of the subject. As moral categories, *good* and *evil* seem to many of our contemporaries too definitive, too transcendent of the freedom and individuality that we all treasure. Can distinctions between good and evil even be suggested without treading on the "rights" of this or that group for free self-expression? Much of what was upheld in the various and successive moral codes by which Western civilization has been guided seems to enlightened postmoderns so restrictive, unbending, and biased towards the privileged that little or nothing can be salvaged from the tradition for present-day use.

Instead, we are encouraged to develop the language and habit of "value-prioritizing"—Nietzsche's concept. The ancients, whether of Athens of Jerusalem, whether Socrates or Christ, did not speak of values but of *goods*. The good, they believed, precedes us. It is a given. What is good is good whether we "value" it or not. Evil is the deprivation or spoliation of the good. And *wisdom*, whether in Greek philosophy or Hebraic-Christian faith, means the cultivation of an understanding of and love for the good—and a concomitant vigilance against its negation by forces of evil within us and around us.

Personally, I do not think that we can dispense with these older traditions without serious consequences. When for the givenness of the good one substitutes the language of human valuation, one ends, surely, with morality by consensus: if enough people value a practice or course of action, it is regarded as good—for the time being. Thus today the effective criteria of acceptable behavior for vast numbers of our fellow citizens are drawn, not from the Ten Commandments of the Sermon on the Mount or the Qur'an or any other traditional expression of good and evil, but from the constantly recurring public opinion polls by which majority values may be ascertained or legitimated.

One consequence of this is of course the lack of any sort of moral stability; for public opinion is remarkably fickle and continually shifting. Suddenly one morning one learns that the majority of one's fellow citizens now favor abortion on demand, or euthanasia, or perhaps (since liberalizing tendencies usually beget conservative reactions) a return to the death penalty. This kind of fluctuation is profoundly unsettling even to those who approve such an approach; because a vital dimension of morality has always been to provide, in the midst of life's flux, a certain sense of normalcy. If good and evil are so unpredictable, what guidelines remain for the living of life, the education of the young, the codification and enforcement of law, and so forth?

But there is an even more questionable side of the "values" approach to morality. For while it may appear highly democratic, as though the entire population were engaged in setting goals and determining appropriate policy, the reality is that public preferences are constantly being manipulated by powerful elements in our midst—especially, today, by global economic forces that, in the age of mass communications, easily and regularly sway whole populations towards preferences favorable to their commercial interests. Thus, with a strange Marxian twist, the power that Nietzsche reserved for his superior intellectuals devolves upon *economic* elites, whose designs are even more detached from moral considerations than were those of Nietzsche's fabled *Übermenschen*.

It will be (and is!) argued that in a pluralistic and multicultural society, a society no longer based on one dominant cultural heritage, there *can* be no other basis for moral decision-making than human valuation. But that conclusion, I believe, is both a deceptive and a dangerous one. Obviously enough, it is neither possible nor desirable today to seek to *impose* upon the whole diverse population moral conventions that derive from one particular cultic and cultural heritage. Christians in North America who attempt to do so are constantly opposed by other who (with right!) complain that the theological presuppositions of Christian morality are not *their* foundational assumptions. And this complaint, we must assume, will only increase with the increasing human and spiritual diversity of our populations.

But while specific moral codes and conventions may belong to particular traditions, the contemplation of good and evil is not reserved for any one culture or cult. It is a *human* undertaking, privilege and responsibility—part, indeed, of what it *means* to be human. And the most vital aspect of such contemplation is not, surely, that out of it there should emerge definitive, immutable codes and systems of morality. What is important, rather, is that both as individuals and societies we should learn through such contemplation to live with the *question* of good and evil— that this question should become a vital aspect of the consciousness that, individually and corporately, we bring to the consideration of every act, decision, or piece of legislation and public policy. To ask whether a thing is *good* is, after all, quite different from asking whether one values it. I may value personal freedom; but if I ask whether, in the context of a complex society, my own unlimited freedom is a "good" that must be sustained at all costs, I shall (hopefully!) come up with a response that challenges my private evaluation of the matter. As nations facing increasingly alarming rates of unemployment and underemployment, most reasonable people *value* the preservation and creation of meaningful work for everyone; but if we ask, as we must, whether such a goal can be attained without placing limits on the growth of human-displacing technologies, our valuational thinking will at least have to be qualified by a more informed regard for the whole. In North America, we obviously value the kind of personal mobility that automobiles provide; but if the threat of global warming is as closely related to the automobile as we are assured it is, we shall very soon have to reconsider a long-term *good* that transcends and 'trumps' our present love-affair with cars.

Indeed, the ecological crisis of our period may be the most effective of all in turning us back to rudimentary considerations of good and evil, and away from purely subjective and majority preferences. For nature, we are learning, represents an *objective* face of reality that will not unquestioningly support the demands made of it by human greed and species domination.

I argue, then, that, far from being passé, the age-old quest for the knowledge of good and evil is still existentially necessary—and necessary, now, not only for the satisfaction of an intellectual or spiritual impulse, but for human and creational *survival*. Civilization will not endure without a lively return to just this quest. In this, I stand with Dostoevsky and against Nietzsche. Dostoevsky's greatest novel, perhaps the greatest novel of Western literature as a whole, *The Brothers Karamazov*, is one long protest against the substitution of ephemeral human valuation for fundamental considerations of good and evil. If no good or evil exists beyond our valuing, then, says Dostoevsky, *everything is permitted*: there is nothing that may not be done. Those "heroic Nietzschean" types, like Dostoevsky's Ivan Karamazov, who feel they are above petty moral considerations on account of their superior intellectual capacities, will reap the whirlwind of their supposed cleverness. For the great question, which Dostoevsky does not hesitate to make the centerpiece of his story, is whether a secular society, a society without God, is capable of sustaining *any* operative and meaningful ethic. How, he asks, is humankind to fare without God? "After all, that would mean that now all things are lawful, that one may do anything one likes."

> . . . if God does not exist, man is the boss of the earth, of creation. Magnificent! Only how will he be *virtuous* without God? That is the question. I think about it all the time. For whom will he love then, whom will man love? To whom will he render gratitude, to whom will he sing his hymn?

This is the *theological* question that underlies all contemporary discussion of the mystery of good and evil. We will not solve it here; yet we must certainly notice it, and mark its continuing presence and unavoidability in all human cultures. Whether our post-Christendom West will be capable of profoundly ethical reflection and behavior remains to be seen. One can hope, however, that the new concern for "spirituality" that has gripped many of our contemporaries is more than just a bourgeois extension of fashionable value-prioritizing rhetoric—that it contains within itself some intuitive awareness of he need for genuine transcendence if we are to survive the self-destructive propensities of our so-called freedom.

Our Moral Ambiguity

Contrary to every type of moral absolutism, good and evil are inextricably <u>*interwoven*</u> *in the fabric of our actual living.*

So far, I have argued—against the present-day drive towards ethical relativism—that we are obliged by the circumstances of our context to return to elementary considerations of good and evil, considerations that are distinct from our immediate personal and societal preferences. We must learn anew to ask about what is *good*, not only what is valuable to ourselves as individuals and societies and a species.

There is, however, a certain *temptation* connected with every attempt to define the good and to distinguish it from evil. It is a temptation into which humankind has fallen time after time, and it is a temptation, moreover, that is so close to our own history as peoples of this so-called New World that it may almost be said to be our natural or habitual inclination. I refer to the temptation to moral absolutism, or, more simply, moralism. Under the spell of this temptation, people conclude that the quickest solution to any sort of moral confusion is to revise old moral codes or construct new ones that delineate *clearly and explicitly* what is good and what is evil, and fashion legislation accordingly. It is not surprising, given the power of this temptation in North American history, that today, in the face of our society's moral lassitude, there should be a vociferous "law and order" element in our midst, continuously clamouring for the reestablishment of a strict codification of good and evil, with all the predictable rewards and punishments thereto pertaining. What is so frustrating about this approach for all who have a modicum of knowledge of its history is that they know how ineffective moralism really is—and how baneful are the moral problems that it introduces in its naïve attempt to solve all moral problems! For serious Christians, moralistic solutions to profound ethical questions are especially frustrating because (usually in the name of true-believing Christianity!) they promulgate simplistic moral teachings that misrepresent and distort the most penetrating moral insights of biblical faith.

That the ethical relativism and confusion of the present should be countered by fresh demands for moral decisiveness is, however, all too consistent with our history as peoples of this continent. The search for moral absolutes inheres in our Puritan and other beginnings. As a new world endeavoring to extricate itself spiritually as well as physically from the centuries of revenge that finally pushed our forebears out of the old European homelands, we tried to establish on these shores a more innocent, more righteous commonwealth—one in which good and evil were plainly demarcated, in which good was honored and evil shunned, in which children were reared in morality as the finest fruits of religion, in which those who governed were *worthy* of governing—not (as for Nietzsche) on account of their intellectual superiority, but because of the superior moral quality of their lives.

It was in many ways a noble vision, and never as wrongheaded as its detractors have regularly claimed. Yet it was, surely, naively idealistic about the *attainability* of authentic goodness, and less than perceptive concerning the subtle character of evil. In particular, it failed to take account of the temptations to *self*-righteousness on the part of the apparently good. Throughout our history, we have been plagued by a moralism that too easily distinguishes between good and evil, overlooking the "mystery" of their combination in the actual living of life. Lured by simplistic definitions of good and of its reward, the greatest surprise that has overtaken us as peoples of this continent (a surprise already visible to many in the previous century but unavoidable by all thoughtful persons in our own century) is the surprise of finding how impossible it is, in fact, to fashion a "new world" free from the sins of the old. As peoples we did not foresee how regularly evil can be and is the consequence of high intentions for good, or how deeply *failure* is bound up with the most determined pursuit of success. As Eugene Borowitz has written:

> We did not anticipate the possibility of deep and lasting failure. We could not believe that our best ideas might be too small, our plans inadequate, our character mean, our will perverse, our human situation too restricted for us to accomplish perfection. And we certainly did not expect that in doing righteousness we might also create evils, that the unintended consequences of our ambitions might add to pain and to misery, might outweigh the good

we had done or sought . . . The result is not only moral malaise but a time in which, amid the greatest freedom and affluence people have ever known, our common psychiatric problem has shifted from guilt to depression. Knowing our failings, we cannot truly believe in ourselves. We cannot even do the good which lies in our power, because failure has convinced us that nothing we might do is worth anything.[2]

And Borowitz goes on at once, significantly, to challenge the *religions* of our society, especially his own Judaism, and Christianity, to provide something better as a spiritual basis for society than predictable reinforcements of conventional morality: "If religion could teach secular society to accept failure without becoming paralyzed through self-abnegation, and to reach for forgiveness without mitigating our sense of ongoing responsibility, we might end the dejection and moral lassitude which now suffuse our civilization." "If religion could restore a social sense of self to secular society, it would heal the narcissistic wound that today enfeebles our corporate identity." "Insisting on the transcendent, on personal dignity, we secure the basis upon which any hope of rebuilding the morale of our civilization must rest."[3]

To take up this challenge, Christians (to speak only for my own tradition) must begin by distinguishing biblical faith from the *biblicism* that usually fires the passions of those who demand the reinstatement of "the old morality." Biblical faith does not disdain the attempt to distinguish good from evil, and to spell out the difference in specific commandments (over six hundred of them in the older Testament)! In this respect, the newer Testament may be thought even more stringent than the older; for it dares not only to name good and evil, but to specify the *attitudes and motives* by which good and evil are inspired. Thus, in the Sermon on the Mount, Jesus insists that it is not enough that one should refrain from murder or theft or adultery; true righteousness must refrain from thinking murderous, covetous, or prurient thoughts as well. And it is not enough that one should perform externally good works: the God whose will for us is summed up in the commandment to *love* requires of us an obedience that is free of pride, and is not motivated by the hope of reward and the avoidance of punishment. It is mistaken to consider the old cov-

2. Borowitz, *Exploring Jewish Ethics*, 65–66.
3. Ibid., 66, 65, 62.

enant one of law and the new one of freedom; both make high demands of us; neither offers an easy forgiveness. "Not an iota, not a dot, will pass from the law," declares Jesus, "until all is accomplished" (Matt 5:18).

What biblical faith understands, however, in a manner that no moralism ever has, is that while good and evil may and must be named, and while we must seek always to realize the good and eschew evil, our lives in the actual living of them are inevitably strange admixtures of good and evil. The reason for this is not to be found in the nature of good and evil as such, but in the ambiguity and duplicity of our human spirits. Even when we are drawn to the good, which is by no means consistently the case, we are enticed by feelings, leanings, and questionable motives that detract from its pure enactment. Our conscious intentions are often worthy enough: there is that in most of us, I believe, that would truly like to be good—not only to do the right thing, but to do it "for the right reason" (T. S. Eliot), selflessly, rejoicing only in the knowledge that we are participants in an authenticity that is close to the heart of things, tasting as it were that "original righteousness" to which our Creator gave expression in pronouncing all that had been made "very good." Few human beings, I think, are actually drawn to deliberate, obvious, and sustained evil. But even while we, most of us, know something of the impulse to goodness, honesty compels us to confess that the goodness we intend is continuously inhibited by antithetical desires and predispositions. Who among us is not able at some deep level of comprehension to sympathize with the frustration of the Apostle Paul when he cries out, "The good that I would, that I do not, and the evil that I would *not* –that is what I do . . . Wretched man that I am!" (Romans 7:15, 24).

Precisely this, however, is the *self*-knowledge that biblical faith seeks in us; and it is the surest sign of the lack of such self-knowledge when human beings imagine that they are wholly acceptable to God and the world because of their untainted goodness. Jesus's great quarrel, accordingly, was not with the obviously wicked but with the apparently good—those especially whose very religion functioned to prevent genuine awareness of their moral ambiguity. Those enmeshed in evil, whether through their own wrong turnings (like Judas Iscariot) or because their public offices plunged them into the systemic evils of the age (Zachaeus, Pilate)—such persons, the New Testament suggests, are often more conscious of their inauthenticity than are the seeming righteous, whose external correctness blinds them to their very real though subtle internal contradictions. Taking inordinate pride in their goodness, they demonstrate their basic incapacity for the "wholeness" (*salus*) that is offered by the Christ; for that salvation can only be received as gift, and only by those who have come to know something of their great need for it—"the sick who have need of a physician."

Indeed, when it comes to genuine goodness, the newer Testament is exceedingly sparing. Can anyone be called good, really? The gospels even dare to question whether goodness should be ascribed to their principal subject, Jesus himself! "Why," Matthew's Jesus asks one who has addressed him, perhaps flatteringly, as "Good Teacher"—"Why do you cal me good? One there is who is good" (Matt 19:17). In a fallen world, no good is untouched by evil; no individual, however comparatively pure, can be isolated from the evil that affects the entire historical condition. It is consistent with this when Jesus makes himself at least partially implicated in his own betrayal by Judas: "What you must do, do quickly!" (John 13:27).

In short, throughout the biblical narrative we find ourselves in a world quite different from that moralism—whatever its name, old or new, Victorian or bourgeois, religious or secular—that not only spells out with enviable omniscience what good and evil are, but proceeds, on the basis of its assumptions, to draw clear lines of distinction between good and evil *persons*—children of light and children of darkness, sheep and goats, saved and sinners. In biblical anthropology, goodness and evil are mysteriously present in all and each of us; and the aim of the evangel is to bring about the recognition, within us, of this reality. That, at least, is its point of departure: the whole journey of faith which this message would initiate in us is premised on the condition of this kind of self-knowledge.

It is not implied that there are no distinctions, moral distinctions, between persons and communities. It is not implied that all actions are equally flawed, or that there is no use *trying* to be good—or at least better. The point, rather, is to deliver us (and particularly those of us who do make the effort to be good) from easy distinctions and false conclusions about good and evil as they are compounded within our actual lives. As Rosemary Ruether writes in her *Gaia & God*, the shadowy nature of all human goodness "does not mean that there is no such thing as evil, or that ethical distinctions as such should be repudiated for an acceptance of all that is good, or, at least, necessary. The difference between starving a child or torturing a prisoner and, on the other hand, nurturing their lives, is real, and reflects decisions made by actual people. But," she continues, "the reality of evil does not lie in some 'thing' out there . . . Rather, evil lies in 'wrong relationships.'"[4] And when, through the exaggeration of our own goodness, we elevate ourselves in relation to others (as did the Pharisee who thanked God he was not like "this wretched publican"), we only exemplify how very distorted our relationships can become.

Reinhold Niebuhr, whose sustained examination of the mystery of good and evil is in some real sense *the* great exception to North American religious moralism, made essentially the same point as Ruether in his 1939 Gifford Lectures. Against the background of Jesus's parable of the kingdom in Matthew 25, Niebuhr reflects upon biblical religion's final criteria of human authenticity. To be sure, he notes:

> There are those who serve their fellowmen and there are those who do not. But the ones who do are conscious of the fact that in any final judgement, as Jesus sees it, they are discovered not to have fulfilled the law of life; while the ones who do not are too self-centred to know of their sin. Thus the final judgement actually includes both levels of prophetic Messianism, the more purely moral and the supra-moral. *The distinction between good and evil in history is not destroyed; yet it is asserted that in the final judgement there are no righteous, i.e. in their own eyes* . . . for "whosoever shall exalt himself shall be abased; and he that shall humble himself shall be exalted [Matthew 23:12]."[5]

"The distinction between good and evil in history is not destroyed" (our first point, above); "yet it is asserted that in the final judgement there are no righteous" (our second point). But if righteousness—human authenticity—is unattainable, "who then can be saved?" That was the question of the disciples of Jesus as they watched the sorrowing departure of the one who had called Jesus "good." If that "good" man, who by his own estimate had striven to keep all the commandments from his youth up, could not meet the test of authenticity, then who could? Jesus admits the logic of their concern: yes, human endeavor, even when it is admirable, cannot achieve the moral authenticity that God—or conscience, or life!—

4. Ruether, *Gaia & God*, 256.
5. Niebuhr, *The Nature and Destiny of Man*, 2:44.

requires of us. "With human beings," Jesus tells his puzzled disciples, "this is impossible; but with God all things are possible" (Mark 10:27; par.). And with that we are led to the third point in my thesis: *Human authenticity depends upon a grace that is indeed (but not in Nietzsche's sense)* . . .

Beyond Good and Evil

Decades ago, when I was only twenty, I was asked one night to read aloud to two elderly friends a poem by the remarkable nineteenth-century American poet and abolitionist John Greenleaf Whittier. In this poem (which was set to rather doleful music in the hymnbook of my denomination), the Quaker activist Whittier contemplates his own ending, and wonders what the God before whom he has lived his life could make of it in any "final judgement" (Niebuhr):

> When on my day of life the night is falling,
>   And in the winds, from unsunned spaces blown,
> I hear far voices out of darkness calling
>   My feet to paths unknown,
>
> Thou, who has made my home of life so pleasant,
>   Leave not its tenant when its walls decay;
> O Love Divine, O Helper ever present,
>   Be Thou my Strength and stay!

The poem draws, naturally enough, upon nineteenth-century sentiments that are in some ways (perhaps sadly) scarcely accessible to our late twentieth-century skepticism; yet its fifth stanza particularly gives expression to what Reinhold Niebuhr would have recognized as Christian realism of a type that is permanently illuminating:

> Suffice it if—my good and ill unreckoned,
>   And both forgiven through Thy abounding grace—
> I find myself by hands familiar beckoned
>   Unto my fitting place— . . .

At the age of twenty, I did not know quite *why* I was so drawn to those lines. At eighty I think I have a rather better understanding of the reason. "Suffice it if—my good and ill unreckoned, / And *both* forgiven, through they abounding grace." Youth, with its needful idealism, probably must have difficulty grasping the thought that our *goodness*, and not only our "ill," must be "forgiven." But with the years—especially if, like Whittier the abolitionist, we have tried sincerely to do good and not evil—we are taught in the school of life a wisdom that, even sometimes at twenty, we may intuit: namely, that our goodness is never more than partial and tenuous, noble intentions notwithstanding. Certainly Whittier, a man whose whole life was devoted to causes that must still be regarded as good by all persons of goodwill, did not mean to sanction moral passivity or cynicism when he affirmed that he did not expect approval, whether divine or human, on account of his alleged goodness. What he wants most to emphasize in this poem—this statement which sums up, as it were, his whole experience of life—is that in the last analysis it is not ours to untangle the mysterious intermingling of good and evil that constitutes a life; that the authenticity for which we long and toward which our goodness is indeed a striving, can be realized by us only as a gift—only as a grace that is indeed . . . beyond good and evil.

It is that grace, I believe, that both in our private and our public life we need most to approximate. That, as I interpret him, is also what Eugene Borowitz had in mind when he affirmed that "if religion could teach secular society to accept significant failure without becoming paralyzed through self-abnegation, and to reach for forgiveness without mitigating our sense of responsibility, we might end the dejection and moral lassitude which now suffuse our civilization."[6] Too consistently, too simplistically, religion in our society has functioned merely to undergird the understandable but in the end misguided human quest for moral absolutes. Of true grace we have known too little, and we have resisted, mostly, what we know of it. We have wanted to be worthy and blameless all by ourselves, and to build for ourselves a worthy and blameless empire of the good. So it is not surprising that we are so debilitated by our failure to do so, and so pathetically victimized by our own rhetorical heroism returned to judge us. Grace, contrary to Nietzsche's dismissal of it, does not breed weakness and moral passivity. Only when it is distorted by the human desire to escape our vocation as creation's stewards does it detract from the sense of responsibility that Christians like Whittier have always felt. What divine grace offers (and I doubt if there can be any other genuine source of this)

6. Borowitz, *Exploring Jewish Ethics*, 66.

is a new freedom: the freedom to end preoccupation with one's own moral condition; the freedom to become ultimately concerned, rather, with the good of *the other*. The disposition of good and evil, including our own, does not belong to us, but to God. And both our good and evil may be used by divine Providence in ways not intended by us. As Joseph of old said to his trembling brothers at the end of that biblical tale of good and evil, "Even though you intended to do harm to me, God intended it for good" (Gen 50:20). Our evil is not thereby justified; but it does not have the last word.

Nor does our goodness.

10

Dietrich Bonhoeffer
and the Ethics of Participation

SIXTY YEARS AGO—ON JULY 21, 1944—Dietrich Bonhoeffer wrote the following paragraph from his cell in the Tegel prison in Berlin to his former student and friend, Eberhard Bethge:

> I discovered later, and I'm still discovering right up to this moment, that it is only by living completely in this world that one learns to have faith . . . By this-worldliness I mean living unreservedly in life's duties, problems, successes and failures, experiences and perplexities. In doing so we throw ourselves completely into the arms of God, taking seriously, not our own sufferings, but those of God in the world—watching with Christ in Gethsemane. That, I think, is faith; that is *metanoia*; and that is how one becomes a [human being] and a Christian.[1]

I quoted this paragraph at the end of my discussion of Bonhoeffer in my book *Remembered Voices*; and then I brought that discussion to an end with the thought from which, today, I should like to begin this essay:

> It is this *worldly discipleship* of Jesus Christ that constitutes the final, mature statement of the thirty-nine-year-old martyr about the meaning of what Luther named *theologia crucis*. To be a disciple of the crucified one, to receive from the Spirit of the risen Christ the

1. Bonhoeffer, *Letters and Papers from Prison*, 369–70.

courage of *Jesus'* kind of suffering love, is not to walk away from this world in search of a better, but precisely the opposite—to proceed more and more steadfastly into the very heart of the *civitas terrena*, like the fleeing Peter redirected to burning Rome by the One he met on the Appian Way. Worldly discipleship: These words of Bonhoeffer must not be forgotten; this discipleship can never be sufficiently learned; this legacy remains largely unclaimed by our floundering churches.[2]

The *thesis* I want to develop here is already implicit in that comment but I shall restate it in a slightly different way simply for the purposes of clarity. It is necessary to see Dietrich Bonhoeffer as a twentieth-century exemplar of what Luther called the theology of the cross. This theological posture, which is still scarcely understood in the Anglo-Saxon world, is what unites Bonhoeffer's earlier and later writings. What is unique in his articulation of this theological tradition is the manner in which, over against the pietistic distortions of the *theologia crucis*, he carried its premises concretely into the context of worldly existence, exemplifying for us the participatory *ethical* consequences of this minority theological approach.

There will be four sections in this brief presentation. They follow the ordering of thought in that statement.

The Theology of the Cross as the Link

One of the perennial questions associated with Bonhoeffer's work concerns what appears to many to be a discrepancy, or at least a significant hiatus, between his earlier and his later works. In the earlier writings—works like *Creation and Fall*, *Life Together*, and (especially) *The Cost of Discipleship* (in German in 1937)—Bonhoeffer seems to many of his readers an interesting yet by no means groundbreaking exponent of European Lutheran piety. These writings interested people largely on account of the life-story that was their background, ending with Bonhoeffer's execution at the hands of the Nazis just one month prior to their total capitulation. To be sure, with the publication of his *Ethics* (in German in 1949; in English in 1955), one saw an academic side of the young scholar that the earlier works didn't manifest. But by the time Bonhoeffer's last sur-

2. Hall, *Remembered Voices*, 74.

viving writings, under the title *Letters and Papers from Prison*, had been digested by a significant number of thinkers, many began to feel that the later Bonhoeffer differed significantly from the earlier. Some were pleased about that, others disappointed. Eberhard Bethge, who became the editor of Bonhoeffer's works, reports that Karl Barth was definitely among the latter. Barth did not dismiss the fragments of the *Letters* that have become most famous, but he cautioned against taking them too seriously. Perhaps, he said, "the lonely prisoner might possibly have 'peeped around some corner' and seen something that was true, but . . . it [is] too 'enigmatic' and . . . it [is] better to stick to the early Bonhoeffer."[3]

On the other side, many (including members of the so-called death-of-God school) took hold of ideas like "religionless Christianity" and "world come of age" as confirmation of Bonhoeffer's repudiation of his earlier, rather Barthian emphases, and an endorsement of their own radical secularity; and this approach was also indirectly confirmed by Bishop Robinson's bestselling book *Honest to God*, first published in 1963, in which the Bonhoeffer of the late fragments played a highly significant role.

It is my belief that neither of these reactions is appropriate. Clearly, the thoughts expressed in Bonhoeffer's letters from the Tegel prison and especially from April of 1944 onwards, contain very serious if fragmentary ideas, and should not be shrugged off as "peeping around some corner." At the same time, while Bonhoeffer made an occasional, mildly critical reference to his own earlier work, it is extravagant and superficial to see his last thoughts as if they were entirely discontinuous with what went before. So I find myself in agreement with those (including both Bethge and W. A. Visser t'Hooft) who say that while there are new emphases and a conspicuous *deepening* in Dietrich Bonhoeffer's last writings, the *essential* thread of thought already present in his earliest writings has been carried through to the end. Indeed, I think that the late Bonhoeffer has taken to its logical conclusion (though it is a conclusion too many have avoided) the theological premises with which the younger theologian was enthralled from the outset. There are not two Bonhoeffers, only one. The story of his life parallels the progress of his thought; both life and thought involve an ever-deepening descent into the meaning of gospel for a world that is no longer Christian or even "religious."

---

3. Bethge, *Dietrich Bonhoeffer*, 889 [2nd ed.].

What Is the Theology of the Cross?

How can we characterize the core of Bonhoeffer's spirituality? What is the "essential thread" that runs through the complex tapestry of his life and work? It is without doubt, I believe, a twentieth-century expression of the theological posture, method and spirit that Martin Luther named *theologia crucis*, theology of the cross.

But long experience has taught me that this term cannot be used without further explanation—and especially in our English-speaking theological and religious circles. As Ernst Käsemann said a few years ago, in the English-speaking world, if it is heard at all, the term "theology of the cross" is usually taken as a synonym for the doctrine of atonement. This is part of a larger problem, namely, the general unfamiliarity with the *Lutheran* side of the Reformation in English-speaking cultures. (I argued in a recent article for *The Lutheran* (the official magazine of the Evangelical Lutheran Church in America) that Luther himself is, of all the major reformers, the least understood in Anglo Saxon Christianity (indeed, a recent poll reveals that 78 percent of Americans don't know who Luther was).

Of all Luther's puzzling and paradoxical ideas, the theology of the cross is the most foreign to the kind of Christianity that has shaped our White Anglo-Saxon Protestant society, whether it be that of Calvin or Wesley or the nineteenth-century Evangelicals.

To be honest, I rather despair of trying to say anything definitive about the theology of the cross in the context of an essay on another principal subject; but I shall have to attempt it all the same because, after more than half a century of living with Bonhoeffer, I have had to conclude that it's impossible to understand him apart from his spiritual and intellectual formation by this theological tradition. So let me offer eight terse observations about the theology of the cross as background for the rest of this discussion.

1. The term *theologia crucis* is Luther's. He certainly didn't invent the idea, but he did invent the terminology—and very . . . inventively. He first used it in 1518 in the Heidelberg Disputation when he was required by the vicar general of his Augustinian order to explain himself after the furor he created over his Ninety-Five Theses. The theology of the cross, Luther says, looks for the invisible things of

God hidden beneath their opposite: God's *glory* is indeed revealed in Jesus the Christ, but it is revealed as something completely antithetical to our preconceptions of divinity and of glory. The revealed God is thus the hidden God.

2. Luther is committed to the christological center of the gospel as testified to by scripture; but he is also committed to an honest realism about the world—a realism that refuses to lie about reality in the service of the triumphant religion. "The theology of the cross," he said, "calls the thing what it is." Luther presented this theology both as a *critical* and a *constructive theology*. It is critical chiefly of what Luther called *theologia gloriae* (theology of glory), which he understood to be the dominant theology of Christendom, and which we could call religious triumphalism. The imperial church requires an imperial theology, the glorious church requires a glorious theology. This glorious theology necessarily distorts the gospel by turning the crucified Christ, who is inglorious by all worldly standards, into a figure of power and grandeur, and thus effectively removes him from the sphere of real life.

3. The *locus classicus* of the theology of the cross in the Newer Testament is found in the first two chapters of Paul's First Letter to the Corinthians: "We preached Christ crucified . . . "—the text that prompted Luther to write, *crux sola nostra theologia* (The cross alone is our theology). But the Professor Luther who introduced term theology of the cross was also teaching the Psalms, and we must recognize as the greater background of this theological tradition the whole prophetic tradition of Hebraic faith, the essence of which (as Abraham Heschel demonstrated in his book *The Prophets*) is the prophetic consciousness of the "divine pathos," i.e., the suffering of God, who suffers on account of the creatures' suffering. Between the "divine pathos" of the prophets and the *passio Christi* of the apostolic witness, there is a direct line of continuity. So this theology unites the testimony of Israel and the Church in a way that ecclesiastical triumphalism has never done. Christian triumphalism has in fact been the theological backbone of Christendom's supercessionist approach to Judaism.

4. Quite unlike Anselmic or Calvinistic atonement theology, Luther's theology of the cross does not see the cross of Jesus as a substitutionary sacrifice on the part of the one good man who in this way placates a wrathful God, but rather in Christ's passion it sees *God* suffering in solidarity with alienated humanity. The sacrificial movement here is not Humanity towards God but God towards Humanity. Grace is "costly." This is very important for understanding the direction of Bonhoeffer's whole theology and ethic.

5. Far from being a statement about the cross of Jesus in any exclusive way, however, the theology of the cross refers to a whole spirit and method of theology. As Jürgen Moltmann put it in his book *The Crucified God*, one of the most important recent books for this tradition, the theology of the cross is not about any particular part of theology; it is rather "the key signature" in which the whole of Christian theology is written.

6. In terms of method, this theology relies heavily on a dialectical approach, as for instance one has it in Nicholas of Cusa or Peter Abelard. That is, it involves a constant interplay between the positive and the negative, the Yes and the No, thesis and antithesis. As in Kierkegaard's rendition of this tradition especially, there is for Luther (nor Bonhoeffer) no Hegelian synthesis: the dialogue continues; theology does not end; there is no completed work. As I have sometimes put it, with Christian theology you have to keep talking, or else somebody will believe your last sentence. Last sentences always require further sentences to prevent their misappropriation. Because what one is trying to describe, in theological work, is not a What, not an object, but a living Subject, and our statements about this subject are doomed to be wrong. All they can do is point to a living Word that defies containment. And this is also a point of connection between Bonhoeffer and Karl Barth—though Barth, in Bonhoeffer's later view, did not abide by this insight but produced a whole system in which everything is accounted for. In particular, the *negative* has a very important role in this theology—as we see from Luther's nomenclature itself. The theology of the cross has constantly to guard against the tendency of all theology, indeed all thought, to become idolatrous and triumphalist. This is why Bonhoeffer is critical of

most resurrection theology; because the resurrection turns out, in the hands of the imperial church and in imperial cultures, to mean the supercession of the cross and the substitution of "heaven" for a salvation that is directed towards this world.

7. Finally, if I were asked to characterize this theological tradition as to its *content*, as distinct from its method and spirit, I would say that its most salient feature is its insistence precisely upon the world-direct-edness of the Christian message. It is really about God's abiding commitment to this world. God is as committed to the life of this world as that cross is stuck in the earth, and precisely in the place of the skull—symbolically, the place where death is apparently victorious. In other terms, the theology of the cross is the ultimate *incarnational* theology; for it spells out the divine identification with and love for the creation in terms not only of God's solidarity with us in life but in a life whose inherent terminus is death. It is only from that perspective that this theology also allows itself to become a theology of resurrection. Bonhoeffer would have agreed with Käsemann that the resurrection is "a chapter in the theology of the cross."[4]

4. In a letter to Bethge written on June 9, 1944, Bonhoeffer reflected on the differences between what he called the "redemption myths" of many religions and the idea of redemption in the Old Testament. The latter, he said, is "*historical*, i.e. on *this* side of death, whereas everywhere else the myths about redemption are concerned to overcome the barrier of death. Israel is delivered out of Egypt so that it may live before God as God's people on earth. The redemption myths try unhistorically to find an eternity after death."

Then he goes on to speak of "the hope of resurrection" in Christianity, which, he insists, is distorted when it is understood as redemption in the non-Hebraic sense of escaping from the "cares distress, fears, and longings [of this world]—from sin and death, [to] a better world beyond the grave":

> "The difference between the Christian hope of resurrection and the mythological hope is that the former sends a man back to his life on earth in a wholly new way which is even more sharply defined that it is in the Old Testament. The Christian, unlike the devotees of the redemption myths, has no last line of escape available from earthly tasks and difficulties into the eternal , but, like Christ himself ('My God, my God why hast thou forsaken me?'), he must drink the earthly cup to the dregs, and only in his doing so is the crucified and risen Lord with him, and he crucified and risen with Christ. This world must not be prematurely written off; in this the Old and New Testaments are at one. Redemption myths arise from human boundary-experiences, but Christ takes hold of a man at the center of his life" (Bonhoeffer, *Letters and Papers from Prison*, 336–37).

Bonhoeffer's Theology of the Cross

From his earliest days as an intentional Christian in a religiously neutral, upper-middleclass, intellectually-sophisticated family, the church—or what (under Bonhoeffer's tutelege) I call 'the disciple community'—was Bonhoeffer's particular theme. But also from the outset he was exceptionally conscious of the temptation of the church to confuse faith with religion. Strengthened by Barth's critique of religion as "unbelief."[5] Bonhoeffer constantly called his fellow-Christians away from religion and the defense of religion to the serious discipleship of Jesus Christ. As Visser 't Hooft writes, Bonhoeffer insisted that "the church must stop defending itself and its particular "religiosity" and simply *be present* in the world for others, as Jesus Christ was."[6]

This kind of distinction between Christian faith and religion (religion as temptation, as the impulse to control) is already of the essence of the theology of the cross in its consciousness of the dangers of religious triumphalism and power-seeking. It is, so to speak, the *critical* side of the *theologia crucis*; and as such it informs all of Bonhoeffer's earlier writings, especially *The Cost of Discipleship*. What the fragments from the final *Letters* indicate, is that to this critical dimension Bonhoeffer's later experience led him to add a more fully developed *constructive* side of this theological tradition, which is bound up with its radical world-commitment [my eighth observation, above]. In other words, this theology not only warns Christians against trying to achieve *mastery* in the world but it fosters in them an ever-greater sense of worldly solidarity and service—indeed, *suffering* servanthood. The gospel of the cross leads all who are touched by it more fully and defenselessly into the heart of the world, and without concealed religious motivation.

Let us recognize, says the imprisoned Bonhoeffer of the fragments, that the world in which we find ourselves now is no longer the "religious" world upon which the entire *corpus Christianum* has depended heretofore. Rather, it is a world "come of age". Much of course hangs on what Bonhoeffer intended this key term ("come of age") to mean. Was he being ironic? –even perhaps sarcastic? Did he have in mind a pseudo-sophisticated world that (in the terms of Voltaire) found the "hypothesis" of God

---

5. Barth, *Church Dogmatics*, 1/2, 297–325.
6. Visser 't Hooft, "Foreword," in *The Steps of Bonhoeffer*, 10.

unnecessary, and did he (with many a preacher) want to mock this kind of secular bravado? I think not, nor does Bethge. Rather, he was using the term "come of age" in a positive sense, meaning that the world had indeed achieved a certain maturity. Behind this idea, Bethge insists, lies Kant's conception of the *Aufklärung*, the Enlightenment: "'The Enlightenment is the emergence of [humankind] from [the] immaturity that [humans themselves are] responsible for. Immaturity is the incapacity to use one's own intelligence without the guidance of another person." Bonhoeffer, says Bethge, did not scorn this declaration, as so many religious people have done, but rather he "welcomed the evolution of secularization" as humankind's recognition that it must now take responsibility for its own future and not presume that God would "do it all for us." The glorious God, the God of power and might, runs the whole show. But the God who is revealed in the crucified one—the God already central to Jewish faith--makes room for serious human stewardship. In short, Bethge says, "Bonhoeffer now takes Kant's irrevocable description of maturity as an essential element of his *theologia crucis*."[7]

> Because Bonhoeffer never stopped thinking dialectically, his statements about the world's coming of age have two levels and do not level out into a positivism. The Gospel of the *theologia crucis* tolerates the world come of age and even accepts that such a world may deny the Gospel—and this in fact helps it find its own position and its essence. The unity and paradox of the *theologia crucis* and the world come of age found its most succinct expression in the now famous passage of 16 July, 1944, when he wrote:
>
>> . . . that we have to live in the world *etsi deus non daretur*. And this is just what we do recognize—before God! God himself compels us to recognize it. So our coming of age leads us to a true recognition of our situation before God. God would have us know that we must live as [people] who manage our lives without him. The God who is with us is the God who forsakes us (Mark 15:34). The God who lets us live in the world without the working hypothesis of God is the God before whom we stand continually. Before God and with God we live without God. God lets himself be pushed out of the world onto the cross. He is weak and powerless in the world, and that is precisely the way, the only way, in which he is with us and helps us.[8]

7. Bethge, *Dietrich Bonhoeffer*, 867 [2nd ed.].
8. Ibid., 868–69 [2nd ed.].

Given this chance of exploring in both directions the knowledge of the theology of the cross and the knowledge of the world's having come of age, Bonhoeffer is even able to venture to state the contrary proposition, namely that the knowledge of the world's coming of age can help us to a better understanding of the Gospel:

> "To that extent we may say that the development towards the world's coming of age . . . , which has done away with a false conception of God, opens up a way of seeing the God of the Bible, who wins power and space in the world by his weakness."
>
> Or, more daring still: "The world that has come of age is more godless, and perhaps for that very reason closer to God, than the world before its coming of age."[9]

Let me try to state all this in other words: God, for Christians, is not identical with the gods of religion, including the Christian religion. As Buber put it, God is more than merely "God." Tillich, similarly, spoke of "the God beyond God." But throughout history until the period of late modernity, Christianity has sought its place in the world by assuming that its God is the true God after whom religion thirsts. Yet the God revealed in the crucified Christ is not only transcendent of this God of religion, but entirely different—different especially in God's complete lack of interest in competing with other religions or in competing with the world itself for preeminence. The God revealed in the cross of Christ is wholly devoted to the future of the world itself, to the fulfillment of the creation. Therefore, so long as people went looking for God beyond the world, in transcendent and glorious Otherness, God could not get through to those most apparently devoted to God, the religious. The 'coming of age' of the world, to the extent that it is realized, means the growing realization that the world itself—and not some unworldly Deity, and not some transworldly heaven—is the proper sphere of human attention and care. In this way, the loss of what Bonhoeffer calls "the religious apriori"—i.e. the loss of the notion that humans are by nature "religious" (*homo religiosus*)—is a positive gain for faith. Instead of pursuing a God who carries us off to some ecstatic supranatural sphere, discipleship means pursuing the God who penetrates more and more deeply into the life of the world. And that God is found, not in the places where religion traditionally has looked for God,

9. Ibid., 869 [2nd ed.].

but in the places where God seems absent: that is, among the abandoned, the abused, the suffering, the marginalized.

The Ethic of the Theology of the Cross

Now if we have been following this theo-logic we shall have been led through a world-oriented *theology* of the cross to an *ethic* of the cross. And the essence of this ethic is its *participatory* character. Bonhoeffer, whose life itself was a gradual but irrevocable progression from the kind of detachment that an economically secure student of theology can know to a greater and ever greater involvement in the life of the world, in his case, a world in terrifying turmoil and danger. One of his poems is entitled 'Stations on the Road to Freedom,' and it details precisely his own descent into the hell of his own worldly context. His theology of the cross could not remain (in that "academic" sense in which we usually use this word) a "theology"; it had to become an ethic of the cross. As Larry Rasmussen remarks at the end of his book on Bonhoeffer, "Luther's initial impulse remains the suggestive one, namely, the theology of the cross. Bonhoeffer's contribution is to envision and embody a community of the cross with an ethic of imitation, or participation, as the church's societal vocation and presence."[10]

Paul Lehman, Bonhoeffer's closest American friend, captured something of what I think Bonhoeffer intended as his ethic of participation. In his book, *Ethics in a Christian Context,* Lehman asserts that the task of Christian ethics is to follow the Christ into the world. Jesus Christ, he says, "is at work in the world to make and to keep human life human", and the task of the Christian community, the community of discipleship, is to ask, where is the Christ now at work in the world?, and to go there and seek to work with the One who is already active in that context.

This approach, I say, captures something of Bonhoeffer's meaning; but I believe that Bonhoeffer's ethical teaching is more radical than Lehman's. For Bonhoeffer, the great clue to the whereabouts of Christ in the world, so to speak, is worldly suffering. The defining mark of God for Bonhoeffer is God's suffering—God's *voluntary* suffering, suffering born not of necessity but of love for the suffering creation. This is why Luther dared to call God (not just Christ, but God!) *der gekreuzigte Gott.* As

10. Rassmussen and Bethge, *Dietrich Bonhoeffer,* 173.

Visser 't Hooft puts it, "The challenge [of Bonhoeffer] means that we must understand the incarnation really radically. Christ did not bear the sins of Christians; he bore the sins of the world. The church must therefore live and suffer in the world, with the world, and for the world."[11]

Thus Bonhoeffer's ecclesiology, as Bethge writes, "seems entirely absorbed within the *theologia crucis* . . . For him everything depends on the *theologia crucis*, but the only form in which he knows this is in its urging us towards the concrete fellowship with those who share Christ's sufferings in the world."[12]

In a manner very similar to that of Simone Weil, Bonhoeffer assumes that the Christian community can only learn what it may have to *bring* to the world's healing by first participating in the suffering that is actually present. The disciple community has in some real sense to know itself bereft of solutions, empty handed in the face of real agony. It will only discern the meaning of gospel, and of love of God and neighbor, as it allows itself to descend into the darkness of human experience, and to do so without the cheap grace of easy religious answers.

It may help our comprehension of what is involved here if we lift this discussion, finally, out of the context of Hitler's Europe and consider what it would mean in our global context today. What would the theology of the cross, in the form of an ethic of participation, mean in the realm of contemporary social ethics?

I think we would be able to discover a great deal about this ethic if at this point, for instance, we were to have the time to stop and listen for several hours to the testimony of General Romeo Dalaire as he recounts the devastating personal consequences of his experiences is Rwanda, or of Stephen Lewis as he relates the frustrations and limited successes of his attempts to interest Western peoples in the plight of sub-Saharan African peoples under the scourge of AIDS, or of those who are trying to make the affluent North more conscious of the poverty of the hemispheric south—for example, the ghastly reality of starvation in Ethiopia. The ethic of the cross, which was the final stage of Bonhoeffer's lifelong preoccupation with this neglected theological tradition, drives towards solidarity with those who suffer; and the ethic that emerges from this participatory involvement, while it may certainly be informed by the great traditions

11. Visser 't Hooft, "Foreword," 11.

12. Bethge, *Dietrich Bonhoeffer*, 887 [2nd ed.].

of biblical and traditional law, will be informed in a primary way by the actual conditions of the sufferers.

Perhaps it is easier to grasp what is involved here if we move from social to personal ethics. Any number of problems could be considered in this case, but in my book *The Cross in Our Context: Jesus and the Suffering World*, I illustrated the meaning of participatory ethics by referring to the question of the church's attitude towards homosexuality—obviously a very 'hot' topic. The usual approach to this question, particularly (but not exclusively) on the part of the more conservative element in the churches, is to assume that the Christian scriptures and tradition already have an explanation of this kind of human behaviour, and all the necessary counsel for those for whom it is an existential reality. This is, in other words, a triumphalistic ethic: an ethic borne of the theology of glory.

Armed with this kind of moral assumption, conservative Christians considering the matter of the ordination of gay and lesbian persons produce biblical and other arguments that in their belief strictly forbid the inclusion of such persons in ministry—and perhaps in the church at large. Liberal Christians, on the other hand, find other aspects of the tradition on whose basis they can endorse gay ordination. I would make no secret of the fact that I am on the side of the liberals in this; but neither group is pursuing participatory ethics in the Bonhoeffer sense. Both are approaching the question theoretically, i.e. from a posture of detached and principled theory. Jesus did not evolve an understanding of the place of women in the community of faith by studying the relevant texts—though he certainly knew the texts! Rather he entered into dialogue with specific women, including ritually excluded women, and left for his followers a way of considering the whole question of the relation of the sexes that is in a real sense "new", though it has certain antecedents in the literature of the Old Testament.

Similarly, the ethics of participation require a prior in-depth engagement with persons and groups whose sexual orientation differs from the behavior of the statistical majority. New and highly pertinent factors have entered the scene of which the Scriptures and the most regnant traditions of Christendom know little or nothing—in particular the entire concept of sexual *orientation*, as distinct from sexual behavior. Until Christians know something of what it means to live as one psychically and perhaps biologically oriented towards one's own sex, and to live under the specific conditions of society here and now (a society, in our case, pervaded by fear of AIDS and the stigmatization associated with that epidemic), they are surely in no position to make concrete decisions that will affect the fate of those concerned.

"The first requirement of the ethic of the cross . . . is that the disciple community must allow itself to be led as deeply as possible into the sphere of *the question*. The question—that is, any matter deserving serious moral deliberation, decision, and action,—is never a merely general one, for example, 'The Human Relation to Nature', or 'Human Sexuality'. It is always specific, for the historical conditions under which it is asked are never incidental to its reality. It is precisely the complex contextual specificity of the question that makes it a real and not merely a theoretical question."[13]

Let me in conclusion simply restate my thesis (I think that I have commented on each part of it, and I hope that the reader will hear it, therefore, in a little more integrated manner now:

> It is necessary to see Dietrich Bonhoeffer as a twentieth-century exemplar of what Martin Luther called 'the theology of the cross'. This theological posture, which is still scarcely understood in the anglosaxon world, is what unites Bonhoeffer's earlier and later writings. What is unique in his articulation of this theological tradition is the manner in which, over against pietistic distortions of the theology of the cross, he carried its premises concretely into the context of worldly existence, thus exemplifying for us the participatory *ethical* consequences of this neglected minority tradition of our Christian heritage.

---

13. Hall, *The Cross in Our Context*, 201.

11

Christianity and Empire

Age after age their tragic Empires rise,
Built while they dream, and in that dreaming weep ...[1]

Christian Empire: An Oxymoron

CHRISTIANITY CAME INTO THE world half a century after the founding
of one of history's greatest empires, the Roman,[2] and throughout most of
its own two-thousand-year history the Christian religion has functioned
as the cultus of imperial peoples. Yet at its biblical and doctrinal roots
Christianity is fundamentally incommensurate with the concept of empire. There is indeed something almost ludicrous about a faith at whose
very center stands the cross of one executed by Rome becoming, in the
short space of three centuries, the official religion of the Roman Empire.
Empires, whether ancient or modern, do not adopt crucified criminals
as their principal symbols—and especially not when they are themselves
the crucifiers. As they regularly are! Empires want symbols of power, triumph, superiority. The eagle, a powerful, flesh-eating bird of prey, has
long been a favorite with empires. How, then, is this centuries-old associa-

1. Clifford Bax, "Turn Back, O Man," 1919.
2. As empire, Rome dates to 31 BCE.

tion of the Christian religion with imperial peoples of the Western world to be explained?

There is, I think, no simple, straightforward answer to that question. History does not answer to logic. Life, whether corporate or individual, is full of contradictory elements and incompatible combinations. Certain observations about the nature of the modus operandi between Christianity and empire may help us, nevertheless, both to understand this relation and to clarify for ourselves ways in which *today*, as precisely this relation comes unraveled, we may as Christian persons and institutions think and act faithfully.

Empire Needs Religion

There is nothing particularly mysterious about the fact that religion— some religion or other—has been a prominent aspect of nearly every empire.[3] From the first intentional *imperium*, that of Sargon of Akkad in Mesopotamia, to the greatest contemporary superpower (America), empire has manifested a vested interest in religion. Superficially considered, this may be attributed to the fact that the bulk of humanity is inherently religious, and political schemes always need as much popular support as they can get. We all know, for instance, how greatly the latest Republican administration of the USA relied on the vote of the so-called Christian Right.

But imperial interest in religion has a deeper explanation than the quantitative. Beneath the rhetoric and the bravado of empire, there is a profound if repressed undercurrent of doubt—as there is whenever human beings set themselves up as bearers of extraordinary power, authority, and permanence. Empires are "tragic" in the same way that the protagonists of Shakespeare's plays are tragic: they court a state of transcendent significance that, subconsciously, they know they're incapable of attaining. Empires are the fruit of human dreaming, but there is a hidden "weeping" in such dreaming because the fragility of what is dreamt of is darkly sensed by the dreamer. Human beings, individually and collectively, are capable of great things; but there is a limit to our greatness, and when our

---

3. Including the USSR. For, as many have observed, the ideology of history's inevitable progress towards the classless society is as much a religious faith as any explicit theism.

pride (*hubris*) tempts us beyond that limit we know, at some deep level of awareness, that we are courting the "fall" that pride "goeth before."

The quest for religious undergirding and legitimation on the part of empire builders is born of that inner knowledge. They seek in religion the security that they know they cannot assume as mere human enterprises. The builders of that mythic city, Babel (Genesis 11), knew intuitively that the kind of ultimacy and certitude they craved for their state required a Guarantor more reliable than themselves or the fortunes of history; thus the *tower* they erected, a specifically religious venture without much *practical* use, became the most important part of their project. They needed access to God, or what they imagined God to be: they needed to control the Controller.

When Emperor Constantine invited the Christians to become, as it were, chaplain to his imperium, he was not just doing a favor to his mother's religion. The diverse and quarrelling old religions of the classical period had failed, and so had the contrived new "state religion" of emperor worship. The empire of the Caesars was beginning to collapse. Constantine saw in the Christian religion some of the ingredients he needed to ward off Rome's decline.

What Empires Find Attractive about the *Christian* Religion

One of those ingredients—perhaps the most attractive of them—was the Christian emphasis upon unity. The unity of the deity.[4] The unity of all things "*under* God." The perceived unity and intelligibility of God's historical purposes (*providentia Dei*). After all, empires are rather artificial and usually enforced collectivities of very diverse elements—diverse historically, racially, ethnically, linguistically, culturally, and religiously. The "natural" tendency of such immense collectivities is for their various components to maintain a stubborn distinctiveness or, having been forced into conformity, continually to resist its constrictions. It is not enough to have conquered other tribes and territories; they must be governed—kept

---

4. A decisive factor in the evolution of the doctrine of the Trinity, which was "settled" only after the Constantinian beginnings of the Establishment of the Christian religion, was the need of Rome to combat the existing polytheism of its territories, and therefore to accentuate the principle of *unity* in the discussion of the triune God. Particularly in the West, the unity principle practically ruled out the notion of distinctive "persons" in the godhead.

in the fold! Like empires before and after it, Rome, we know, expended immense energy and resources on the maintenance of the unification it imposed upon subject peoples. How desirable, then, is a faith which, working *within*, motivates divergent groupings to believe that the greatest good is unity and not distinctiveness.[5]

A second attractive element of Christianity, from the perspective of empire builders, is its potentiality for triumphalism. I say "potentiality", because, in order to actualize this potential, a certain ideological sleight of hand must be performed: that is, those elements of the Christian account of reality that are apparently consistent with the mandatory power-and-glory rhetoric of empire must be accentuated, and those elements of the biblical message that remind us of the vulnerability of the human condition and the ambiguity of all our victories must be deemphasized. A *crucified* Messiah is an embarrassment to empire (as Paul suggests in 1 Corinthians 1–2), but a crucified Messiah *resurrected to ultimate and universal sovereignty* could be a positive boon! Can there be any doubt why Easter Sunday and not Good Friday constitutes *the* religious feast day of the United States of America? Or for that matter why Christmas could be so easily incorporated into the bourgeois triumphalism of the consumer-driven West?

A third advantage empires have found in Christianity (as in some other religions) is its tendency to foster *personal* morality and to downplay or neglect social ethics. This too, of course, requires a generous application of the aforementioned ideological sleight of hand. Yet the transformation is not so drastic as in the previous point; for in the first place the biblical (explicitly the newer Testamental) ethic itself tends to stress the personal and ecclesial, and the "religious impulse" in humans generally manifests itself in a no doubt understandable concern for the self—which is why Marx could call religion "opiate of the people." The Christian faith has been mistrusted (and sometimes persecuted) by worldly powers only

---

5. I am tempted here to comment on the Canada crisis. A forgotten element in the discussion of Canadian unity and the threatened "breakup of the country" is the role that the Christian religion played in the maintenance of confederation. It is not accidental, surely, that the separatist movement has achieved its greatest influence in a post-Catholic, highly secularized Quebec. In this situation, there is no longer an internal, "spiritual" influence quietly at work persuading people to suppress their long-cherished distinctiveness in order that the greater good of human harmony might prevail.

where it has led to radical concern for or interference in social and political conditions—that is, concern for *the world as such.*

Fourthly, empire, having once embraced the Christian religion, could almost always count on that religion to support, encourage, or even enthusiastically promote imperial authority. Indeed, the *potentiality* for such support is already to be found in the New Testament. Not only its concentration on the personal and the ecclesial, but in some explicit directives (notably Romans 13), the New Testament seems to assume, if not positive support of the "governing authorities," a certain political passivity. So much of the spiritual focus of the earliest church was centered in faith's eschatological expectation of the Parousia (the inauguration of the reign of God) that the glory and power of "the kingdoms of this world" could seem ephemeral indeed. Why raise questions? Their prominence was strictly transient; their fate was already sealed.

From such observations, we can appreciate the attractions of Christianity, not only for the *Roman* Empire but for every subsequent imperium with which the Christian religion has comingled. But by the same token we can also notice something of what Christianity had—and has still—to relinquish and deemphasize in order to function in the role of imperial religion. What should astonish us today is not how appealing Christianity could be to empire, but rather how uncritically the dominant forms of the Christian religion have adapted themselves to the roles that successive empires have recruited them to play. Whether in its various de jure (legal) expressions or in the de facto cultural forms of North America and elsewhere, Christian establishment has meant that the whole *prophetic* side of the Judeo-Christian tradition has been greatly reduced where it was not dispensed with altogether.

Empire and Prophetic Faith

By prophetic faith is meant the faith that is exemplified especially by the prophets of ancient Israel as they are testified to in the Hebrew Bible, and in the New Testament's witness to John the Baptist and Jesus of Nazareth. Contrary to the tendency of conventional Christianity to relegate prophecy to the past,[6] however, responsible Christian theology today insists

6. This tendency can be noted already in the New Testament, which values Old Testament prophecy for its (real or imagined) "predictions" of the events on which the

that the prophetic calling is essential to the very being and mission of the church.[7] Jesus Christ, especially in the classical Protestant theological tradition, is understood to be the inheritor and (for Christians) supreme exemplar of the *three* Old Testament "offices" of prophet, priest, and king.[8] From its fourth-century inception onwards, Christendom was prone to covet for itself both the priestly and the kingly aspects of its christological foundation, though often in questionable forms; but, precisely on account of its close ties with "the governing authorities" (Rom 13:1), established Christianity found it awkward if not impossible consistently to take up the prophetic office that belongs to the church's participation in the being and work of the Christ. For that vocation presupposes an exceptional spiritual and intellectual independence of existing structures and a courageous readiness to critique the status quo.

Prophetic faith clashes with empire almost inevitably because of the priorities inherent in it. Without exhausting these, we may name some of the most elementary:

First, prophetic faith is oriented towards truth.[9] The prophetic community does not claim to *possess* the Truth (for Truth biblically understood is a *living* reality and does not admit of possession), but prophetic faith is driven by an insatiable *thirst* for truth that cannot be satisfied with half truth or comforting fictions any more than with deliberate falsehood. As suggested earlier, the dream of empire as such involves a certain suppression of truth, or at least a willing suspension of disbelief. Questions about the desirability and even the feasibility of such extensive power, or the potential for evil within it, or the worthiness of those who wield it, or the discrepancy between its rhetoric and its reality, must always be repressed. The propaganda of empire (for instance, the incessant use of the word *freedom* in present-day America!) invariably cloaks reality. Prophetic faith

Christian message is based, and their meanings, but does not sufficiently stress the prophetic vocation of the church as participant in the same work of witness as that to which Israel was called.

7. This is true not only of Liberation and other explicitly "political" theologies; it belongs to the Social Gospel of the late nineteenth and early twentieth centuries and (what is often overlooked today) the so-called Neo-Orthodox renewal of Christianity spearheaded by Karl Barth, Dietrich Bonhoeffer, Paul Tillich, Reinhold Niebuhr, and others, all of whom confronted "the powers" of the turbulent mid-twentieth century.

8. The "threefold office" (*Munus Triplex*) of the Christ—prophet, priest and king—was a particularly important teaching in the Reformed tradition.

9. There is a German word for this: *Wahrheitsorientierung*.

cannot maintain silence in the face of such distortions of actuality. From Amos to John the Baptist, prophetic consciousness is impelled to name deception, even when it seems innocent or unintentional—and especially when it finds echoes in the religious community itself. Jesus was crucified not only because he threatened the oppressive hegemony of Rome but also because he named the hypocrisy of the religious who made an easy alliance with Rome.

Second, the prophetic tradition never allows its hope in the ultimately benevolent purposes of God to blind it to the actual negations that mar existence under the conditions of history. Not only in Jeremiah and the so-called pessimistic Wisdom literature (Job, Ecclesiastes) but in the Psalms, Second Isaiah, the Pauline letters, and most of the other biblical writings, there is a remarkable and sustained testimony to the suffering, evil, finitude, death, and despair to which human life is heir. Overtly optimistic Christianity, which empire invariably prefers, has characteristically neglected or expunged whole sections of the Bible for this very reason. (They do not sing the hymns of Passiontide at the Crystal Cathedral!) But prophetic faith knows that when the depth of creaturely vulnerability is denied expression, the gospel that speaks to it will also be cheapened. The great problematic of imperial peoples, especially visible in our time, is their psychic imprisonment in ideologies of success. They cannot face the data of despair, and therefore it plays havoc with them all the more—for instance making it necessary for them to locate the sources of their fear and insecurity outside themselves. In contrast, prophetic faith gives open expression to all forms of human and creaturely pain; the language of lament is not only allowed, it is nurtured; for prophetic faith locates its hope precisely in the belief that God *participates* in this suffering and is redemptively at work within it.

Third, it follows that prophetic faith manifests a particular awareness of and concern for those whose suffering is greatest: the poor, the excluded, the infirm and all whose condition is at least partly a consequence of their victimization by the dominant culture. The liberationist motto that the biblical God has "a preferential option for the poor" is the other side of the truth that the biblical God has an abiding *suspicion* of the rich and powerful. ("He hath put down the might from their seats and exalted the humble and weak . . .")

Living on the Edge of Empire

For these and similar reasons, prophetic faith has always recognized that it cannot be part of the human fascination and experimentation with empire. *Christendom*, namely, the alliance of the Christian religion and imperial cultures, was always something of a contradiction in terms, itself an oxymoron![10] But throughout the fifteen or sixteen centuries of Christendom in the Western world there were also Christian individuals and movements that recognized this fundamental incompatibility. They include not only martyrs and saints but theologians, activists, and ordinary folk who sensed in the gospel of the cross a Way radically different from the way of power and glory.[11] This recognition meant that they would have to live on the edge of empire—even when, as was the case with many of them (like St Paul!), they were citizens of some imperium.

Today, and in consequence of a transformation that has been occurring in the West for two centuries or more, Western Christendom is in its final stages of decay. Predictably enough, this prompts some to make extraordinary—and even frantic—attempts to reinstate Christianity as the dominant religion of our civilization. But those who have taken seriously both biblical and traditional warnings against the assumptions of imperial *religion* experience the end of Christendom as opportunity, and not defeat. From now on, all serious Christians will know themselves to be living on the edge of empire. This is not a positioning they shun or resent: it is the stance that prophetic faith finds most natural. It is not accidental that the prophetic consciousness of the biblical tradition evolved precisely in a small nation that found itself on the edge of one empire after another.

In this new, post-Christendom situation, the question arises, as it did for the early Christians and for many at the time of the Protestant Reformation, what attitude ought to be taken by Christians towards empire generally, and specifically towards the empires on whose edges they actually find themselves? From what I have said heretofore, it will be obvious to readers that I am among those who believe that Christians cannot embrace the ideology of empire as an acceptable way of organizing public

10. On Christendom, see Hall, *The End of Christendom*; and also Hall, *Thinking the Faith*, 200ff.

11. Luther named these two ways *theologia crucis* (theology of the cross) and *theologia gloriae* (theology of glory, i.e., religious triumphalism). For details, see Hall, *The Cross in Our Context*.

life. I believe that Christian faith engenders in one a deep suspicion of the dream of empire, including an informed awareness of empire's inherent weaknesses and contradictions, and (especially) an active vigilance in behalf of empire's victims.

But precisely as natural critics of the ideology of imperialism, Christians should be careful to avoid ideology themselves—the ideology of an *a priori anti*-imperialism, that is, a rejection of empire at the level of abstract theory that is not sufficiently grounded in existing conditions. There is an ideological component in all human thought, including theology; but Christian theology differs from ideology specifically in its commitment to *this world*, that is, to actual *contexts*. Because of its inherent contextuality, this theology constantly involves the submission of its theoretical ideas, doctrines, concerns and hunches to the realities of the here and now. Therefore it is ready to make distinctions and to entertain paradox and nuance.[12] It knows that thought, however impressive and compelling, must be tempered and corrected by history.

Thus, with respect to the discussion of empire, this theology recognizes that not all empires are the same, nor is the activity of empires—from the perspective of Christian faith—always only evil or unacceptable. Rome, by comparison with some other empires, manifested a surprisingly liberal tolerance of most religious and ethnic groupings, and often prevented their wrathful treatment of one another. Important distinctions are being made today between the British Empire, which at its best evidenced a certain maturity of world-citizenship, and the American Empire as presently governed, which by comparison many believe to be impulsive and naïve. Yet few would deny that even the American Empire serves humane and far-reaching global needs—needs for aid and order that cannot be met by less powerful nations.

The dream of empire is a dangerous dream—dangerous not only to the conquered but to the conqueror. But there are degrees of danger. The well-known aphorism of the nineteenth-century historian John Lord Acton is instructive here too: "Power tends to corrupt, and absolute power

---

12. Perhaps the most telling statement of George W. Bush was his quip, "I don't do nuance." Interestingly, a recent biography of Abraham Lincoln pointed out that Lincoln, on the contrary, was "comfortable with ambiguity" (White, *A. Lincoln*, 5). Ideology knows what is there in the world before it actually takes a look. It functions in the same way that religious fundamental functions, namely, to keep its adherents from the unsettling experience of realizing that life is far more complicated than their theories about life.

corrupts absolutely." Empires always *court* imperial*ism*; but the degree to which powerful nations are swayed by imperialistic ambition is not predetermined or fixed. Even though the *tendency* to pursue power excessively is always present in the dream of empire, there may be countervailing forces at work. For instance, in the history of the United States of America there has always been (and continues to be) a persistent protest against imperial ambition on the part of an articulate and significant segment of the population that remembers the *republican* (small *r*!) intentions of the architects of the Union.[13] And while the media make much of the "Christian Right" in that country, there is a much older and much deeper form of Christian influence in the USA that is keeping alive that particularly classical-Protestant witness which *protests* against the identification of purely finite institutions and philosophies with the infinite, and draws attention daily to the hypocrisies, failures, and corruptions perpetrated by government, business, industry, and the military.

Indeed, if I were asked to illustrate what I mean by Christians living "on the edge of empire today," I think that I would be more apt to point to American than to European or Canadian examples. Serious Christians in the United States know themselves to be "on the edge" of their dominant culture today, in a way that Europeans and Canadians, whose nations are certainly on the periphery of power physically speaking, on the whole do not. For it is too easy for Europeans and Canadians self-righteously to attribute innocency and wisdom to our own less prominent, less powerful societies—which, however, are most of them as deeply implicated in the injustices and vulgarities of the possessing peoples of the earth as are the Americans. It would speak more appropriately of Christian contextual responsibility in such a world if Canadian Christians (to speak only for my own nation) spent less of their time and energy pointing the finger of guilt at the United States and devoted more of it to the support of their fellow Christians in the USA, who must live spiritually and intellectually "on the edge of empire" whilst being physically and as citizens part of it.

There have been at least sixty intentional empires in recorded history; no period has been free of them, and it is unlikely that the quest for empire will disappear in future. The task of prophetic faith is to capitulate neither to a fatalism that bows to the inevitability of imperial*ism*, nor to a

13. A fascinating treatment of this theme in US history is found in Gore Vidal's historical novel, *Empire*.

utopianism that imagines that the dream of empire will vanish from the earth. Our task is rather to continue faithfully to name the evils that unchecked power regularly evokes, whilst encouraging the good that power trained and corrected by virtues nobler than itself sometimes makes possible.

12

Many Churches * Many Faiths * One Planet

The Perils and Possibilities of Religion in a Fragile World

Introduction

The Ambiguity of Religion in the Light of the New World-Consciousness

THE CONCERN THAT DROVE me to prepare this lecture was articulated in the starkest manner conceivable in two words scrawled, a few years ago, on the graffiti-inviting outer wall of the Presbyterian College in Montreal. These words, written in large, black, angry letters appeared in the immediate wake of the events of September 11th, 2001, and they were obviously intended as a militant challenge to all of us in the region of the McGill University's Faculty of Religious Studies, with which the Presbyterian College is affiliated. The two words were: "*Religion Kills!*" I am sure that all of us who taught or studied in the Faculty of Religious Studies at that time felt the sting of this accusation. I know that, as a Christian, I did; and I suspect that the same sense of judgment was felt by my colleagues and students who were Jewish, Hindu, Buddhist, Muslim, or members of other faith traditions.

"Religion Kills!" The same sentiment was expressed more gently, and at greater length, in a letter to the editor of the *International Herald Tribune*, and it seemed important enough to the moderator of the Central Committee of the World Council of Churches to be cited early in his official Report, delivered in Geneva in the fall of 2003. "The fundamental problems we are facing today," the letter declared, "derive from religion. Most of the terrorism and counter-terrorism in the world are based on religious fanaticism and extreme belief systems."[1]

These sentences are not the ravings of secular exhibitionists or disgruntled atheists. The accusation they level at "religion" is representative of thought entertained by significant numbers of our civilization's most concerned citizens. And do they not represent, also, the spoken and unspoken anxieties (perhaps even the shame) of those of us who, to a greater or lesser degree, regard ourselves, and are regarded by society at large, as *being* "religious"? Few thinking persons would be ready to consider religion *wholly* detrimental to the life of the world. Yet it would be difficult indeed, in today's global village, to ignore the role of human religious fervor in the many and various threats to planetary existence that shout at us from every news broadcast and look out at us through the eyes of many who are the most obvious and immediate victims of those threats.

The threats of which I am thinking include not only terrorism and counterterrorism but economic injustice and the maldistribution of global resources, environmental degradation, the oppression of women and children, globe-encircling diseases, and many other impediments to creaturely well-being that use and misuse the religious impulse for their inspiration. The day is over when "religion" could be thought an unambiguously Good Thing, as many in the past believed it to be. Informed and sensitive members of every faith tradition today are likely to think twice, if not explicitly to demur, when they hear themselves described as "religious" persons.

It may be that the human being is by nature religious: Dietrich Bonhoeffer's well-known remarks notwithstanding, *homo religiosus* may still be a more accurate generalization about humankind than is the rather pretentious designation *homo sapiens*. But it is no more self-evident that

1. Aram I, "Report of the Moderator," *The Ecumenical Review*, October 2003; p. 378.

our religious impulse will actualize itself in ways that are recognizably good and life-giving than that our human instinct to self-preservation or sexual expression will actualize themselves in a benevolent manner. At very least, religion, like sexuality and self-preservation, seems to be an ambiguous quality in the human. Its actualization will depend upon many influences, internal and external, that are not necessarily implicit in the impulse to religion as such.

Among those influences is what might be termed the "world-consciousness" that pertains in given historical settings. In the relatively small and homogeneous geographic units that were dominant in premodern periods, and, in varying degrees, until very recent times even in the so-called developed world, there was little—relatively speaking—to challenge a religion that assumed the right to pursue its own interests without considering the implications of its beliefs and pursuits for the larger community of human and extrahuman life. Like some of you, I am old enough to remember a time when most Canadians and Americans lived their lives and thought their thoughts almost entirely within the confines of their villages, towns, or townships. The great world (Asia, Africa, Latin America, even Europe) was of course there—"out there"—for them, for us; but with few exceptions it was not part of our immediate and involuntary consciousness. Most people not only acted locally, they also thought locally.

The realities of the past half century have changed all that. Not only the communications revolution but frequent travel, the mobility of entire populations, the presence in our midst of large numbers of non-European peoples, the fact that the vast majority of our population now lives in sizable multicultural cities, the swiftness with which communicable diseases in human and animal life affect us all, and many other factors have produced in most of us a degree of world-consciousness unheard of in my childhood and youth. As many have pointed out, the most important consequence of postwar space exploration has probably been the subtle but entirely effective manner in which it has engendered in all of us an awareness of our common and unalterable location within the biosphere of a small blue-green planet, beautiful and fragile, floating in an unbounded sea of space. I do not for a moment suggest that everyone has fully absorbed the ontological and ethical implications of this new world-consciousness—hardly! But I do believe that it affects all of us at an appreciable level of awareness, and—more important for our present topic—I feel sure that the extent to which it *has* entered one's conscious-ness will inevitably be reflected in one's understanding of and attitude toward religion. In a manner that was simply not true of our society prior to the mid-twentieth century, most North Americans today are apt to re-gard religion from the perspective of its actual performance on the global stage. There can be no doubt, I think, that for many of those who in the most recent surveys declared "no religious affiliation,"[2] a prominent factor in their thinking is the suspicion that religion is inherently divisive if not inimical to world peace and order.

Can Religion also Contribute to Planetary Well-Being?

The question that this new world-consciousness raises for those of us who *are* in some meaningful sense of the word "religious" is whether religion—and specifically our own religion—is, or has the potentiality for being, also a *positive* contributor to the well-being of the planet; and of course, beyond mere speculation, whether such a potentiality, if it is present, can be more fully realized in the actual living out of faith in the tradition in question.

The answer to this question is bound up with religious plurality and the readiness of the religions to engage in dialogue aimed at greater mu-tuality. No specific religious faith may be pursued *seriously* today in isola-tion from the lived awareness of a multitude of religions other than, and perhaps at odds with, one's own. Part and parcel of our expanded world-consciousness is our increasingly existential awareness of the plurality of religions. In the very—indeed the exclusively!—White Anglo-Saxon Protestant village in southwestern Ontario in which I grew up, one could be "Christian," *Protestant* Christian, in a nonchalantly isolated way. That kind of innocence (which was never guiltless!) has been impossible now for decades. As Wilfred Cantwell Smith put it in his 1962 CBC lectures published under the title *The Faith of Other Men*, "The religious life of mankind from now on, if it is to be lived at all, will be lived in a context of religious pluralism . . . It will become increasingly apparent . . . that to be a Christian in the modern world, or a Jew, or an agnostic, is to be so in

---

2. In the 2001 Canadian census 20 percent of Canadians, as compared with 13 per-cent in 1991.

a society in which other [people], intelligent, devout, and righteous, are Buddhists, Muslims, Hindus."[3]

The more conscious we become of the physical unity and the vulnerability of the one planet, the more pressing is our need to come to terms with Earth's many religions. While ordinary (or perhaps one should say extraordinary) human tolerance and liberality, where it exists, can provide a reprieve from intellectual and spiritual struggle with the reality of religious plurality, serious faith of whatever specific brand, cannot for long avoid the need for understanding where this multiplicity is concerned. And in significant portions of the globe, by which nonetheless the whole is affected, such tolerance and liberality cannot be counted upon.

There is an urgency, therefore, about interfaith understanding and dialogue, and this is widely felt. Yet the actual *experience* of such dialogue is still severely limited. By comparison, dialogue within the divided and once militantly independent faith communities of Christendom has by now accumulated a century's worth of encounter and struggle towards greater unity—and I refer only to the modern ecumenical movement, which should be dated from the Edinburgh Missionary Conference in 1910, which led to the establishment of the International Missionary Council in 1925. The World Council of Churches grew out of these deliberations, and was actually conceived in 1937, though on account of the Second World War, its inauguration was delayed until 1948. Despite the acknowledged fact that ecumenism has never been able to overcome the entrenched and stubborn divisions of the churches, and despite the fact that still today its course is characterized by an alternating "ebb and flow" (as the recently published *Encyclopaedia of Protestantism* puts it), no one can gainsay the extent and depth of a hundred years of concrete experience in the quest for Christian unity. All who are able personally to remember the ecclesiastical situation that pertained prior to (let us say) 1950 can only marvel at the distance we have come, in fifty or sixty years, from that kind of noncommunication between the churches. With the Second Vatican Council in 1962 and beyond, a whole new era in Christian life opened up almost overnight, and those of us who experienced it at close range are still, many of us, in a state of happy astonishment. The question, therefore, to which I should like to address myself in the main part of this essay can be stated thus: *Is there in this extended <u>Christian</u> experience of ecumenical*

3. Smith, *The Faith of Other Men*, 11.

dialogue any wisdom to be gained that is applicable to the larger diversity of religious faiths? In putting the question that way, I am assuming (and of course not everyone assumes this) that Christians *ought* to be committed to a serious quest for understanding and mutuality between the religions of the world. Personally, I find myself in wholehearted agreement with the great Jewish thinker, the late Abraham Heschel, who in his address before the Congress on the Theology of the Renewal of the Church convened by Roman Catholics during Canada's centennial year, 1967, announced: "I believe that one of the achievements of this age will be the realization that in our age religious pluralism is the will of God."[4]

How Can Christian Ecumenical Experience Facilitate Interfaith Dialogue?

Christianity *can*, I believe, make an enormous contribution to the "realization" of such an "achievement." It is in fact the central conviction of this paper that <u>Christian</u> *ecumenical experience has provided a background of both theoretical and practical wisdom from which it is possible to derive certain principles that could prove invaluable in inter<u>faith</u> encounter and dialogue.*

More to illustrate than to exhaust the possibilities, I will describe *four areas* of ecumenical Christian experience from which such principles may (I repeat, *may*) be deduced. If I speak tentatively here it is of course because Christians themselves have by no means fully accepted or exemplified any of these principles; yet, in the most profound expressions of Christian ecumenism in all branches of the universal church, these principles have been present both clearly and centrally. Thus they represent what may at least be termed tried-and-true *guidelines* for any discourse between persons and communities of diverse religious conviction.

First: The Well-Being of the World as the Foundational Rationale of Ecumenical Endeavor. This first principle (and therefore I have put it first) speaks directly to the background concern with which I have begun this address, namely, the fear that religion is inherently divisive and prone to violence. One may readily draw such a conclusion about religion, alas, even about religions, like Christianity, that emphasize such virtues as

---

4. Congress on the Theology of the Renewal of the Church, *Renewal of Religious Thought*, 110.

peace and justice and love, when religion is driven exclusively or chiefly by its own internal dynamism and quest for survival and enhancement. But what may occur when a faith community embraces a *raison d'etre* larger than itself?—when it comes to regard as the primary rationale for its existence, its mission, its struggle for integrity, a *world* that vastly transcends its own existence and is deemed by its own authoritative scriptures to be the chief object of the sacrificial love of God? Obviously, such a vision will exercise both a self-limiting and an expanding influence upon its entire life and outreach.

And that, I suggest, is precisely what the Christian ecumenical movement of the twentieth century came to realize as it gradually worked its way into its task. It discovered that, so long as the churches were concerned chiefly for their own security and influence, dialogue between them was bound to flounder. But when they felt themselves led by the divine Spirit and by the gospel itself to discern and develop a genuine regard for the fate of the earth, they experienced the grace of a sufficient self-forgetfulness to be in dialogue with one another as participants in a common task: namely, the peace, prosperity and flowering of God's beloved world. While ecumenical deliberations over these hundred odd years have frequently degenerated into preoccupation with narrowly conceived ecclesiastical relationships, the great exponents of Christian ecumenism (like W. A. Visser t'Hooft and Karl Rahner) have always reminded the churches that the fundamental rationale of the movement towards unity is not the well-being of the church but the well-being of God's beloved world. I suppose that the biblical text most frequently quoted in ecumenical discussions over the past decades has been the twentieth and twenty-first verses of the seventeenth chapter of the Gospel according to St. John. There, in his so-called High Priestly Prayer, the Christ is represented as praying for the unity of his little band of followers to the end "that the world may believe." The oneness of the church, said the great ecumenists, is not and must not become an end in itself; it is only a means—for Christians the most pressing means—to a right and credible communication *to the world* of the truth and trustworthiness of God's abiding love for and commitment to creation. A gospel of reconciling love proclaimed by a church notoriously divided within itself is a contradiction in terms. If the world is to take seriously the message that it is greatly loved, and that the lived experience of its Creator's love effects a wondrous new mutuality among creatures who hear and believe that message, then *the apostolic messenger* must at least approximate such "new creaturehood" in its own life.

While John's account of Jesus's Gethsemane prayer can be read to support Christian exclusivity (as seems to be the case in Christian fundamentalism), and while authentic Christian concern for the world has always been tainted by a lingering constantinian expansionism that wants to *conquer* the world, the programs and pronouncements of the main ecumenical bodies of the churches manifest a genuine and consistent world-orientation that is not marred by excessive self-interest. Personally, I feel that this kind of world-orientation was most concretely articulated in the decision of the Vancouver Assembly of the World Council of Churches in 1983 to adopt as its working theme for the next seven years, "Justice, Peace and the Integrity of Creation."

There is, it seems to me, a principle here that can be applied in both theoretical and practical ways to inter*faith* discourse; for while, like Christianity, every religion no doubt manifests a certain all-too-human desire for preeminence, it is also true of most great world religions (and therefore they may be thought great!) that they contain dimensions of generosity and vigilance for universal peace and justice, which, when stimulated by awareness of the great need and vulnerability of the world as a whole, are able to exercise a countervailing influence in the face of religious isolationism, exclusivity, and chauvinism. With its long and studied experience of the manner in which world-orientation modifies and guides religious discourse between historically divided faith communities, Christianity *could* help to make such commitment to the well-being of the planet more effectively present in other religious bodies and in our encounter with one another.

Second, particularity as entrée to Universality. At the center of the Christian confession of faith there stands the figure of an historical person, entirely human, yet representing in the very fullness of his humanity a transcendence that has prevented the church, even in its more humanistic expressions, from describing him in human terms alone. This christocentric concentration is not optional for Christians. What would Christianity mean without Jesus as the Christ at its center and core? As Paul Tillich affirms in the christological section of his influential *Systematic Theology*, "Christianity is what it is through the affirmation that Jesus of Nazareth, who has been called 'the Christ', is actually the Christ, namely, he who brings the new state of things, the New Being. Wherever the assertion that Jesus is the Christ is maintained, there is the Christian message; wherever this assertion is denied, the Christian message is not affirmed. Christianity was born, not with the birth of the man who is called 'Jesus,' but in the moment in which one of his followers was driven to say to him, 'Thou art the Christ.'"[5]

There can be no Christianity, then, that is not bound up with this *particular* person and event. That realization led theologians in the first half of the twentieth century to introduce the phrase "the scandal of particularity." The term *scandal* in this usage of course derives from St. Paul, who in 1 Corinthians speaks of the *skandalon* of the gospel of the crucified Christ (1 Cor 1:23).

For many Christians both yesterday and today, belief in and about the Christ, often defined in very explicit and doctrinaire forms, is treated as the great test of authenticity. Many of those who have refused membership in the World Council of Churches, for instance, have done so on the basis of the Council's alleged failure to be sufficiently centered in Christ. And even within the World Council itself there has been a never-ending debate between those who stress a strong, definitive christology, to the point of suspecting all who do not embrace their definitions, and others who are vigilant against the substitution of christomonism for christocentrism.

Among the latter group there has emerged what I would like to call a new awareness of the role of particularity in religious faith. There is no entrée to the universal—and faith is ultimately bound up with universals, including the understanding of deity—there is no entrée to the universal that does not pass through the particular. I only encounter childhood or womanhood through my meeting with particular children and particular women. I only encounter Deity, or transcendence, or the Holy through particular beings, symbols, events, texts, or oral testimonies that authenticate themselves to me as being bearers of ultimacy.

The question that must be asked of all particulars is how they function for us. Attachment to a particular child *could* (and often does) produce indifference—or worse!—towards other children. On the other hand, profound knowledge of and love for a one child may so enlarge the imagination and compassion of the knower that he finds himself introduced in a new way to the whole world of children—and thus to a concern for "the

---

5. Tillich, *Existence and the Christ*, 97.

future," a future that surpasses his own futurity. The question about the particulars that are always present in religion is, surely, how they function for believers. Do they function to exclude and circumscribe, or do they function to include and enlarge the range of human awareness and care?

It has been the discovery of those most deeply involved in Christian ecumenism, I believe, that the particular called Jesus—if he remains *person*; if he is not reduced to mere dogma; if the ineffability of his historic personhood is sustained; if he is encountered as the Word *incarnate* who defies retranslation into mere words!—that this particular "particularity," while "scandalous" in terms of the usual presuppositions about deity, nevertheless does not function for true faith as an excluding factor but rather opens faith to the other, to difference, to the mystery of the whole, and in a manner that is both new and, often, radical. The greatest symbolic representations of Christian faith in our time (including those of Martin Luther King Jr., Mother Theresa, Bishop Oscar Romero, Dietrich Bonhoeffer, Jean Vanier, and others) *are* the symbols that they are precisely because their Christian faith has expressed itself in exceptionally nonpartisan and inclusive ways.

Now, *every* religion—even those which assume direct access to the absolute—is involved with particularity, whether that be the particularity of a person (Mohammed or Moses or Baha Ullah), the particularity of a text, particular historical events or experiences, or whatever. And what one may ask, out of Christian ecumenical experience, is whether the particularities associated with other religious traditions do not *also* contain or suggest openness to the other that Christian ecumenists, in their internal debates, have found to be the case in a Christology that is pursued at depth. Perhaps no religion has been so intensely focused on its particularity as has Christianity upon Jesus Christ—and often, to be sure, with dire consequences for others. Yet in the most searching christological contemplation in and around the modern ecumenical movement, precisely Jesus the Christ—the "scandal of particularity"—has proven the very doorway of many Christians of all persuasions to a universality that, otherwise, they would not have known. It is therefore possible for Christians to encourage representatives of other religious traditions to explore as fully as possible the potentiality of *their* particularities to give birth to similar expressions of inclusivity. It is, in short, not a matter of abandoning the particular foci of our traditions, but of allowing them to *deepen* our awareness of their grounding in a universal transcendence that cannot be possessed exclusively by any or by all religions.

Third, the quest for power always impairs ecumenical discourse. It has been the experience of Christians involved in interchurch dialogue that there can be no dialogue when the bodies represented approach the ecumenical task with a prior and adamant commitment to the maintenance of their own preeminence. This refers not only to the determination to control discourse and to exercise political power in all decision making; it refers also, and more important, to the assumption that a particular doctrinal tradition has captured truth and must therefore maintain itself intact over against all alternative perceptions. Ecumenical dialogue comes to a standstill whenever its participants act on the assumption that they alone are in possession of ultimate verity.

The actual experience of the breakdown of dialogue whenever that assumption is present, either openly or (which is more often the case) covertly, has led in ecumenical circles to a more modest—and I would say a more profound and biblically-informed—understanding of the nature of theological truth. It has done so, not as a triumph of Christian humility or bourgeois niceness, but for the very practical reason that without such a critique of truth and of the human and institutional relation to truth, ecumenical dialogue could not have proceeded. In the meeting of ecclesiastical bodies that had for centuries been almost totally isolated from one another, and that in their isolation could pursue their various "orthodoxies" without reference to or challenge from other versions of Christian truth—in the actual *meeting* of these long-separated groupings it was necessary to rediscover an understanding of the nature of truth which, though never wholly neglected by theological scholarship, could remain a pious sentiment without exercising its innately critical function with respect to the truth claims of the churches.

I am referring to the biblical conception of Truth as a *living* reality. "No one," wrote Paul Tillich, "not even a believer or a church, can boast of possessing the truth, just as no one can boast of possessing love."[6] Jesus did not offer his disciples a systematic theology; he offered them himself. "*I* am the Truth," St. John's gospel has him declare, thus capturing the livingness of truth as it is understood to be throughout the older and newer Testaments. Whoever hears this *I* knows that the entire assump-

6. Tillich, *On the Boundary*, 51.

tion that theological truth can be possessed, owned, and used to confound every rival claim is false and idolatrous. At most, we may be oriented towards truth; and insofar as we are so oriented we shall be open to others in whom we may perceive the same orientation. In specifically Christian parlance: *Those who are turned towards the truth that Jesus "is" will be able to recognize others who also look beyond themselves for what is ultimate, even when these others are not looking specifically towards Jesus.*

Christian ecumenicity has been able to function—not, often or consistently, to flourish, but at least to function!—for a hundred years only insofar as it has been capable of realizing the modesty factor inherent in this principle. Cynicism might write such modesty off as being nothing more than the influence of modern humanism and liberalism; but it is in fact the consequence—I would say the absolutely necessary and self-evident consequence—of a faith that is founded, not on propositional truth, but the truth of encounter with Person, with "the eternal Thou" (Buber). Under the impact of diverse and sometimes antithetical testimonies to the meaning of that encounter, Christians in ecumenical conversation had once more to realize that their *doctrine* can only *point* to ultimate reality, and therefore cannot and must not be regarded as a source of power over others. This realization is plainly present in the concluding words of the report of the moderator of the World Council of Church's 2003 address, from which I quoted briefly at the outset: "Any religion that aims for power loses its *raison d'être*. God is the owner, protector, sustainer, and reconciler of the whole humanity and creation. Religion is the servant and agent of God's universal plan."[7]

Again we may ask, is there not in other religious traditions also, and perhaps in the religious impulse as such, something comparable to this recognition of the transcendence of ultimate power, especially the power of truth? And may not Christians, on the basis of their own experience of the ways that such a recognition, stimulated by diversity, exercises a qualifying effect on religious discourse, exemplify and encourage members of other faiths to explore their own traditions for such insight? If the assumption of power, its possession and retention, has proven a sure barrier to interchurch discourse, it will certainly prove a barrier to serious attempts at inter*faith* discourse. Can the concrete ecumenical Christian experience of the transcendence of power, especially the power of truth,

7. Aram I, "Report of the Moderator," 391.

find an echo in all religions as they seek to enter into new relationships with one another?

Fourth, hospitality towards and dialogue with other traditions does not diminish but can in fact enhance one's knowledge and appreciation of one's own tradition. It has been a source of hesitation on the part of many Christians and ecclesiastical groupings that the prospect of ecumenical encounter, if entered into earnestly, could have the effect of distancing them from their own tradition—who knows (?), of incorporating them into a kind of globalized spirituality, a superchurch, in which the familiar comforts and challenges of their own established tradition have been absorbed and, for all practical purposes, forgotten. There are still denominations and elements within all of our denominations that fear and distrust ecumenism, especially at the local level, for precisely that sort of reason.

Yet most of us who have actually been involved in ecumenical discourse for several decades realize, I believe, that such fear is unfounded. In fact, with few exceptions (in my experience at least), the exact opposite is the case. Not only do we become more knowledgeable of our own ecclesial tradition when we enter into dialogue with persons of other heritages; we frequently find ourselves appreciating aspects of our own tradition that had eluded us heretofore. The presence and testimony of the others has illumined both positive and negative qualities in our own received faith. We *change*, in consequence of such illumination; but we do not feel that we lose what is essential to our own historic faith; rather, we find ways of sharing that essence with the others, and of being enriched by what they bring. Thus, as countless Christians of all historic persuasions have found over the past hundred years, while ecumenical discourse introduces something new to all who undertake it sincerely, it does not destroy but puts into wider circulation emphases and concerns that are the treasures of the whole, varied testimony of the ages.

In quite practical terms, ecumenical Christian experience throughout these decades has helped immensely to overcome the forgetfulness, not to say the plain ignorance, of many with respect to their own ecclesial traditions. You cannot sit in theological or ethical discussions that are representative of many doctrinal and moral traditions without sooner or later being brought to the point of asking yourself, what *does* my church teach on that subject? In the post-Christendom era that is now the social and cultural context of all Christian groupings, there is a growing awareness of the often-appalling lack of knowledge (scriptural, doctrinal, historical) that characterizes most of our churches. Yet without such knowledge faith itself will not survive, to say nothing of specific communities of faith. Churches will not be kept going by sentiment or ritual, or hereditary custom. Anselm's dictum, *Fides quaerens intellectum*, has a new currency and urgency among us now. In churches that face the demise of automatic religiosity, there is among those who remain a felt need to *understand* what they believe. And that need is nowhere more in evidence than in the meeting of once-separated Christian bodies with one another.

This experience of Christian ecumenicity, namely, that hospitality towards and discourse with the other, does not diminish but can enhance knowledge of one's own, has immediate applicability—a fortiori!—to interfaith encounter. Conscientious Christians often tell themselves and one another that their knowledge of other world religions is appallingly slight. But whenever interreligious dialogue is attempted, especially though not exclusively at the congregational level, Christian participants have realized, often to their chagrin, that their knowledge of *their own* tradition is almost as minimal as their knowledge of other faiths. Heretofore, they have been satisfied with generalities and pious clichés and "favorite Bible verses"; in interfaith discourse they now find themselves incapable of articulating Christian belief in an informed and nuanced way. The presence and testimony of the other, especially when the other—whether Muslim, Jewish, Hindu or whatever—*is* religiously informed and articulate, often goads Christians into deliberate and disciplined attempts to comprehend their own tradition in ways that might never have occurred apart from this encounter with religious difference.

I must conclude therefore that another contribution that ecumenical Christian experience can make to interfaith dialogue is the confidence that opening oneself to the faith of others, far from risking the loss or relativization of one's own tradition, much more consistently results in a deepening of one's understanding of one's own, while at the same time being the occasion for greater knowledge of and compassion for other faith tradition.

This is perhaps the most important lesson to be learned by all of us, especially, who live in conspicuously multireligious cultures. For the great fear of those most committed to a particular religious tradition, I think, is that close encounter with religious diversity will rob them of their assumption, nurtured in more homogeneous contexts, that their own religion is the best, the truest, the ultimately approved. Genuine and sustained interfaith dialogue, which surely must include those most committed to their specific religion and not only persons of a liberal frame of mind, will only be feasible where there is some assurance that the encounter with difference will not result in the loss or relativization of the faith one has known and loved. Christian ecumenical experience can contribute much to the building of such assurance.

Conclusion

My contention, then, to sum up, has been that there are numerous ways in which the ecumenical experience of Christians over the past century particularly can facilitate dialogue between the various religions that are present in our world and, especially, in multicultural and religiously pluralistic cultures like that of our own country. By way of illustration, I have described briefly *four* of these ways: (1) that the well-being of *the world* is the foundational rationale of ecumenical endeavor; (2) that particularity profoundly appreciated is our entrée to a deeper universality; (3) that the quest for power always impairs ecumenical discourse; and (4) that hospitality towards and dialogue with other traditions does not diminish but can in fact enhance one's knowledge and appreciation of one's own tradition. There are of course many other principles that could be derived from a century of Christian ecumenical experience.

Now, it would be false and misleading to exaggerate the potential Christian contribution to interfaith relationships, for not only have Christians themselves failed to appropriate fully or consistently any of the principles I have named, but in addition to that there are of course barriers to interfaith dialogue that are not present in interchurch dialogue. But we must not wait to be perfect before we attempt to apply whatever wisdom we have learned about seeking understanding and unity between religious communities. For the alternative to such a quest is a world that is already, and will increasingly be, victimized by religions that *refuse* dialogue and court the kind of intransigence that is inherently belligerent and, ultimately, violent. The quest for harmony and trust between religions, even if it can only hope for approximation, is no longer an option for serious persons of every faith posture. For the one planet cannot for long contain the human suspicion, envy, competition, and revenge that are augmented and emboldened by a religious fervor that lives exclusively within its own "dividing walls of hostility" (cf. Eph 2:14). While keeping our eyes wide open to the conflicts that religion inspires or is caused to sanction, we should never lose sight of the blessings that all humankind's great faiths, at their best, wish to bestow upon the world.

13

A Latter-Day Kierkegaardian
Visits a Megachurch

"Come hither all"—the invitation is undeniably for all, but when it comes to the pinch and it has to be determined to what it is that Christ invites us... then, as in the age of Christ, all most heartily decline with thanks ....[1]

HE WENT THERE EXPECTING to be repulsed, and then disliking himself afterwards for having once again played the critic. He was not repulsed. So at least he was spared the orgy of self-examination that his 'negativity' too consistently engenders. What the experience produced in him, however, was almost as excruciating as self-flagellation: How is one to comprehend a phenomenon like that? Had the megachurch service evoked in him mere aversion, he'd at least have known how to deal with it. As it is, he couldn't dismiss it out of hand. Much of the service had surprised him in a quite pleasant way. Occasionally he even found himself smiling. Once he laughed openly—at not *at* them, *with* them.

All the same, something quite wrong—bogus—was going on in that place, he felt. Not obviously wrong, yet wrong nonetheless. Subtly, quietly,

---

1. Kierkegaard, *Attack upon Christendom*, 286–87.

and very, very *nicely* wrong. He wrote the following piece primarily to try to tell himself what he meant by that.

A novelist, or even a clever journalist, would approach such a task indirectly; but he—for better or worse!—is a theologian, so he had to be content with . . . *dialectics*. Like Peter Abelard's *Sic et Non—Yes and No*.

Affirmation, *Sic* / Presumption, *Non*

The entire first part of the service (no, let's be accurate: the *program*) was devoted to the sweet belief that God Almighty, Creator of all things visible and invisible, is positively obsessed with "you." "You're great! You're wonderful!" we were told by the performer-*cum*-evangelist who directed the singing and praying that preceded the taking up of our offerings in large baskets. I suppose the cynical might put that down to a good sales pitch, coming as it did just at that particular juncture in the proceedings; but the same theme of our enthusiastic personal affirmation by the Master of the Universe persisted (with a little fuzziness that I'll mention later) in the sermon.

"I love my kids," declared the preacher, "because—well, because they're . . . my kids!" We are all, he said, "God's kids"—each one of us so unique and precious to our heavenly Father that He'll just "bolt out the door after any one of us who strays."

So what is wrong with that? I've said something like it myself often enough—and in much less colorful language! My esteemed teacher Paul Tillich, notorious for his own "straying," named the sermon that many regard as his greatest, "You Are Accepted." It was Tillich's way of translating into contemporary language the rather inaccessible concept that lies at the heart of the Protestant Reformation: justification by grace through faith. So why quibble?

Well, there's a difference, surely, between saying, "You are accepted" and saying, "You're great!" Acceptance presupposes the experience and acknowledgement of a negative condition—possible or actual nonacceptance, maybe even plain rejection. Justification by grace through faith assumes that negation. You are accepted—*unacceptable as you actually are!* I know that contemporary citizens of a mass culture that doesn't care a damn for their precious uniqueness, need to be assured that they matter, each one. But the line between acceptance and presumption, affirmation and smugness, while thin as a razor's edge, is nevertheless an important line. It is especially important for *us*, who are first among the materially favored peoples of the earth, and who in that respect are affirmed and accepted beyond all deserving! There was so much "You, You, You" in this spiritual agenda that one lost all consciousness (supposing one had it in the first place!) of "Them, Them, Them"—the impoverished, marginalized, and forgotten of the planet. (Significantly, there were no prayers of intercession at all, let alone any other mention of "Them.")

Glancing around the immense auditorium, I realized that the hearers of this wonderfully positive message about themselves were not, *Deo gratia*, the movers and shakers of our society; yet neither were they in any sense a cross-section of the meek and lowly. Collectively, they obviously represented a great deal of wealth and power. Some of them in all probability lived in high-priced homes of the gated communities that encircle this new and much touted exemplification of Christendom's perennial fascination with property. Churches, *mega*churches! Odd, this obsession with buildings—put up for a God who "does not dwell in houses made with human hands" (Acts 7:48).

Isn't it possible that while affirming persons as "God's kids," even the gospel of the megachurch might incorporate a modicum of social consciousness—something a little more far-reaching than food baskets in the parking-lot? One does not expect American middle-class Christianity to go in for Christian socialism; but surely an institution that wants to retain the adjective *Christian* ought to wonder sometimes about a message of personal affirmation that so easily and regularly turns into *class, gender, racial and national* affirmation.

Immediacy, *Sic* / Folksiness, *Non*

Everything that happened in that place, from the moment we entered its shining corridors until we made our way back into the crowded parking lot, was calculated to make Middle America feel entirely at home. To begin with, it resembled a modern shopping mall—minus, to be sure, a food court, but replete with boutiques and an information center and coffee (free, if you were ready to chat with the well-wishers who dispensed it). The auditorium, sometimes anachronistically called a sanctuary, was as familiar as any posh, comfy, spectator-accommodating cinema.

By a providential mistake, our party sat just behind the "control center," where four busy technicians operated a complex, multilevered panel managing the sound and color in which, that morning, we would encounter the Eternal. "It's like being an audience in a TV studio," my wife whispered. But of course an Oprah-educated clientele would find that the homiest thing in the world.

The endeavour to make us all feel at home, however, extended well beyond the physical environs. The music was the same music you hear (correction: you cannot avoid!) in elevators, department stores, on radio programs, and from the i-Pods of teenagers sitting next to you on the subway—though oddly combined with lyrics emanating from the most sentimental of yesteryear's pietistic hymns.

The illustrations chosen by the preacher were so simplistic, often to the point of ludicrous incongruity, that it made the Kierkegaard in me squirm when I considered that the biblical text they were supposed to illuminate was Abraham's call to sacrifice Isaac. The distraught, God-fearing patriarch, driven by his strange faith to slay his long-awaited and beloved and *only* son to his demanding Deity was compared to a modern-day father refusing to let his teenager use one of the family cars. ("Ah, come on Dad. That's not fair!") Perhaps, in the Age of ADD, the preacher had to stoop to this kind of homespun stuff to retain the interest of his huge audience—he preached for forty minutes (a feat rarely achieved today in our once-mainline churches, which go in for seven-minute sermonettes and meditations). But what happens to the biblical story when we try to make it ours by drawing upon the more mundane, less complex and serious occurrences and relationships of daily existence?

Otherwise stated: Is it impossible to achieve points of contact with "real life" while retaining some sense of the ineffability, mystery, otherness, and holiness of the Transcendent? Shouldn't anybody who comes within shouting distance of the Bible suspect that the tradition of Jerusalem really does introduce a "strange, new world," as Karl Barth insisted in one of his early essays?[2] The Bible certainly knows about the marketplace, but it looks at the marketplace from a perspective that it does not gain from the marketplace itself! The Bible isn't much interested in teenagers who want to get hold of the family car, or the ancient equivalent thereof. Or if it sometimes seems to be—for instance if the Prodigal Son parable might

2. Barth, "The Strange New World within the Bible."

lend itself to that kind of parallel—it soon takes the story well beyond the point of "Come on, Dad!"

The "strange, new world" in the Bible is simply *not* the shopping-mall world in which, at the level of the superficial, North Americans live and move and have their being today. It is a world filled with characters stranger than Dostoevsky's, and more like the people in those bleak and dark Hollywood films that megachurchgoers don't like. *American Beauty. Brokeback Mountain. There Will Be Blood.* Shouldn't the bearers of the biblical narrative expect to find *that* world even in the midst of their well-clad, compulsively smiling congregations, just a little—*a little!*—under-neath the surface?

In any case, is it really the object of Christian worship to make people feel at home? Recently I heard a person praising a certain minister who conducted her services "just as if she were in her own living room." Kierkegaard nearly made me cry out on that occasion. But I suspect this does, nevertheless, define today's religious norm—and not only for the megachurch. "God," declared our preacher (defying, without knowing it, not only poor SK but that champion of the *Deus absconditus*, Martin Luther)—"*God* is not hidden! God is as familiar as our best friend." But maybe that's the trouble. Haven't I heard somewhere that familiarity breeds contempt?

Jesus, *Sic* / Jesus-ism, *Non*

A friend of mine came storming out of a liberal church service once mut-tering that he had not heard the name Jesus once in the entire hour. It was right for him to bluster. Jesus is not incidental to the Christian faith!

That was not the problem at the megachurch. Jesus was conspicuous-ly present and accounted for from the word *go*. While my poor friend SK died of embarrassment, we were asked to sing love songs to Jesus—songs that the crooners of the 1950s would not have sung to Amy or Laura or Georgia or any their other real or imagined lovers. The names Jesus and God were used interchangeably. What prayer there was (and it all came from the stage) alternated between private whisperings to "Jee-zus" and private whisperings to "Gah-odd", with "Lord" and "Father" functioning in the usual way—i.e., as mantras to fill in the blanks.

Perhaps fortunately, the preacher did not explain to us his Trinitarian and christological preconceptions; but one could be pretty sure, if one knew any of the code language, that he would have come down heavily on the side of divine unity and the sovereignty of the Son. And in that he'd have been right in step with the most popular Christianity on this continent, and with Western Christendom generally. For, as historians of dogma have long pointed out, the West has always preferred to err on the side of Sabellianism. New World Christianity, however, having seldom exercised itself over the intricacies of Trinitarian theology, has characteristically assumed, simply, that "Jesus is God"—a formula that you can hear on television or radio religious broadcasting twenty-four/seven. As H. Richard Niebuhr rightly asserted, North American Christianity in both conservative and liberal dress characteristically replaces a genuine Trinitarian understanding of God with a "Unitarianism of the second person of the Trinity."

In the presence of this kind of Jesus-ism, my inner Kierkegaard found himself somewhat uncomfortable. For he himself had been capable of a certain preoccupation with Jesus. But in the multiculture of today he found himself surrounded by many other voices—Jewish and Muslim and Buddhist and other voices that wanted to know whether he still wishes to make the same kind of unconditional connection he used to make between the Absolute (God) and the Particular (Jesus). Would there have to be any alterations in the text of the *Concluding Unscientific Postscript*—for example, would it still be quite right to say that "the Teacher" (Jesus) has not only to bring "the Truth" but also "the condition necessary for understanding the Truth"? *That* teacher only? Jesus only?

Seeing the blatant, unqualified way in which the West's propensity to Christo*monism* played itself out in such religious environs as this, my Kierkegaard had to ask himself whether theological emphases are not more *contextually* determined than even he, the father of existentialism and champion of "the Moment," had perceived. He had been struggling, back there, against an Enlightenment rationalism whose denizens felt they had immediate access to the Truth, the Absolute; so he howled about this scandalous Particular, Jesus. But mid-nineteenth-century Copenhagen was not early twenty-first-century Atlanta or Chicago. There are other skirmishes that must be joined in our context; and while one of them may indeed be a crassly technicized rationalism more pretentious than anything flowing from the pen of Hegel or Voltaire, another is certainly the *anti*-rationalism and exclusivistic *fideism* that makes the rhetorical and doctrinalized "Way of Jesus" the *only* way. A more nuanced Trinitarianism, in which God the Father/Mother and God the Spirit have at least little 'offices' of their own might facilitate dialogue with the other faiths that are not going to go away just because Christians are still capable, here and there, of making a lot of noise.

The Cross, *Sic* / Substitutionary Atonement Theory, *Non*

According to my own manner of regarding it, the cross of Jesus Christ was not a reality *at all* in this service. Certainly it wasn't present symbolically. There were no symbols of any kind—unless one thinks of artificial shrubbery as a symbol (and, to be sure, it may be a very accurate symbol of our culture!); for the only item on the stage besides a gargantuan grand piano and the singing, swinging songsters were five or six large, very uniform, very symmetrically placed plastic plants. Still, symbols as such guarantee nothing. In themselves, artificial crosses say no more about the crucified Christ than do plastic shrubbery about Life. The Christ of Bethlehem and Golgotha can be as absent from a cross-bedecked Gothic cathedral as from a stainless-steel and broadloom-covered auditorium with complicated electronic machinery for sound and lighting!

Or as present. I am sure that Christ *was* present among those apparently well-heeled and doggedly cheerful "winners"; because finally we are none of us winners, and the largely unspoken pain of the American middle classes may be as unbearable, in the last analysis, as that of "the poor" for whom "God has a preferential option." But the pathos of humanity in which, one way or another, we are all wrapped, was decidedly *not* the anthropopolitical keynote of this gathering, and in fact everything possible was done to mute the covert despair that is so patently a feature of the American middle classes—the despair, as Kierkegaard said with devastating insight, that cannot and will not name itself as such. That is the despair in which the crucified One participates; it is the spiritual space where He tries to meet us, for only there can he engender in us the hope that is beyond despair. And so much *religion*—perhaps religion *as such*—seems designed to prevent just that meeting!

I am saying that the cross wasn't really present at all in this service, theologically understood; but of course it was abundantly present at the rhetorical level. It's hard for Christian churches to avoid cross-talk altogether (though some even manage that!)—it's so much part of the language of Christendom.

As noted earlier, the preacher had chosen an Old Testament text, a familiar one: the near sacrifice of Isaac by his obedient father Abraham. As usual, this story provided a fertile text for the usual, predictable reiteration of the Latin atonement theory. Unlike Father Abraham, whose costly sacrifice God stayed at the last minute, *God-the-Father* had to go all the way with his beloved Son! Because only in that way could God save *us* from . . . God's wrath. Anselm of Canterbury capped the theory with his impeccable logic in the eleventh century, and the Christendom West has rarely questioned it since, or looked elsewhere for an explanation of the meaning of the cross. Even Kierkegaard sometimes talks in those terms.

So my Kierkegaard took a backseat to my Bozo at this point. Bozo, as the initiated will know, is the fictitious monk who "dialogues" with Anselm in the tract *Cur Deus Homo?*, that is the *locus classicus* of this substitutionary atonement theory: Jesus had to die on the cross in order to make satisfaction for the sins of humankind. Bozo, Anselm's straight man in this quaisi-Socratic booklet of St. Anselm, wanted to know why God had to go to all the trouble of becoming human, suffering rejection and death and all that, when quite clearly all God really *wanted* to do was to accept and forgive us—again and again, if necessary; "seventy-times-seven," as Jesus said ordinary believers ought to do for one another!

Bozo's question took on new weight for me in this setting, because the theological *premise* of the whole presentation (as I've noted in the first point, above) was the declaration of a divine affirmation of "you and you and you"—an affirmation so unqualified that I had to wonder (to quote a well-known psychologist) "whatever became of sin?" The conflicting message of this whole service came to a head in this dichotomy between a love-besotted deity and a deity needing human sacrifice to look twice at us distorted creatures! The theological contradiction was so naively and blatantly stated in this megachurch service that it clarified for me, once again, the questionable character of the whole Anselmic/Latin theory, which has so captivated Western Christendom. Jews, it seems to me, are right, when they claim that the Abrahamic story of the near sacrifice of Isaac is a better demonstration of the love of God than a Christian doctrine that has the heavenly Father going all the way with the killing. Until we can overcome the strange fascination of the West with Anselmic atonement theology, which conveys very conflicting messages about the kind of God Christians worship, we shall have to flounder about, as this preacher did, trying to assure us that although God loves us unconditionally (because "we're his kids"!), he can only do this because his real, flesh-and-blood Kid took the rap for us! As readers of my books will realize, I do not want to trash Anselm altogether, but (a) the exclusive attention Western churches have paid to the Latin theory is not warranted, either doctrinally or psychologically; and (b) this theory lends itself, as the other two theological traditions of soteriology do not, to such simplistic interpretation that the above-named contradiction is almost unavoidable in popular communication.

Conclusions

What I learned from the megachurch experience is a lesson directed, not at the megachurch and its excited developers, but at all of us who still claim some rootage in classical Protestant traditions—as represented, for example, by Søren Kierkegaard. If I ponder why it is that so many of my clerical and lay friends who visit American megachurches come away glowing, the only explanation I can offer is that they discover, in these settings, ways of doing *better* the very things they are trying to do, alas, in their own bailiwicks. The marketplace successfulness of the Big Church confirms them in their theological innocency and inspires them, not to rethink their gospel, but to refurbish their skills as communicators and promoters.

The point, however, is to ask *what* is being offered in these new temples (*and* our duller, less successful, and often nearly defunct churches)—*not* how it is *packaged!* *What* is it, and how does it stack up against the Bible, Augustine, Luther, Calvin, Barth, Tillich, Ruether, Soelle—and (*sic!*) Kierkegaard. And others. Concretely speaking, in view of the four previous observations, I ask the following four questions:

First, can Christians in North America today affirm and encourage the much beleaguered and belittled human individual without, in the process, implying that the lifestyle, together with the racial, sexual, economic and other assumptions and pursuits of persons shaped by our consumer society, is just what is ordered by the Master of the Universe?

Second, how can Christian communities be hospitable without reducing faith to sentimentality, mystery to ordinariness, truth to slogan, hope to optimism, love to *luv*?

Third, is it possible to perceive and present Jesus as the representative and revealer of true God without making of him all the God of God there is?

Fourth, how shall we keep the cross at the center without turning God into a transcendent Shylock and relegating humankind and all the rest of creation to the status of a failed experiment?

Afterword

THE THIRTEEN ESSAYS IN this book are revisions of essays and lectures written over a fifteen year period from about 1995. They were selected from a large accumulation of such (mostly unpublished) writings because I felt they could give substance and concreteness to the theme announced in the book's title and elaborated in the *Introduction*.

As separate and independent pieces, the essays do not, of course, pursue a single thesis; rather, they address aspects of the theme of *Gospel* as I understand that term: (1) its meaning, intent, and mystery; (2) its most basic claims (Jesus Christ, the Cross, the human self, human vocation); and (3) the ethic to which it leads.

Anyone who wishes to ascertain the 'systematic' theological foundations out of which these essays emerged, and on which they are based, is invited to consult my most comprehensive theological opus, the three-volume work subtitled, *Christian Theology in a North American Context*. Volume I, *Thinking the Faith*, concerns theological method including the necessity for *contextuality* in Christian theology; Volume II, *Professing the Faith*, addresses the three principal doctrines of Christian faith (Theology, Christology and Anthropology), and Volume III, *Confessing the Faith*, concerns the Church, its struggle to move beyond 'Christendom,' and its message and mission today.

This larger work of comprehensive (systematic and contextual) theology is encapsulated and developed further in a single-volume work titled *The Cross in Our Context: Jesus and the Suffering World*.

D. J. H.
Notre-Dame-de-Grace,
Montreal, Quebec, Canada

Bibliography

Aram I. "Report of the Moderator." *Ecumenical Review*, October 2003, 378–91.

Aulen, Gustaf. *Christus Victor: An Historical Study of the Three Main Types of the Idea of Atonement*. Translated by A. G. Hebert. 1961. Reprinted, Eugene, OR: Wipf & Stock, 2003.

Bailey, J. Martin, and Douglas Gilbert. *The Steps of Bonhoeffer: A Pictorial Album*. Foreword by William A. Vissser 't Hooft. Philadelphia: Pilgrim, 1969.

Baird, Daniel. "The High Ground." *The Walrus Magazine*, June 2011. Online: http://www.walrusmagazine.com/articles/2011.06-religion-the-high-ground/.

Barth, Karl. *Church Dogmatics*. Translated by G. T. Thomson et al. Edinburgh: T. & T. Clark, 1936–77.

———. *Evangelical Theology: An Introduction*. Translated by Grover Foley. New York: Holt, Rinehart and Winston, 1963.

———. *Karl Barth, Church Dogmatics*. A selection with an introduction by Helmut Gollwitzer. Translated and edited by Geoffrey W. Bromiley. Louisville: Westminster John Knox, 1994.

———. "The Strange New World within the Bible." In *The Word of God and the Word of Man*, 28–50. Translated with a new introduction by Douglas Horton. New York: Harper, 1957.

———. *Witness to the Word: A Commentary on John 1*. Edited by Walther Fürst. Translated by Geoffrey W. Bromiley. Grand Rapids: Eerdmans, 1986.

Bax, Clifford. "Turn Back, O Man." London: Stainer & Bell, 1919. [Hymn]

Bernanos, Georges. *The Diary of a Country Priest*. Translated by Pamela Morris. New York: Macmillan, 1937.

Berry, Wendell. *What Are People For?: Essays*. San Francisco: North Point, 1990.

Bethge, Eberhard. *Dietrich Bonhoeffer: A Biography*. Rev. ed. Translated by Eric Mosbacher et al. Edited by Victoria Barnett. Minneapolis: Fortress, 2000.

Bonhoeffer, Dietrich. *The Cost of Discipleship*. Translated by R. H. Fuller, with some revision by Irmgard Booth. 2nd rev. ed. London: SCM, 1959.

———. *Ethics*. Translated by Reinhard Krauss et al. Edited by Clifford J. Green. Dietrich Bonhoeffer Works 6. Minneapolis: Fortress, 2005.

———. *Letters and Papers from Prison*. Edited by Eberhard Bethge. Translated by Reginald Fuller and revised by Frank Clark and others. 3rd ed. rev. and enl. London: SCM, 1967.

Bibliography

Borowitz, Eugene B. *Exploring Jewish Ethics: Papers on Covenant Responsibility*. Detroit: Wayne State University Press, 1990.

Brown, Robert McAfee, editor. *The Essential Reinhold Niebuhr: Selected Essays and Addresses*. New Haven: Yale University Press, 1986.

Carroll, James. *Constantine's Sword: The Church and the Jews; A History*. Boston: Houghton Mifflin, 2001.

Congress on the Theology of the Renewal of the Church. *Renewal of Religious Thought*. Introduction by Paul-Émile Léger. Theology of Renewal 1. Montreal: Palm, 1968.

Gollwitzer, Helmut. *Karl Barth, Church Dogmatics*. A selection with an introduction by Helmut Gollwitzer. Translated and edited by Geoffrey W. Bromiley. Louisville: Westminster John Knox, 1994.

Greene, Graham. *The Power and the Glory*. New York: Viking, 1946.

Hall, Douglas John. *Confessing the Faith: Christian Theology in a North American Context*. Minneapolis: Fortress Press, 1996.

————. *The Cross in Our Context: Jesus and the Suffering World*. Minneapolis: Fortress, 2003.

————. *The End of Christendom and the Future of Christianity*. 1997. Reprinted, Eugene, OR: Wipf & Stock, 2002.

————. *Imaging God: Dominion as Stewardship*. 1986. Reprinted, Eugene, OR: Wipf & Stock, 2004.

————. *Lighten Our Darkness: Toward an Indigenous Theology of the Cross*. Rev. ed. Lima, OH: Academic Renewal, 2001.

————. *The Messenger: Friendship, Faith, and Finding One's Way*. Eugene, OR: Cascade Books, 2011.

————. *Professing the Faith: Christian Theology in a North American Context*. Minneapolis: Fortress Press, 1993.

————. *Remembered Voices: Reclaiming the Legacy of "Neo-Orthodoxy."* Louisville: Westminster John Knox, 1998.

————. *The Steward: A Biblical Symbol Come of Age*. 1990. Reprinted, Eugene, OR: Wipf & Stock, 2004.

————. *Thinking the Faith: Christian Theology in a North American Context*. Minneapolis: Augsburg-Fortress Press, 1989.

Heschel, Abraham Joshua. *The Prophets*. New York: Harper & Row, 1962.

Hillerbrand, Hans J., editor. *The Encyclopedia of Protestantism*. 4 vols. New York: Routledge, 2004.

Holloway, Richard. *Doubts and Loves: What Is Left of Christianity?* Edinburgh: Canongate, 2001.

Jenkins, Philip. *The Next Christendom: The Coming of Global Christianity*. Oxford: Oxford University Press, 2002.

Kierkegaard, Søren. *Attack upon Christendom*. Translated by Walter Lowrie. Boston: Beacon,1944.

Kittelson, James M. *Luther the Reformer: The Story of the Man and His Career*. 2nd ed. Minneapolis: Fortress, 2003.

Lehman, Paul L. *Ethics in a Christian Context*. Library of Theological Ethics. Louisville: Westminster John Knox, 2006.

Lewis, Alan E. *Between Cross and Resurrection: A Theology of Holy Saturday*. Grand Rapids: Eerdmans, 2001.

Lifton, Robert Jay, and Richard Falk. *Indefensible Weapons: The Political and Psychological Case against Nuclearism*. New York: Basic Books, 1982.

Loewenich, Walter von. *Martin Luther: The Man and His Work*. Translated by Lawrence W. Denef. Minneapolis: Augsburg, 1986.

Moltmann, Jürgen. *The Crucified God: The Cross of Christ as the Foundation and Criticism of Christian Theology*. Translated by R. A. Wilson and John Bowden. New York: Harper & Row, 1974.

———. *Theology of Play*. Translated by Reinhand Ulrich. New York: Harper & Row, 1972.

Niebuhr, Reinhold. *Beyond Tragedy: Essays on the Christian Interpretation of History*.

———. *The Nature and Destiny of Man: A Christian Interpretation*. 1964. Reprinted with an introduction by Robin W. Lovin. 2 vols. Louisville: Westminster John Knox, 1996.

———. *The Self and the Dramas of History*. New York: Scribner, 1955.

Rahner, Karl. *The Spirit in the World*. 2nd ed. Translated by William Dych. London: Sheed & Ward, 1968.

———. "A Theological Interpretation of the Position of *Christians in the Modern World*." In *Mission and Grace: Essays in Pastoral Theology*, 1:3–55. 3 vols. London: Sheed & Ward, 1963.

Rasmussen, Larry, with Renate Bethge. *Dietrich Bonhoeffer: His Significance for North Americans*. Minneapolis: Fortress, 1990.

Ruether, Rosemary Radford. *Gaia & God: An Ecofeminist Theology of Earth Healing*. San Francisco: HarperSanFrancisco, 1992.

Robinson, John A. T. *Honest to God*. Philadelphia: Westminster, 1963.

Simons, John. "The Next Christendom: Prospect and Challenge." Montreal: Diocesan College of Montreal, n.d.

Smith, Wilfred Cantwell. *The Faith of Other Men*. Harper Torchbooks. New York: Harper & Row, 1972.

Sobrino, Jon. *Christology at the Crossroads: A Latin American Approach*. Translated by John Drury. Maryknoll, NY: Orbis, 1978.

Taylor, Charles. *A Secular Age*. Cambridge: Belknap, 2007.

Tillich, Paul. *The Courage to Be*. The Terry Lectures. New Haven: Yale University Press, 1952.

———. *Existence and the Christ*. Systematic Theology 2. Chicago: University of Chicago Press, 1957.

———. "He Who Is the Christ." In *The Shaking of the Foundations*, 141–48. New York: Scribner, 1955.

———. *On the Boundary: An Autobiographical Sketch*. New York: Scribner, 1966.

———. *The Protestant Era*. Translated, with a concluding essay by James Luther Adams. Chicago: University of Chicago Press, 1948.

———. "You Are Accepted." In *The Shaking of the Foundations*, 153–63. New York: Scribner, 1955.

Toffler, Alvin. *Future Shock*. New York: Random House, 1970.

Tranströmer, Tomas. *The Half-Finished Heaven: The Best Poems of Thomas Tranströmer*. Chosen and translated by Robert Bly. St. Paul: Graywolf, 2001.

Tuchman, Barbara W. *The Guns of August*. 1962. Reprinted, with a new Foreword by Robert K. Massie. New York: Ballantine, 1994.

Vidal, Gore. *Empire: A Novel*. New York: Random House, 1987.

Bibliography

Visser 't Hooft, William A. "Foreword." In *The Steps of Bonhoeffer: A Pictorial Album.* Edited by J. Martin Bailey and Douglas Gilbert. Foreword by William A. Visser 't Hooft. Philadelphia: Pilgrim, 1969.

———. *Rembrandt and the Gospel.* Translated by K. Gregor Smith. Philadelphia: Westminster, 1958.

White, Ronald C., Jr. *A. Lincoln: A Biography.* New York: Random House, 2009.

Wiesel, Eli. *The Gates of the Forest.* Translated by Frances Frenaye. New York: Holt Rinehart and Winston, 1966.

Wright, Ronald. *A Short History of Progress.* New York: Carroll & Graf, 2005.

Index of Scripture

Index of Scripture

Index of Names

Index of Names

53860108R00135

Made in the USA
Middletown, DE
30 November 2017